INDIAN KĀVYA LITERATURE
Volume Three

INDIAN KĀVYA LITERATURE

A.K. WARDER

VOLUME THREE

THE EARLY MEDIEVAL PERIOD
(ŚŪDRAKA TO VIŚĀKHADATTA)

MOTILAL BANARSIDASS PUBLISHING HOUSE
SINCE 1903

MOTILAL BANARSIDASS
PUBLISHING HOUSE • DELHI
Email: naraina@mlbd.in • Website: www.mlbd.in
@mlbdofficial
+91 89 2999 9000

3rd Reprint: Delhi, ***2024***
2nd Revised Edition: Delhi, 1994
First Edition: Delhi, 1977

ISBN: 978-93-5966-629-7 (Hardcover)
ISBN: 978-93-5966-861-1 (Paperback)
ISBN: 978-93-5966-191-9 (Hardcover set)
ISBN: 978-93-5966-694-5 (Paperback set)

Printed & Published by
Rajendra P Jain *for*
Motilal Banarsidass Publishing House
A-44, Naraina Industrial Area, Phase I,
New Delhi–110 028 (INDIA)
Email: naraina@mlbd.in Website: www.mlbd.in
Tel.: (+91-11)4751 1592
Showroom:
4637/20, F-2, Hari Sadan, First Floor, Ansari Road, Daryaganj
Delhi–110 002 (Opp. Fire Station) ***Tel.***: (+91-11)4559 7999

CONTENTS

Chapter XX

DRAMA IN THE +3 : ŚŪDRAKA; CONTEMPORARY LYRIC POETRY

1152. The +3 inaugurates a new period in the political and social history of India. When it began, the Kuṣāṇa Empire was already in decline and the Sātavāhana Empire was about to follow suit and collapse more swiftly and completely. During its second quarter the remnant of the Kuṣāṇa domains in the North West submitted to the overlordship of the Persian Sāsānian Dynasty, whilst most of the former Indian provinces of the Kuṣāṇas, such as Avanti under Śaka governors, Vatsa under the Maghas and Magadha under the Muruṇḍas, had become independent. Rudrasena I Śaka, the successor of Rudrasiṃha I, entered into a marriage alliance with the Muruṇḍas [835, 1102], who then had their capital at Vaiśālī, and probably became the greatest power in India (+200 to +222—for the historical sources, see e.g. *A Comprehensive History of India*, II, pp. 104, 286f., 772, 774). The Kuṣāṇas did not disappear but remained as vassals of the Sāsānians and from time to time reasserted their independence. Many centuries later the Ṣāhi Dynasty of Gandhāra claimed direct descent from them. Yajña (śrī) Śātakarṇi at the end of the +2 was the last powerful Sātavāhana Emperor, ruling from sea to sea across India. At the beginning of the +3 his successors suddenly collapsed before the Ābhīras in Mahārāṣṭra and the Ikṣvākus in Āndhra, both former feudatories of the Sātavāhanas, who then divided most of the Empire between them.

1153. These political revolutions were preceded and probably precipitated by internal developments in both the great empires, which distinguished them from the earlier empire of Magadha. Whereas earlier the governors of provinces had been appointed for limited periods, rotated from place to place and paid cash salaries, a new system of hereditary vassal rulers had appeared under both the Kuṣāṇas (e.g. the Śakas) and the Sātavāhanas (who in fact to our knowledge went further in making grants of land even in small fiefs, giving up the administrative rights with at least part of the revenue—see D.C. Sircar, *Select Inscriptions*, pp. 198, 200-1, 208). In fact it seems proper to speak of a feudal revolution, leading to a society of local lords drawing revenues from their lands, instead of salaries, and passing on as little as they could to their overlords. The surrender by the central government of administrative rights, and of the power to enforce them by armed action, leads to the formation of private local armies by the lords. Though this change was a gradual one, by +200 it had produced a society whose outlook was very different from that of the old one.

1154. We may expect the change in social ideals to be reflected in literature: the heroes in fact tend to become protecting lords offering security to those who commend themselves to them. The change of outlook is nowhere clearer than in religion, where the theistic trend becomes dominant, influencing even Buddhism (the Mahāyāna), and the hierarchical ideal is symbolised by a supreme deity who shelters the world and realised in human society by the various secular powers. Both the ideal and the real powers expect reverence and loyalty, though the traditional tolerance of India preserves a fairly harmonious balance among the numerous alternative versions of the ideal. The change was gradual and proceeded without any decisive break: the traditions of India were reinterpreted and then reaffirmed, though there was extensive rewriting of *Purāṇas* in the +4 and later and much new production of theistic scriptures. In *kāvya* too the well known themes of Tradition and mythology retain their popularity but are freshly interpreted according to the new perspectives of the writers.

1155. However, Indian literature remains endlessly various in outlook, expressing many different views and not subject to any oppressive orthodoxy. The tendency we have just indicated must therefore not be pressed to a rigid generalisation: *kāvya* remains a great debate, essentially secular and autonomous. The new empires of medieval India were rather less successful than the old in uniting large areas under a single power, apparently as a natural result of their decentralisation of administrative power; writers always had a choice of patrons and could never be subjected to any single, all engulfing censorship and direction. Their laws were their own, those of literary criticism, which enjoyed a great efflorescence during these centuries.

1156. The Ābhīras were originally nomadic pastoral tribes from the lower Indus valley, who migrated Eastwards and Southwards across Avanti. They were warriors, and after serving in the armies of various states, especially of the Śakas, some of their leaders set up as independent princes at mountainous strongholds in Southern India. The historical traditions concerning them are unfortunately vague, but according to the *Purāṇas* an Ābhīra Dynasty ruled for sixty-seven years between the Sātavāhanas, whom they overthrew, and the Vākāṭaka Dynasty (founded about +250 or a little later), in the Vindhya region and probably in some adjacent areas (Pargiter : *Dynasties of the Kali Age*, p. 46). The period of rather more than half a century fits reasonably well between the dwindling away of Sātavāhana power *c.* +200 and the establishment of the Vākāṭakas, particularly when we remember the *Purāṇa* method of sometimes allowing an overlap of dynasties in time (which has hopelessly entangled their chronology), when two dynasties claimed hegemony simultaneously. The earliest Ābhīra king whose reign was counted in the sixty-seven years may therefore have been a contemporary of one or more of the last Sātavāhana rulers, at first subordinate to them; later he or a successor revolted and reversed the situation. It seems possible that the Śakas of Avanti also were subordinate to the Ābhīras for a time, since Śūdraka sets his plays in Ujjayinī, their capital as well as a great centre of the drama in this period. Unluckily the *Purāṇas* do not record the name of any Ābhīra king, probably dismissing them as non-Aryan upstarts (the Epic refers to them as Dasyus, i.e. non-Aryan original inhabitants of India, and as *śūdras*, 'helots'). From inscriptions (see the references under 'Ābhīra' in the *Comprehensive History of India*) we learn that Ābhīra generals such as Rudrabhūti were in the service of the Śaka Rudrasiṃha I and that an Ābhīra named Īśvarasena ruled as an independent king at some subsequent time (undetermined) over a region including Nāsikā in Mahārāṣṭra. Since the latter's father, Śivadatta, is mentioned without a royal title it would appear that this Īśvarasena was the founder of the dynasty. His inscription at Nāsikā, like those of the Śakas of Avanti, is in Sanskrit.

1157. Śūdraka seems nowhere to be given any dynastic name, except that in one legend (*Skandapurāṇa*) he is called an Āndhrabhṛtya, i.e. vassal of the Āndhras, which in fact the

Ābhīras once were as well as the Ikṣvākus and others (Pargiter p. 46). The *Skandapurāṇa* also gives (I.ii.40.249 f.) the date of King Śūdraka as Kali 3290, which corresponds to +188 if no correction is required. The legends make him a king in Vidiśā (so Bāṇa, *Kādambarī*, p. 6, in Daśārṇa, adjacent to Avanti on the East)or in Ujjayinī, ('Mālavarāja', ***Avantisundarīkathāsāra*** V.144). 'Sātavāhana' is said to have given him half his empire (Jaina tradition, see Upadhye's Introduction to the *Līlāvaī*, p.50; Jinaprabha: *Vividhatīrthakalpa*, p. 63); alternatively, on the premature death of a Sātavāhana Prince Svāti, he succeeded him (at Pratiṣṭhāna?); or he fought against Svāti and defeated him, but as he had formerly been a friend he reinstated him in his father's kingdom (Daṇḍin, *Avantisundarī*, p. 201) but ruled himself as emperor for a hundred years over the whole Earth (*Avantisundarīkathāsāra*, IV 201). According to Daṇḍin, or at least his paraphraser (*Sāra*, IV 175), Śūdraka's original name was Indrāṇīgupta and he was born in Aśmaka (this agrees with Jinaprabha, p. 61 : born in Pratiṣṭhāna). Born a brahman, he despised his class and was consequently cursed, but after many misfortunes acquired the status of a noble (warrior) and royal fortune. [3279, 4400, 4474, 4476].

1158. From these scraps of information we can perhaps infer that Śūdraka was in fact an Ābhīra, as Konow first suggested (*Das indische Drama*, p. 57), and possibly the successor of Īśvarasena who greatly extended the Ābhīra power. The name Śūdraka suggests the *śūdra* class of the family (and the ancient Śūdra tribe of Sindhu or NW Rājasthān, which has been supposed to have been connected with the Ābhīras when they were in the same region—*Comprehensive History* II, p. 331; cf. D. C. Sircar, *Successors of the Sātavāhanas*, p. 242, for references). The names of the Ābhīras known from inscriptions indicate that they were Śaivas and Śūdraka likewise invokes Śiva in his plays. Like the Ābhīras, the Śūdraka of legend supplanted or subjugated the Sātavāhanas. He perhaps ruled at the time of weakness of the Śakas in and after the second quarter of the +3. It might seem to confirm his association with Aśmaka and the Sātavāhanas that he is the first dramatist known to use Māhārāṣṭrī in a play, responding to the growing popularity of verses and songs in that language. A novel on Śūdraka was written *c*. +400 [1297], but it appears to have been lost. A highly fanciful story of the hero, as a perfect lover, will be found in Vidyāpati's *Puruṣaparikṣā* (+15).

1159. Śūdraka is one of a great many royal authors of *kāvyas*, it having been very much the fashion for kings to display command of cultural as of political matters. Rather naturally, these royal authors have been suspected of merely buying *kāvyas* from writers of repute. However, in no case has this supposed purchase of literary fame been established beyond doubt and accepted generally by the critics. Under the conditions of the royal 'halls' *sabhās* of scholars and writers, with discussions of new works, such a total fraud might have been difficult to keep secret, but on the other hand a king would have the best advice always at his command to smooth the path of composition, as well as plenty of secretaries. Rājaśekhara (*Kāvyamīmāṃsā* p. 55) notes that Śūdraka was a famous patron who presided over a literary circle.

1160. The figure of Śūdraka, a legend even in the earliest sources which name him, is thus very much under suspicion. A date in the +3 does not go against the probabilities indicated by the style of the works ascribed to him and their relation to other literature, but it remains a hypothesis. Whoever the real Śūdraka was, if there ever existed such a person, the name 'Śūdraka' has to serve us as a convenient designation for the author of a set of plays, marked by an individual and brilliant style, which we have now to examine.

1161. The Vīṇā Vāsavadattā *Viṇāvāsavadatta* is a *nāṭaka* in more than eight acts, which has been imperfectly recovered as yet from the manuscript tradition. The first eight acts are apparently intact as we now have the play, but the action is not finished, requiring either one or two more. The play was popular with some dramatic critics, including those of Kerala in recent times, where alone it has been preserved at least in this incomplete form. As a dramatic more than a literary work it suffered like all such plays from the persecution of the Indian theatre in the +2nd millennium, along with Śūdraka's other plays.

1162. The title of the play, like that of Bhāsa's Dream Vāsavadattā, refers to a special feature of a new drama on a story previously staged, in this case the prominence of the *viṇā* or lute and the heroine's lesson on it. The story in this case is the same as that of Bhāsa's Yaugandharāyaṇa's Vows, namely of the capture of Udayana by Pradyota and his escape taking Vāsavadattā with him. The earlier play was a *nāṭikā* or 'light play', the later version a full scale play in every sense. As in the Bhāsa plays, the author is not named in either the prologue or the available manuscripts, but his name happens to be given in an anthology which quotes a verse from it (Vallabhadeva's *Subhāṣitāvali*, Krishnamachariar pp. 378f.: manuscript T. 989 in Kerala University Library, p. 20). Despite the common subject matter, Śūdraka's play is entirely different from Bhāsa's. In the Vīṇā Vāsavadattā Udayana is the hero and plays a leading part (in Bhāsa's play he never appears on the stage), and the scene after which the play is named is one in which Vāsavadattā (who likewise does not appear in Bhāsa's play) receives her first *viṇā* (lute) lesson from Udayana, though the *viṇā* also appears conspicuously in the other decisive scenes.

1163. The play opens with Mahāsena (Pradyota) anxious to get Vāsavadattā suitably married. He has just seen Śiva in a dream, who has told him his daughter will be married to a husband with ideal qualities, but "....unwillingly" (it is not clear who is "unwilling"). In a discussion with his ministers in council he finds all the available kings and princes ineligible. One hunts and gambles, one drinks, another is a fool, another is cruel, another avaricious, and so on. The minister Vasuvarman ventures to suggest that Udayana is Śiva's choice, but Mahāsena is absolutely opposed to this because Udayana is too proud. After further discussion it is suggested that Śiva's utterance may be interpreted as a command to bring Udayana against his will (i.e. by force). The prime minister, Bharatarohaka, who in fact is convinced that Udayana is Śiva's choice, suggests that capturing him would cure his pride. Bharatarohaka recalls that in his boyhood Udayana, when playing at being an elephant, with his friends threw dust at a *ṛṣi*, who cursed him to fall into his enemy's power through an elephant. Pradyota is pleased at this idea, though, regarding the marriage, he fears he may be committed to the consumptive drinker Sañjaya of Aśmaka, from whom he has accepted a gift. Bharatarohaka undertakes to remedy this : Śiva's command must prevail.

1164. The introductory scene *praveśaka* to Act II shows one of Pradyota's spies, disguised as an ascetic, in an elephant forest extracting information about Udayana's forces and movements from one of the latter's soldiers. Another spy tells him of the deployment of an Avanti force led by the minister Śālaṅkāyana, near the Yamunā, with an elephant painted blue : he goes there to report Udayana's movements. Then Udayana is seen in the forest at the beginning of the Act proper, with his fool *vidūṣaka* Vasantaka. This is a classic example of the latter character: to the king the forest appears to consist of elephants, but to the fool of rice; his hunger was aroused early by the wild cocks in the forest who woke them. Udayana has his forces deployed to round up a nearby herd of elephants, when one of Pradyota's agents, disguised as a forester, reports seeing a blue elephant at two leagues' distance. With only his personal attendants and twenty soldiers, Udayana mounts his horse and rides off with the spy, disregarding all advice, leaving the rest of the army, and the fool, behind to finish capturing the herd.

SPY. Master ! There is the elephant, in the shade of a jasmine creeper !

KING (UDAYANA). He

Has hooves and tusks entire, a backbone like a bow,
a brow with good jaws and temples, a long tail, firm shoulders,
Very broad mouth and ears, a trunk developed and turned up,
a body lofty in front—and dark as a cloud heavy with its load of water ! (II.10)

SPY [*aside*] Now I have succeeded ! [*Aloud*] I will rest a moment in the shade of these ebonies. [*Exit.*

KING [*dismounting*] The pitcher, now !

SERVANT [*entering with pitcher*] Victory to the master ! Here it is.

KING [*sipping*] Musician ! Bring me Ghosavatī [986] !

MUSICIAN [*entering*] Master ! Here is Ghoṣavatī.

The King takes the vīṇā *and tunes it.*

SERVANT. Now I will sit down over there. [*Exit.*

KING [*aside*] My arm is weak and my left eye trembles !

MUSICIAN. O fie ! A crow is cawing in a thorn tree against the Sun. The forest thicket is the home of many bandits. Now what will happen ?

Then enter a bandit general and his servant bearing a sword.

BANDIT GENERAL. Ah ! The power of kings ! Merely hearing that the King of Vatsa had entered this forest, our multitude broke !

Both walk on.

KING [*playing the* vīṇā *and singing*]

Of incomparable strength, vigour, might and courage !
of body blue as a waterlily, O ! Of handsome back !
Hear my words, O destroyer of many ramparts !
my friend, come under my influence, let us be friends ! (11)

Off stage is made a noise of kettle drums, conches and big drums being sounded.

KING. Oh ! We are deceived ! This elephant of the blue waterlily body is a fake ! Someone has employed that spy to draw me !

Who are these with bow and arrow readied at the leather sword-hilt ?
eager, they encircle me many times, taking various weapons.
In dress or speech they seem like heroic men of Avanti—
I know ! It's the wicked plot of Pradyota, animal king, against me ! (12)

1165. In Act III Yaugandharāyaṇa in Kauśāmbī receives a spy bringing a letter from his agent in Ujjayinī, the nun Sāṅkṛtyāyanī. This brings warning of the blue elephant plan, but the spy has been delayed on the roads blocked by Avanti troops and it is too late. Before Yaugandharāyaṇa can move, Haṃsaka, who had escaped after the fight, in which he had been knocked out by a sword blow on the head, arrives with the news of Udayana's capture. Recovering from the shock, Yaugandharāyaṇa at once conceals his nascent counter plan. First he orders Haṃsaka, who had entered the city secretly, to go out and enter again publicly, bewailing the 'death' of Udayana. Then Yaugandharāyaṇa simulates his own death, as a loyal minister following his master and acknowledging no other. He orders his funeral pyre prepared, dismisses his followers one by one, asks the citizens to forgive his mistakes, and at sunset circumambulates the blazing and smoking pyre : then leaps to a safe place and slips away in the dark. Udayana has three brothers, who may succeed him, whilst the government is entrusted by Yaugandharāyaṇa to other ministers, to one of whom he sends a cryptic message. The main task appears to be defence against King Āruṇi of Pañcāla, who is expected to invade a weakened enemy country. Apparently Yaugandharāyaṇa's aim is to convince the Avanti agents and ministers that no action is being taken about the imprisoned King, whereas this is precisely where he is directing his main resources. He tells the audience (verse 17) he will go to Ujjayinī disguised as a lunatic and come back with his master.

1166. In an introductory scene to Act IV we see some of the Vatsa agents in Ujjayinī in a brief variation on Act III of Yaugandharāyaṇa's Vows. Haṃsaka enters disguised as a crazy beggar *ḍiṇḍika* and finds the fool Vasantaka in the same disguise, dancing to entertain people at a temple. After getting away from their audience they exchange information. Vasantaka has amused King Pradyota with his fooling and been received in the palace, subsequently he has been able to see Udayana in prison; he has also met the disguised Yaugandharāyaṇa. Haṃsaka reports that Āruṇi has captured Kauśāmbī after killing Udayana's brothers in battle. The minister Rumaṇvant is holding the fortress of Lāvāṇaka [968] as his headquarters after the defeat, keeping secret agents in various villages. Haṃsaka explains Yaugandharāyaṇa's escape plan: five hundred Vatsa soldiers are hidden in Ujjayinī and the elephant Nalāgiri has been made excited, which is expected to lead to Udayana's being asked to pacify him, whereupon he can mount the elephant and ride off as his soldiers seize the streets.

1167. In the Act proper Pradyota receives Śālaṅkāyana as a hero, who had been wounded in the fight and has just recovered. The King and ministers discuss Udayana's qualities and Pradyota would now like to release him, thinking he has suffered enough. They think precisely of the wild Nalāgiri as offering a suitable pretext for bringing him out of prison, but also, on Śālaṅkāyana's advice, send ten thousand men to block the roads in case Udayana should try to escape. Pradyota gives the order for Udayana to be brought out and at once goes to watch the scene from the balcony of his Diśāmukha Palace, in the company of his Queen and the Princess Vāsavadattā. Śālaṅkāyana sends the *viṇā* Ghoṣavatī brought as a trophy from the forest fight, and Vāsavadattā, who is interested in learning the *viṇā*, at once likes it as a perfect instrument. Pradyota sends it for Udayana to use in his exploit. Then roars are heard from the street as the people of the city, from the safety of walls, palaces, trees, etc., watch the wild elephant approaching and Udayana alone with his *viṇā* entering the street. The Queen watches Udayana with great excitement and alarm and Pradyota comments as the enraged elephant runs towards him. Vāsavadattā calls to her father to stop the elephant and the roars of the people *off stage* are heard all round. Pradyota tells his ladies not to be disturbed: Udayana's music has calmed the elephant. Udayana hands the *viṇā* to Bharatarohaka (who had brought him from the prison) and mounts it. Vāsavadattā says she is covered with sweat and goes close to the rail.

Then the King of Vatsa enters mounted on the elephant.

KING OF VATSA. Ho !

Hear my words, O son of Mahāpadma !
best of elephants ! You have nothing to do with the sage's curse !
Proceed to its necessary sequel, leave this bad behaviour !
and once more, free from the curse, you will find a good place ! (IV.20)
(Mahāpadma is the Southern celestial elephant.)

KĀÑCANAMĀLĀ (VĀSAVADATTĀ'S CONFIDANTE). Princess, the Moon is rising even in the daytime !

VĀSAVADATTĀ [*aside*] But he is sweeter than a thousand moons !

KING OF VATSA [*approaching*] Victory to the King !

KING (PRADYOTA) [*rising and going to the rail*] Dear Vaidehīmātṛ (Udayana) !

This act of yours though actually seen with the eyes
could not be conceived of in others even with the mind !
Is it a dream or illusion ? With wonder
my intellect delights again and again. (21)

KING OF VATSA. O King ! Indeed the heart of an elder is easily satisfied !

QUEEN. His words are worthy of his appearance.

VĀSAVADATTĀ. Today I have recognised that only a man is pleasing to look at !

KING OF VATSA [*seeing Vāsavadattā, aside*] Who is she ?

With affection and playfulness,
with modesty, a significant gesture and confusion,
Casting her glance
on me as I wait in front, she is gentle as a gem ! (22)

QUEEN. Daughter ! Vāsavadattā ! Come here !

KING OF VATSA [*aside*] So she is Vāsavadattā !

Pradyota asks Udayana if the elephant can be made disciplined and Udayana says he will soon do it. Then Pradyota dismisses him and leaves, with his retinue, telling Bharatarohaka to treat him like his own sons. Udayana remaining alone quickly decides that when he leaves he must take Vāsavadattā with him, moreover it would not be proper to retreat without inflicting some loss on his enemy. At this moment the disguised Yaugandharāyaṇa enters and approaches him, ready to effect the rescue. Udayana refuses to come, thinking of Vāsavadattā, saying he is tired but speaking a verse in appreciation of his devotion. Then he enters the palace with Bharatarohaka.

1168. An introductory scene to Act V reports through a conversation between Kāñcanamālā and a maid that Vāsavadattā is not well. The maid tells the confidante that Sānkṛtyāyanī claims to know a 'science' whereby she can become possessed by a goddess, who will then answer the Queen's questions as to what should be done for her daughter. The nun has already gone to a temple for this purpose, after telling the Queen, who has told the King about it. Kāñcanamālā and the maid decide to go there.

1169. In the Act proper we see Sāṅkṛtyāyanī preparing to fake the oracle : she has understood that what is wrong with Vāsavadattā is simply that she has been in love with Udayana since seeing him tame the elephant; she also knows that Udayana declined to escape when Yaugandharāyaṇa had everything ready, from which she infers that he is detained by his heart since seeing the Princess. All this Sāṅkṛtyāyanī reports in a monologue, as she watches the light of dawn coming through the windows of the temple. She also expresses her devotion to all three: Vāsavadattā, Udayana and Yaugandharāyaṇa (the latter two on account of her past life in Kauśāmbī, we learn elsewhere), and her determination to save them. But she also wants to save herself from her divided loyalty. Hearing the temple gate being opened, she then takes up her sitting posture as a priestess possessed by a goddess. A chamberlain enters first, conducting Vāsavadattā and Kāñcanamālā. This Sāṅkṛtyāyanī finds fortunate, as she can reassure Vāsavadattā, speaking as the goddess and telling her that her desire for the King of Vatsa will be fulfilled. Then she dismisses her.

1170. The Queen enters, with King Pradyota and Bharatarohaka. Pradyota consults the oracle and is told that once Vāsavadattā was watching the moonrise from the rail of the balcony, when she was seen by a celestial musician *gandharva*. Since then her heart has been 'bewildered' and she has a 'longing' for the celestial musician. We may interpose that all this is perfectly correct because Udayana himself belongs to the Lunar Dynasty and is an extraordinary musician : it is therefore good oracle, true but dark. The oracle then continues that celestial musicians have no power where the King of Vatsa lives, because he is their teacher : indeed he is their king, Citraratha, born as a human being through a curse of Tumburu (his cousin). This is enough : Pradyota obeys the oracle as a divine command to admit Udayana to the palace of the Princess; Bharatarohaka suggests music lessons for her as a pretext to satisfy the public about Udayana's movements.

1171. In Act VI Udayana, freed by Pradyota but bound

by the Princess, reflects on the enmity between their families, though noting Pradyota's apparent friendliness. His fool Vasantaka enters, having got into Pradyota's service, as noted earlier, and being now sent by his new master to insinuate himself into the ex-prisoner's intimacy and find out all he can about him : Pradyota offers him to Udayana as a crazy beggar to amuse him. In his disguise Vasantaka has assumed the name Mattavilāsa. The fool now teases his old master about the drama he is meditating, regarding himself and Vāsavadattā, and they discuss its construction and possible conclusion. Udayana will not just think the drama, he will act it : Yaugandharāyaṇa is the producer, Sāṅkṛtyāyanī the actress (in the prologue), himself the hero and so on. This incidentally gives us useful information on the author's ideas of dramatic construction, though they are perfectly regular according the *Nāṭyaśāstra*. Then the fool tells Udayana the latest news of Pradyota. Āruṇi has sent an envoy who has been very attentive to him and brought a message suggesting that Udayana should be closely guarded, because he is brave and has devoted friends. Because of this (danger of his escape and rallying Vatsa), Āruṇi says, he has occupied Kauśāmbī; now Pradyota must decide what should be done. At this, Pradyota had only smiled to Bharatarohaka. As the fool concludes, Bharatarohaka arrives to conduct Udayana to the Princess for her music lesson. The Act ends with the chariot drive to her palace.

1172. In Act VII Sāṅkṛtyāyanī takes Vāsavadattā to the Emerald Pavilion for her music lesson. Udayana arrives and the lesson takes place in the presence of Sāṅkṛtyāyanī, Kāñcanamālā, the fool 'Mattavilāsa' and a chamberlain who brings the *viṇā*, Bharatarohaka having left to supervise a festival in the city. After tuning the *viṇā*, Udayana first plays and sings at the nun's suggestion, by way of demonstration. She thinks it appropriate to start with a benediction, so he sings a verse on Viṣṇu (as the Dwarf) and one wishing that the King (Pradyota, or just any king ?—the verse is such as one finds as the concluding benediction of plays)—should protect the whole Earth (Goddess). This second is a rhyming *aparavaktra*, a fixed metre of semi-musical origin (VII.6) [583, 660]. Meanwhile, he falls more and more in love with Vāsavadattā as she watches him, which he expresses in a verse aside. Then he sings a verse in the delightful *pṛthvi* metre, clearly of musical 'bar metre' origin and very suitable for singing :

Love, the charioteer, joyfully drives the great chariot of desire
to the best city of meeting, where the dear festival of love is,
For lovers; who inflame the fulfilment of full grown new youth,
each tender with the abundance of mutually increasing love's delight. (VII.8)

SĀṄKṚTYĀYANĪ. Good ! May it be even so !

UDAYANA. Princess ! Give your attention to this. [*Develops the* madhyama grāma *gamut of notes*] Princess ! You should make just a beginning in this.

SĀṄKṚTYĀYANĪ. My dear. Take the *viṇā*.

VĀSAVADATTĀ. Yes, sister. [*Taking the* vīṇā] What should I do now, sister ?

SĀṄKṚTYĀYANĪ. What the King (Udayana) has demonstrated.

VĀSAVADATTĀ. There's no escape !

She plays very slowly.

UDAYANA. Ah ! Wonderful ! Sister, the Princess is a good student, for her

Brilliant finger-shoots touching
successively the honey-streaming reddish strings
Suggest the wandering beak-play
of parrots in a rather reddish *bakula* cage. (VII.9)

(The *bakula* is the tree Mimusops elengi, whose hard wood is useful in house building and evidently for parrot cages also; it is better known for the fragrance of its flowers.)

As a pretext to keep Udayana longer, Sāṅkṛtyāyanī suggests that the crazy beggar 'Mattavilāsa' should entertain them by dancing. Vāsavadattā doesn't watch him, but nevertheless honours him with a ring afterwards, which Udayana at once takes possession of since the fool prefers sweets.

1173. After the Princess and her retinue have left, Udayana thinks of the danger of his attachment to her becoming known to Pradyota (we remember of course that he intends to abduct her, by way of retaliation against Pradyota, his old enemy; secrecy is therefore a primary concern). The fool agrees that Pradyota and Bharatarohaka are utter rogues. Then Udayana asks him if there is some other woman in the city to whom he could pretend to be attached, by way of cover. The fool suggests a famous harlot, Narmadā. Udayana decides to send her a present, whilst the fool in his new office as Pradyota's spy will make the affair known.

1174. In Act VIII a maid brings the lovelorn Vāsavadattā the rumour, told her by Pradyota's chowrie bearer, that Udayana loves Narmadā. The Princess is angry as well as upset and succeeds in maintaining her dignity. According to the rumour, Narmadā rejected Udayana's advances, despite his presents. Then Pradyota, hearing of the matter from his spies, gave Narmadā to Udayana (this presumably means that Pradyota released her from her status as a government servant, her profession being controlled by the state, and approved her marrying Udayana). But Narmadā still rejected him and threatened to commit suicide, so Udayana sent her to the women's quarters (presumably of his own palace). After the maid has left, the confidante Kāñcanamālā tries to reassure Vāsavadattā by saying that Udayana could not possibly love such a woman, but the Princess thinks that lovers make no distinctions. She reproaches herself for having let Udayana enter her heart. Then Kāñcanamālā suggests consulting Sāṅkṛtyāyanī. They find the nun in the gardens, waiting in a pavilion with jasmine creepers [969] with a letter from Udayana for Vāsavadattā. Sāṅkṛtyāyanī finds out why Vāsavadattā is sulky and overwrought and declares that it is impossible that Udayana could love Narmadā, it must be a sham to conceal his real love. The Princess should not be deluded by this : rather it is Bharatarohaka who has been deluded about Udayana's real wishes. Here Vāsavadattā asks why Sāṅkṛtyāyanī is so partial to Udayana and the nun tells her he had once saved her from drowning in a lake by the Yamunā. This should enable Vāsavadattā to understand everything, including the nun's real rôle, and to clinch the matter Sāṅkṛtyāyanī produces Udayana's letter. Eventually Vāsavadattā is persuaded to sing Udayana's verses with the *viṇā*, first this one :

> When you were seen, O girl whose face is like the King
> of Stars !
> since then my sleep at night has been destroyed;
> In all my pleasures there has been only discontent,
> my sighs have become like the days of summer. (VIII.9)

(The King of Stars is the Moon; summer days of course are hot.)

The Act ends with Vāsavadattā preparing to receive Udayana for her music lesson.

1175. There seems to be no direct indication of how the play should end. The closing verse of Act VIII, spoken by the nun, says simply that Udayana will be delighted when she reports this news to him (i.e. how Vāsavadattā feels). From the action so far, with Pradyota and Bharatarohaka convinced that Udayana loves Narmadā, we must expect a fresh royal council on what now can be done. The situation favourable to Udayana can hardly continue: it is time to act, to avert the obstacle of Pradyota's probable dissatisfaction. Udayana has declared his intention of abducting Vāsavadattā, which will be facilitated if she agrees to elope with him. He ought by now to have informed Yaugandharāyaṇa that he is at last ready for the escape. Perhaps the music lesson about to take place will provide the opportunity for the lovers together tc evade Pradyota and his ministers, if Yaugandharāyaṇa and his men can create a situation in which such an evasion is possible. One further act would be sufficient to conclude the play, with Pradyota and his court on stage and Udayana's escape with Vāsavadattā reported. At the conclusion we would expect Pradyota, reconciled to the inevitable and Śiva's command, to approve his daughter's marriage to Udayana and to order it celebrated (which could be done with paintings as in Bhāsa's version of the story). Alternatively Udayana and Vāsavadattā could be on stage, escaping, and Pradyota's reaction reported at the end, when the fugitives have reached a safe place. This second alternative is perhaps more probable, both in consideration of the technique displayed earlier in the play, of actually showing the most important and exciting events, and because it seems necessary to have the hero and heroine on stage at the conclusion, even at the cost of Pradyota's absence. Given the situation which has been built up, and especially Udayana's attitude of maintaining his proud independence of action, a different ending, with all the misunderstandings cleared up between Pradyota and Udayana without the necessity of the defiant escape, does not seem feasible. It would in any case seem too great a disappointment to the audience to depart so far from the traditional story as to eliminate the elopement. Consequently it does not seem possible that the play could have ended with all the main characters, Pradyota as well as Udayana, on stage together. There is one further point to be cleared up : Kauśāmbī is in the hands of Āruṇi. Before the conclusion can be complete, Udayana must know that Āruṇi has been defeated, or has announced his voluntary withdrawal. After escaping (to Lāvāṇaka ?), he might be brought some news of a victory by Rumaṇvant, as well as of Pradyota's friendship and support.

1176. The editor of the play (K. V. Sarma, in his Introduction, p. 10) has pointed out that the Tamil version of the *Bṛhatkathā* [667] contains a version of this adventure of Udayana very similar to that of the Vīṇā Vāsavadattā. In particular the characters of Sāṅkṛtyāyanī and Narmadā, apparently ignored in all other extant versions of the story of Udayana's capture and escape, are found there playing the same parts. In this version, Yaugandharāyaṇa through a faked oracle engages the Avanti court in a water festival on the outskirts of Ujjayinī, Udayana having the use of the elephant Bhadravatī [696]. Then he raises a fire alarm in the city and Udayana is able to escape, with Vāsavadattā, in the ensuing confusion, the minister and his men covering them from pursuit. This version may have been in the original *Bṛhatkathā*, which could thus have been Śūdraka's direct source. Though there is no probability that the dramatist followed any previous version faithfully, it is at least possible that he retained here the main event of the escape, as we have just suggested, and that he used the device of Yaugandharāyaṇa starting a fire to provide Udayana with his opportunity.

1177. We seem to have no analysis of the Vīṇā Vāsavadattā by an old critic, but its main structure appears reasonably clear. The objective is the marriage of Vāsavadattā—to

Udayana. This is suggested in verse 10 of Act I, which accordingly provides the 'seed'. The ensuing action bringing the couple together offers sufficient 'continuity'. As a sub-plot we have the actions of Sāṅkṛtyāyanī wishing to escape from her situation of divided loyalty (afterwards she will apparently leave Ujjayinī following Vāsavadattā—she appears in some later *kāvyas* on subsequent episodes in the adventures of Udayana such as Mātrarāja's *Tāpasavatsarāja*, +7). She sends a letter to Yaugandharāyaṇa in Act III, but appears on stage and takes a leading part from Act V to Act VIII. An 'intervention' would be Haṃsaka's arrival in Act III, bringing news to Yaugandharāyaṇa and also making possible his disappearance. Of the stages, the commencement is in Act I with the seed. The 'undertaking' will be the capture of Udayana in Act II. The 'possibility of attainment' could be where, in Act IV, Udayana having seen Vāsavadattā decides not to escape yet. The 'certainty of attainment of the fruit' may be in Act VIII, when Vāsavadattā is at last convinced by Sāṅkṛtyāyanī that Udayana loves her. The 'attaining the fruit' is of course the missing final union of the lovers.

1178. The 'opening' conjunction appears to coincide with Act I (production of the seed, plan to capture Udayana). The 're-opening' may similarly coincide with Act II, but perhaps include Act III also. The 'embryo' should include especially Act IV, where Vāsavadattā and Udayana fall in love, but also the following developments up to the music lesson in Act VII. The 'obstacle' is evidently the affair of Narmadā, beginning at the end of Act VII. The 'conclusion' again is missing.

1179. A noteworthy feature of the Vīṇā Vāsavadattā is the repeated references by the characters to the action of 'fate' *daiva* [1010], which at the same time appears to be the will of Śiva. Pradyota's dream of Śiva and the question of the divine command have been noted above in outlining the play, whilst the references to 'fate' are more in the nature of asides by some of the characters as they contemplate the sequence of events which seem beyond human control. The Producer in the Prologue, though without using the word 'fate', anticipates such a sequence by uttering a fatalistic verse:

Marriage, birth or death—where, how and when it must be;
There, thus and then only it happens, surely, and not otherwise! (I.2)

He is discussing the marriage of their daughter with the actress, his wife, who is not satisfied with this because the girl is already of marriageable age. Consequently he undertakes to propitiate Śiva to discover the intended husband, like King Pradyota, thus leading into the play proper by parallelism *avalagita* [139]. In the first Act (after verse 7), Śālaṅkāyana, commenting on Pradyota's dream as he speaks of the appearance of Śiva, remarks that this is the accomplishment of fate *daiva*, where *daiva* might equally mean the 'divine' providence. Again after verse 14 Bharatarohaka, in assuring Pradyota that he need not consider himself committed to Sañjaya, refers to Śiva's command as 'fate'. At the end of Act II the Bandit General, seeing Udayana taken prisoner, though his power was considered unequalled, comments that 'fate' *vidhi* is hard to pass by. In Act III Yaugandharāyaṇa, hearing Haṃsaka's report, laments that no power or policy, nothing in the world of the living, can oppose 'fate' or 'the inevitable' *bhavitavyatā* (verse 5). Through fate *daiva* Rāma and Lakṣmaṇa were bound by Indrajit, according to Vālmīki, the First Kavi, but also afterwards freed (verse 6). This latter is perhaps more consistent with the character of Yaugandharāyaṇa as depicted by Bhāsa [993]; there is always room for optimism and one must keep on trying. When Pradyota describes his changing feelings towards Udayana to Bharatarohaka (IV.2), the minister comments that Udayana has been brought by fate (or divine providence) *daiva*. The fool Vasantaka declares, when making his entrance in Act VI, that it is 'fate' *bhavitavyatā* that Pradyota has employed him in his disguise to spy on his own old master Udayana. Udayana seeing that Vāsavadattā looks lovingly at him thinks that 'fate' *daiva* is looking on him (*unmukha*, more freely 'smiling on' him) (VII.13). When Sāṅkṛtyāyanī reminds Vāsavadattā that she gave her ring to Udayana (VIII.11) the Princess denies it (she gave it to 'Mattavilāsa'), whereupon the nun says that it was given (to Udayana) by the gods *devas* (which, if not actually a scribal error for *daiva*, has similar implications).

1180. We have already noted how different this play is from Bhāsa's drama on the same subject. Practically everything is here represented on the stage, whereas in Yaugandharāyaṇa's Vows several most important scenes are merely reported. The scene of Udayana's capture here is particularly fine. Bhāsa merely presents it as a report, and it seems to be this reported scene which was criticised by Bhāmaha (*Kāvyālaṅkāra* IV, 39ff.) as impossible. Here the capture is made more convincing. Udayana approaches the blue elephant (not a dummy, but a real one painted) playing his *viṇā* and singing, then he hears the drums and conches of the enemy off stage and knows he is trapped. He calls for his horse and closes his men to fight. The actual fight is reported, in accordance with the convention of no bloodshed on the stage, his capture alive seeming feasible because he is wounded whilst still mounted and then taken prisoner after his horse is killed under him (the Avanti troops in any case had orders to take him alive). Śūdraka thus seems to aim at greater realism than Bhāsa, or at least to have taken much greater care of details which seemed open to criticism.

1181. Still more noticeable, even if we allow for substantial cuts in Bhāsa's play as now available to us, as well as the difference of dramatic types, is the far greater length of the Vīṇā Vāsavadattā: the details are worked out more fully and many more scenes are developed out of the story. This will heighten the effect of the various episodes and perhaps produce a more brilliant play, though one might expect it to lead to problems in production on account of the time required. However this was solved, the enlarged scale in fact became standard after Śūdraka. An entertainment spread over a series of evenings evidently became extended to whole nights [160-1]. Perhaps with a growing public appreciation of the theatre increased length was readily accepted and did not upset the connoisseur's sense of the unity of the action.

1182. The relationship of Śūdraka to Bhāsa is extremely close, despite Śūdraka's innovations of scale and more carefully realistic detail. Śūdraka took up Bhāsa's Impoverished Cārudatta and enlarged it—or completed it—as his masterpiece, the Toy Cart *Mṛcchakaṭika*. He interwove a new action into the plot and produced a brilliant 'fiction' in ten acts. Bhāsa's play was on his usual relatively small scale and would probably be complete in about seven acts. Śūdraka's Toy Cart is immensely long. He has retained most of the old play (especially the verses), but has enlarged every act with more detailed action and substantial additional scenes. Numerous additional verses develop the emotional *bhāva* content of the scenes. In general, Śūdraka's acts are longer and contain more incidents than the acts of Bhāsa's plays and he presents more characters than Bhāsa in corresponding plays.

1183. This is indeed the founding of the newer phase of drama, which will culminate in Bhavabhūti's masterpieces in the +8, in which the aesthetic theory of the *Nāṭyaśāstra* is more consciously and literally applied, with the elaborate delineation of emotion as the basis of the maximum aesthetic experience *rasa* which can be generated in the audience. Only the increase in incidents and characters is usually not followed by later dramatists, who prefer to concentrate on the emotional delineation, at length, of a few characters in a few scenes. We are as yet still not far from Bhāsa and the Toy Cart is uniquely rich in action, but the new grander scale of presentation gives full scope for Śūdraka's insistence on the complex intertwining of aesthetic experiences : the sensitive (which is the main one), the compassionate, the comic, the furious and the heroic. To some extent the remaining apprehensive, marvellous, horrific and even the calmed are produced in this extraordinarily rich play. The sensitive predominates but the compassionate also is highly developed.

1184. The play is also remarkable for the great variety of Prakrit dialects used in it, eight altogether : Śaurasenī, Māhārāṣṭrī, Avantikā, Prācyā, Māgadhī, Śakārī, Cāṇḍālī and Ḍhakkī (so the commentator Pṛthvīdhara). The Śaurasenī speaking characters here use Māhārāṣṭrī for their verses, in other words they resort to the famous language of the lyric. This introduction of Māhārāṣṭrī seems to have been an innovation by Śūdraka : it does not appear to have been found in any earlier play.

1185. The first four acts of the Toy Cart correspond exactly to those of Bhāsa's play, ending with Vasantasenā's resolve to visit Cārudatta and the approaching storm. The additional scenes inserted include that of the superintendent of gambling's pursuit of the gambler Saṃvāhaka in the streets in Act II and the latter's escape to Vasantasenā's through the intervention of another gambler, Darduraka. This brings the first mention, except for a hint in the Prologue, of the new action which Śūdraka has woven into the play, a political subsidiary plot. Darduraka, having offended the superintendent by helping the gambler, resolves to join the rebels : a young cowherd, Āryaka, has been declared the future king by soothsayers and all those in trouble under the present rëgime are joining him. It is possible to see in this cowherd hero an allusion to the traditionally pastoral Ābhīras, who may have come to power through this kind of revolt against a corrupt government. Perhaps Āryaka represents Śūdraka himself.

1186. In Act IV we hear that Pālaka, the present king, has imprisoned the cowherd. Sajjalaka, or rather Śarvilaka as he is here renamed (some other names are slightly changed, either by Śūdraka or through textual corruption), is a friend of Āryaka's and on hearing of his imprisonment is determined to start an insurrection to liberate him.

1187. Also in Act IV, when the jester goes to Vasantasenā to return the necklace, we find a scene inserted which describes her palatial abode : conducted by a maid and a bastard (*bandhula*, 'little kinsman') the jester proceeds through eight courtyards before reaching her in the garden. In the first courtyard he sees the storeyes of the white palace with golden and jewelled stairs, their balconies glazed with crystal and draped with pearls as if contemplating Ujjayinī through their Moonlike arches; the porter sits drowsing like a learned brahman. In the second are the draught oxen, an elephant, horses and other animals. In the third, inlaid seats are prepared for high class guests, a half read book lies on a stone table and a gaming table has chessmen of natural (uncut) gems; some geishas and old parasites are wandering about carrying paintings. In the fourth, with musicians and singers some geisha girls are rehearsing a play; drinking water is cooling in the breeze in the windows. In the fifth courtyard servants are preparing food with spices, fine aromas come from the entrances to the kitchen and the jester finds with some geishas a group of bastards, who describe their mode of life to him. In the sixth, jewellers and perfumers are at work and visitors are drinking with geishas. In the seventh are pet birds, singing, talking, fighting, dancing or simply ornamental, many in cages but doves, a peacock and others at large. In the eighth the jester sees the mistress' (Vasantasenā's) brother, expensively dressed, overloaded with jewellery and walking shakily, and her mother, bloated and alcoholic. The *Nāṭya-darpaṇa* (p. 119) quotes from the dialogue here as an example of a 'joke' *vyāhāra* as a limb of the street play [326], with considerable variations from the edition of the play we are using :

JESTER. Who is that female bastard ?
MAID. That is our mistress' venerable mother.
JESTER. If she dies, there will be enough for a thousand jackals ! But of course they built the beautiful gateway after bringing her in? Or did they bring her down from above ?
MAID. Sir ! Don't search so far : the venerable lady is afflicted with quartan ague.
JESTER. Lord Quartan Ague ! Have pity on me too, a brahman !

When the jester finally reaches the garden, he finds it surpasses the garden of Heaven with its many flowers and its pool with red lotuses and waterlilies.

1188. In Act V, beginning the continuation of the play for which we lack Bhāsa's version, Cārudatta is waiting for the jester to return after taking the necklace to Vasantasenā. In the scene (p. 116) where he arrives, Bhoja (*Śṛṅgāraprakāśa* II p. 496) points out an example of 'ironical flattery' *prapañca* as a limb of the street play [326] :

CĀRUDATTA [*seeing Maitreya*] I'm glad to see you ! Welcome, friend. Sit down.
JESTER. I'm sitting.
CĀRUDATTA. Friend, tell me about that business.
JESTER. That business is lost.
CĀRUDATTA. What, didn't she accept the necklace ?
JESTER. How could we have so much luck ? She raised a salute as tender as a fresh lotus and accepted it !

1189. Now Vasantasenā enters, dressed brilliantly as a woman going to meet her lover *abhisārikā* [802] and escorted by the parasite and a maid carrying an umbrella. They continue some time on their way through the stormy night, which Cārudatta has already described, whilst the hero and the jester are still sitting in another part of the stage. This arrangement is parallel to that in Act II, where Vasantasenā sits with her maid whilst the long scene of the pursuit of the gambler Saṃvāhaka is played. Vasantasenā and the parasite describe and discuss the storm with many verses, in relation to the feelings and actions of lovers, a storm being simultaneously an obstacle to them and a cover for them with its darkness. The imagery of mythology, and poetic fancies regarding animals, are invoked and we are in the domain of lyric poetry. Such descriptive scenes are rare or short in Bhāsa but a regular and much appreciated feature of later plays. As a clue to the acting here, Sāgaranandin (285 ff.) finds an example of the *sthitapāṭhya* [363] dance as a limb of the *lāsya* (p. 124):

VASANTASENĀ [*to the parasite*] Sir, what is the use of censuring the foolishness of a woman's nature? See, sir:

The clouds may rain or thunder,
or even let loose a thunderbolt;
—Women going to their lovers
do not consider cold or heat. (V.16)

If Sāgaranandin is right, this one verse represents a complete dance, with changing rhythms, or perhaps the prose sentence is part of the dance too. It is not easy to be certain at present about the interpretation of the brief statements of such writers as Sāgaranandin concerning these now obscure dances, but, since he adds that the *sthitapāṭhya* is adorned with a *carcarī* [359] recitation, it may be that the verse represents the latter, like a refrain, 'preceded by dance steps representing walking' (?—*bhaumacārī*).

1190. The parasite's description of the sky introduces the poetic and sometimes mythological fancies about nature:

As if flaming with its lightnings, as if mocking loudly with its hundreds of egrets,

as if leaping with its rainbow discharging the shower-
arrows,
As if roaring with the sound of its sharp thunderbolts,
as if staggering with its winds,
as if full of indigo dragons, the sky is as if burning
incense with its clouds. (V. 27)

1191. When they reach the house, the parasite calls out to announce her arrival :

Ho there ! Let the honourable Cārudatta be informed:

She has come to the house of her lover, loving, joyful,
her hair moist with water,
at the time fragrant with flowering *kadambas* and *nipas*,
resplendent with clouds ;
Alarmed by the thundering of the clouds with their
lightning, desiring to see you,
she waits, washing her feet covered in mud sticking
to her anklets ! (V.35)

On being let in, Vasantasenā politely gets rid of the parasite by offering him the services of the maid with the umbrella. She is then kept at Cārudatta's house overnight on account of the storm.

1192. Act VI begins with the scene which gives Śūdraka's play its name. Vasantasenā in the morning sees Cārudatta's son with an earthenware toy cart, complaining that he no longer has a gold one (as when his father was better off), and she gives him her jewellery to buy a gold one again. She is now supposed to follow Cārudatta to the old Puṣpakaraṇḍaka Park in his bullock carriage, but the empty carriage of the *śakāra* happens to be stopped outside, also on its way to the Park. Its driver is assisting another driver and while he is away Vasantasenā gets into that carriage by mistake. Meanwhile Āryaka has escaped from prison with Śarvilaka's help and hurries past. Seeing the side gate of Cārudatta's desolate house open, he slips in and hides, then hearing Cārudatta's carriage being got ready for the Park he climbs in while the driver is holding the bullocks, hoping to get out of the city. Hearing someone, and seeing the carriage settle under its load, the driver thinks Vasantasenā has got in and drives off.

1193. In Act VII Cārudatta meets his carriage at the Park, finds Āryaka and helps him, letting him keep the carriage and make good his escape.

1194. In Act VIII the *śakāra* is displayed in all his vileness. After a preliminary exhibition of crudeness and ignorance in an encounter with the Buddhist monk (ex-gambler Saṃvāhaka), who gets away as soon as possible, he waits with the parasite for his carriage to take him to the city. When it arrives, Vasantasenā is in it, realising too late that she is not in Cārudatta's carriage. At first the *śakāra* is afraid, thinking a demoness has taken possession of his carriage. The parasite for a moment hopes to save her, but fails to persuade the *śakāra* to walk instead, which the great man considers shameful. When he knows it is Vasantasenā and thinks she has at last consented to meet him, the scoundrel attempts to woo her, but she angrily rejects him, giving him a kick when he tries to touch her. He is more enraged when his servant, driving the carriage, tells him she has come only by mistake, and a furious altercation *sampheṭa* follows (this is an example of the limb of the *śilpaka* [348] according to Sāgaranandin, 3130ff.).

ŚAKĀRA. Get down, slave girl, get down! You are riding with my bullocks! (p. 178)

1195. Finally the parasite helps her down.

ŚAKĀRA [*aside*] The fire of my anger, kindled when she disregarded my words, is now blazing because of that kick. Therefore it is time for me to kill her. Very well. Even so, now. [*Aloud*] Sir! Sir!

If you'd like a mantle with abundant hanging fringes,
woven with hundreds of threads,
And meat to eat and make you satisfied—
scrumptious! Scrumptious! Scrumptious!
(VIII.22)

PARASITE. What then?
ŚAKĀRA. You do what I want.
PARASITE. Certainly I will, except anything improper.

ŚAKĀRA. Sir ! There isn't even a whiff of anything improper. There isn't any demoness....

PARASITE. Then tell me what it is.

ŚAKĀRA. Kill Vasantasenā.

PARASITE [*stopping his ears*]

A young woman and the ornament of the city,
suitable for love—a harlot who is not like a harlot;
If I kill that blameless woman,
by what boat shall I cross the river of the other world ? (23)

ŚAKĀRA. I will give you a boat. Besides, here in this secluded park who will see you killing her ?

Bhoja (*Śṛṅgāraprakāśa* II p. 499) quotes this passage as an example of the 'other conjunction' gift *pradāna* [141], though the parasite refuses all inducements.

1196. The *śakāra* then turns to his servant and slave Sthāvaraka, trying to induce him to commit the murder, which Sāgaranandin (3122ff.) notes as the limb 'enticement' *pralobha* [348] of the *śilpaka* :

ŚAKĀRA. Little son Sthāvaraka, my servant, I will give you golden bracelets !

SERVANT. And I will put them on.

ŚAKĀRA. I will have a golden seat made for you !

SERVANT. And I will sit on it.

ŚAKĀRA. I will give you all the left overs !

SERVANT. And I will eat them.

ŚAKĀRA. I will make you the head of all the servants !

SERVANT. Master, I will be that.

ŚAKĀRA. Then mind my words !

SERVANT. Master, I will do everything except anything improper.

ŚAKĀRA. There isn't even a whiff of anything improper.

SERVANT. Speak, master.

ŚAKĀRA. Kill this Vasantasenā.

SERVANT. Please, master ! I, unworthy, brought the lady because of the change of carriages.

ŚAKĀRA. Hey ! Servant ! Can't I control even you !

SERVANT. The master can control my body, not my character. Therefore, please, please, master, I am afraid !

ŚAKĀRA. When you are my servant who are you afraid of ?

SERVANT. Master, of the other world.

ŚAKĀRA. Who is this other world ?

SERVANT. Master, the result of good and bad actions.

ŚAKĀRA. What is the result of good actions like ?

SERVANT. Like the master, adorned with lots of gold.

ŚAKĀRA. What is that of bad actions like ?

SERVANT. Like me, eating another's alms. Therefore I won't do anything improper.

ŚAKĀRA. Hey ! You won't kill her? [*Beats him all over*].

SERVANT. The master can beat me and kill me, but I won't do anything improper :

Since I was born a slave,
destined by the faults of my luck,
And I will not buy more,
therefore I avoid anything improper. (25)

1197. The *śakāra* then orders the servant to go to his palace and wait for him there. He gets rid of the parasite too by asking him to fetch the servant back. The parasite hesitates, wishing to prevent the murder and begged by Vasantasenā to protect her, but the *śakāra* declares he didn't really intend to kill her but only to make her love him. The parasite does not trust him and lingers nearby, hiding and watching to see what he really intends to do. The cunning *śakāra* pretends not to see him and proceeds to act the part of a lover, gathering flowers and offering them to Vasantasenā. This satisfies the parasite sufficiently for him to go and fetch the servant. Whilst he is away the *śakāra* beats and strangles Vasantasenā and leaves her for dead. When the parasite and servant return, they find the scoundrel delighted with his crime, and with having out-witted the parasite, and boasting openly of it. The parasite at last decides to finish with the *śakāra* and the court and to join the rebels. The servant is again sent to the *śakāra's* palace, where his master intends to put him in irons so that he can't reveal the secret. The *śakāra* now meditates his plan of accusing Cārudatta of the murder. However, Vasantasenā is not dead. The monk Saṃvāhaka finds her, revives her and takes her to be looked after by a nun.

1198. In Act IX Cārudatta is accused by the *śakāra* of murdering Vasantasenā for the sake of her jewellery, and brought to trial. She is known to have spent the night at Cārudatta's house, the *śakāra* says he saw the murder and a policeman reports finding a woman's body in the Park (in fact it was another woman, killed in the storm by a falling tree). The judge knows Cārudatta's character and hesitates, but the *śakāra* complains that he is partial. The jester arrives and angrily accuses the *śakāra*: there is a scuffle between them in which he drops Vasantasenā's jewellery, which Cārudatta had taken from his son and asked his friend to return to her. The possession of her jewellery is regarded as conclusive evidence against Cārudatta and he is sentenced to death.

1199. In the final Act Cārudatta is led through the streets of Ujjayinī by two executioners, who beat a drum and proclaim his name, his crime and the sentence at appointed places on the way, which will end at the Southern Cemetery outside the city gate. The scene is effectively protracted and the same proclamation relentlessly repeated as the victim is taken along to die as decreed by the law. Dhanika quotes (p.24) Cārudatta's reflections on hearing the proclamation, as an example of 'ancestral pride' *prasaṅga* [149] as a limb of the obstacle :

> My clan was illustrious, completely purified by
> hundreds of rites,
> with the sounds of sacred texts at the firm shrine in
> front of the assembly;
> Now I am at the stage of dying, through demerits,

it is proclaimed by incongruous men in a proclamation. (X.12)

The jester runs after him, bringing his son, but they cannot deter the executioners from carrying out their orders.

1200. Sthāvaraka from his place of imprisonment hears the proclamation and heroically throws himself from a window when his cries that Cārudatta is innocent are not heard. The fall fortunately breaks his fetters and he follows the executioners and stops them. He explains to them what happened and they hesitate. But the *śakāra* was watching, and exulting at the scene, and now rushes after Sthāvaraka, pushing through the crowd. His servant accuses him of the murder, and now of murdering Cārudatta too. The crowd shout at the *śakāra* that he is the murderer and he shrinks back in fear. Then he again tries to seduce the servant, this time to stop talking, offering him a golden bracelet. Bhoja [1195] notes this as another example of 'gift' as an other conjunction. The servant shows the bracelet to the crowd and says he is being enticed with gold, but the cunning *śakāra* cries out that that was the gold, for stealing which he had been fettered. He thus persuades the executioners that the slave's accusation is only the talk of one who has been punished, against his master. The servant deplores his slavery, which causes people to disbelieve him when he tells the truth. Cārudatta sees that even such a heroic effort by the slave to free him is useless when fate *daiva* is opposed (X.31). The march continues until they reach the Cemetery.

1201. Meanwhile the monk is escorting Vasantasenā to Cārudatta's house. They hear the uproar and see the crowd on the royal highway. The monk hears one of the executioners making the last proclamation and they rush through the crowd to save Cārudatta. They are just in time. Seeing that Vasantasenā is alive and Cārudatta therefore innocent, the executioners release him. The *śakāra* runs away.

1202. There is an uproar off stage and Śarvilaka enters. The uprising has succeeded : Pālaka is dead and Āryaka consecrated King. Śarvilaka hurries to rescue Cārudatta. The *Nāṭyadarpaṇa* (pp. 96-7) quotes his words for the limb 'agreement' *samaya* [150] in the conclusion :

Let the villains get away ! Get away ! [*Seeing, with joy*] Cārudatta is alive, with Vasantasenā ! The wish of our master is indeed fulfilled :

It's wonderful, sir, that I see you escaped from the fathomless ocean of disaster !
—united with your beloved
Who is chosen by good qualities and most virtuous ;
—like the Moon rich in moonlight, freed from eclipse. (X.48)

(The translation follows the *Nāṭyadarpaṇa* readings.)

1203. The *Nāṭyadarpaṇa* (98-9) also quotes some of the following passages, for the limb 'conversation' *bhāṣaṇa* [150] in the conclusion, showing that this is speech with conciliation, gifts and other agreeable things and benefits. By command of King Āryaka, Śarvilaka says to Cārudatta :

He who formerly rode in your carriage
and found refuge through you
Has today killed Pālaka
like the animal when the sacrifice is accomplished. (X.51)

CĀRUDATTA. Śarvilaka ! What ? That Āryaka, who by King Pālaka's proclamation was taken for no reason and bound in fetters in the gabled house, had been freed by you ?

ŚARVILAKA. Truly. And as soon as he had mounted the throne in Ujjayinī your friend, King Āryaka, bestowed on you the kingdom on the slopes of the coast !! Thus the first favour of a friend must be honoured.

Again Śarvilaka says to Vasantasenā (see *Mṛcchakaṭika* p. 259: this does not follow immediately, showing how the 'limbs' may be mixed with others [152]):

Lady Vasantasenā ! The King, delighted with you, favours you with the title of 'bride'.

VASANTASENĀ. Noble Śarvilaka ! I am satisfied.

Again Śarvilaka says to Cārudatta (same page):

Sir ! What should be done for this monk ?

CĀRUDATTA. Monk ! What would you esteem most ?

MONK. Seeing impermanence, I have come to esteem 'going forth' most.

CĀRUDATTA. Friend ! His resolve is firm. Therefore let him be made patriarch of all the monasteries on Earth !

ŚARVILAKA. So be it.

CĀRUDATTA. I am delighted !

VASANTASENĀ. Now my life is restored to me !

ŚARVILAKA. What should be done for Sthāvaraka ?

CĀRUDATTA. Let this good servant be freed from slavery.

ŚARVILAKA. As the noble one says !

1204. After the first of these quotations, the *śakāra* is dragged back, bound, with demands for his execution in the most painful way that can be devised. He begs Cārudatta to save him and the generous hero insists that he be released.

1205. There is a cry that Cārudatta's wife is trying to commit suicide by throwing herself into a fire (as *satī*, good wife), in order not to hear the news of his death: her maid and the jester are holding her back and Cārudatta rushes to show her he is alive, embracing his son who is clutching the hem of her garment. After they are reunited, and the jester has complimented the wife on her virtuous resolution which has brought back her husband, she sees Vasantasenā and welcomes her as a sister, embracing her. It is now that Śarvilaka reports that the king has bestowed on Vasantasenā the title of 'bride', in other words that she is released from the status of geisha and can become Cārudatta's lawful (second) wife. The play concludes thus with Cārudatta suitably rewarding some of the other characters, reaffirming his favour to the *śakāra* who has sought his protection and expressing his satisfaction at all his wishes being fulfilled, though adding a verse on the changes wrought by fate *vidhi*, who plays with us like buckets emptied and filled at a well. He recites a typical final benediction invoking prosperity and just rule.

1206. The critics have pointed out a few other elements in the construction of this play, showing further how the dramatic tension is maintained. Rāmacandra and Guṇacandra (*Nāṭyadarpaṇa* p. 77) find the limb 'alarm' *udvega* [148] of the embryo conjunction arising from Cārudatta being accused of theft and consisting in fear of the King. They do not quote. If this refers to the accusation in Act IX, then it is in the obstacle and illustrates Abhinavagupta's remark [152] that the limbs need not be confined to their proper conjunctions. More probably, however, it refers to Cārudatta's fear, at the end of Act III (verse 24), when he is told Vasantasenā's jewellery has been stolen from his house: no one will believe the truth, because of his poverty. In this case the 'alarm' foreshadows the eventual false accusation, though the immediate danger is averted when the thief, Śarvilaka, takes the stolen jewellery back to Vasantasenā in Act IV.

1207. The same critics then find (p. 87) an example of 'panic' *vidrava* as a limb of the obstacle conjunction in the resolve to kill Cārudatta : 'panic' is given by some writers in place of 'contradiction' *virodhana* which we now read in the *Nāṭyaśāstra* [149]; Rāmacandra and Guṇacandra mention this view and the example, but do not themselves accept it.

1208. Sāgaranandin (2815) notes a different kind of 'panic' *vidrava* in the Toy Cart, namely panic as proper for a cooperation [330]. Of the three kinds of such panic recommended by the *Nāṭyaśāstra* (Kāśī XX.66, 70, 74), Sāgaranandin points out an example of that arising from the blockade of a city when Āryaka is being pursued (this is developed at the end of Act VI: after his escape from prison all the city gates are guarded and persons passing through checked, but Āryaka is driven through in Cārudatta's carriage, the driver telling the guards that his passenger is Vasantasenā on her way to the Park).

1209. Rāmacandra and Guṇacandra (p. 43) name Śūdraka's Toy Cart as providing a good example of a play in which the sub-plot *patākā* [122] plays a dominant part in the action, as compared with the other elements of the matter. It is Āryaka's support, brought about through Cārudatta's having helped him earlier, which brings about the complete success of his friend at the conclusion (the appearance of Vasantasenā still alive no doubt saved him from imminent execution, but without the political revolution he would have remained at the mercy of his powerful enemy, who would surely have found some other way to do away with him; thus the conclusion would not have brought the action to an end, besides which only the King could make Vasantasenā Cārudatta's legal bride).

1210. These two critics have also (p. 45) discussed the role of 'fate' *daiva* in this play. In any play, the activities of the hero, his friend, his opponent and fate are shown in the five successive stages of the action, either singly or in combination. The action is in the unfolding of these four kinds of activities in one, two, three, four and five stages, successively (p. 44). But in the last stage, the 'attaining of the fruit', only the leading hero's activity is shown. Rāmacandra and Guṇacandra would not approve of a play in which fate, in the absence of human action, dominated the whole development from the 'commencement' stage onwards. Fate (or 'divine') and human activity should have regard to one another in bringing about good and bad results. Even in plays where the 'fruit' is supposed to depend on fate, that fate should have regard to human activity, the plays being composed for the development *saṃskāra* of the intellects of the audience (this may mean simply sharpening their intellects or being more positively educational, and we may think here of the Jaina insistence on the value of human action, since these are Jaina writers). As examples they name the Toy Cart and the *Puṣpadūṣitaka* [1367].

1211. In other words, although Śūdraka seems to lay considerable stress on the power of fate in the Toy Cart, these critics are satisfied that there is sufficient human action and that the human action is convincing and will thus develop the interest of the audience. If such critics, committed to the importance of the free human will, are satisfied, we may be satisfied too. Nevertheless fate is powerful in this play and has the last word, or rather is the last word, spoken by Cārudatta at the end (only the final benediction follows, which is not really part of the play, being the speech of an actor, not of a character). Fate *bhavitavyatā* is also mentioned in the Prologue (verse 7), when the Producer summarises the action. There is so much human activity in the Toy Cart, however, that the hidden ways of fate seem more than matched. It would appear to be a point strongly in favour of the attribution of the Vīṇā Vāsavadattā to this same Śūdraka, that in that play we find a similar combination of a powerful fate and strenuous human activity.

1212. The critics make a number of points on the Toy Cart as a fiction *prakaraṇa*. Rāmacandra and Guṇacandra are the most detailed here. After noting the main differences between a fiction and a *nāṭaka* ('history'), including their doctrine of degrees of inventedness and the types of hero, they say (II.4) that for the rest the fiction is like the *nāṭaka* but 'without fulness of the tender *kaiśiki*' [181] (mode of stage business). This of course does not mean that the tender, appropriate for the sensitive experience especially, is lacking in a fiction. On the contrary, as the *Nāṭyaśāstra* points out, both the fiction and the *nāṭaka* are distinguished by it, as compared with the other types of play. But, whereas in a *nāṭaka* the tender may be fully developed (for example in the plays about Udayana by Bhāsa and Śūdraka), these critics consider that in a fiction there is less scope for it, chiefly because of the types of characters and scenes portrayed. They even criticise a later dramatist (Bhavabhūti, +8) for developing too much of the tender in a fiction, or at least say this is contrary to the old method. They name (p. 106) the Toy Cart, along with the *Puṣpadūṣitaka* and *Taraṅgadatta* [1374], as examples of fictions of the regular kind in which the tender, though present, is restricted. The action of the Toy Cart, in fact, does not allow much scope for this mode. The scenes between Cārudatta and Vasantasenā are brief and Cārudatta, being poor, cannot be shown elegantly dressed; on the other hand in Act V Vasantasenā is required by a stage direction to be brilliantly dressed and there is a little development of the tender. The Vīṇā Vāsavadattā, with its music lesson and so on, shows the contrasting full development in a *nāṭaka*. [2264]

1213. In their preceding discussion on the types of fiction, Rāmacandra and Guṇacandra take up the different ideas about the 'mixed' type. According to Dhanika (p. 72), there are three kinds of fiction depending on the character of the heroine :

she may be a 'family' woman (as in the *Puṣpadūṣitaka*), or a geisha (as in the *Taraṅgadatta*), or there may be both kinds as in the Toy Cart (meaning Cārudatta's wife and Vasantasenā). He then adds that in a 'mixed' *saṃkīrṇa* fiction there is a 'rogue' *dhūrta* (as well as the usual minister, brahman or merchant hero), such as a gambler who cheats. He names the Toy Cart again as an example of this. This is not clear, because although there are gamblers in the play the only one who is prominent in the action is Saṃvāhaka, who is hardly a 'rogue'; on the other hand is the *śakāra* intended as the 'rogue', as seems more likely? Rāmacandra and Guṇacandra give the same threefold division according to the heroines, with the same examples for the first two (p. 104). For the third, with both kinds of heroine, they refer instead to a play with Mūladeva as hero and a parasite arranging affairs for him, probably the play we have referred to above [1142]. This kind of play they call 'mixed'. They then add that 'some' critics consider a play with a merchant as hero, if involved with a rogue, also as 'mixed', with the Toy Cart as an example. This appears to be a reference to Dhanika. They do not accept his view, retaining three kinds of fiction according to the heroines and seven divisions according to the degrees of inventedness.

1214. Śāradātanaya (p. 243) mentions the Toy Cart for having both kinds of heroine. Also the hero is a merchant. He also mentions the flamboyant dress and ornaments of a *śakāra* (p. 242) as a point of interest in a fiction, which we may understand as being of the utmost extravagance and bad taste. Śiṅgabhūpāla expresses a similar view (p. 285) of the Toy Cart as 'mixed', but the text is corrupt here (he appears to be following Dhanika).

1215. Dhanika has some more references to the Toy Cart. The hero (Cārudatta) is of the 'calmed' *śānta* type (p. 37; followed by Hemacandra, *Kāvyānuśāsana* VII.14) [99], to illustrate which he quotes the verse X.12, to which we have already been referred by the same critic [1199]. The heroine Vasantasenā loves Cārudatta (p. 48), a loving heroine being a necessary feature of a fiction and of most other types of play. Only in a comedy *prahasana* is it appropriate to have a heroine who does not love, for the sake of the comic effect this will produce. Rāmacandra and Guṇacandra make the same point (p. 179).

1216. Sāgaranandin (294-5) notes that the play concludes with the making of peace between Cārudatta and the *śakāra* (i.e. Cārudatta's enemy is not killed or otherwise disposed of). This is of course a perfectly regular type of ending, the example being adduced as a particularly good case to illustrate it (the Toy Cart is not actually named here, so that the reference could be to Bhāsa's play or to both).

1217. The construction of this play is so perfect that if we did not have the four available acts of the Impoverished Cārudatta we could not have suspected that the Toy Cart was not an entirely original composition. Perhaps there were even other plays on the story of Cārudatta. In fact we can be reasonably certain only that the scene which gives its name to the play—that of the toy cart in Act VI—is Śūdraka's own contribution. From this play we may learn that a 'fiction' may become sufficiently popular to stimulate the production of new versions of it, becoming thus, it would seem, a 'well-known' story and threatening the theoretical distinction between *nāṭaka* and *prakaraṇa*.

1218. A third play by Śūdraka (according to its manuscript tradition) is the satirical monologue *Padmaprābhṛtaka*, The Lotus Gift. The 'hero' of this play is Mūladeva, the legendary king of thieves (see towards the end of the last chapter, where a lost fiction on him is referred to [1142]). In this episode he is engaged in an affair with Devasenā, a sister of his better known mistress Devadattā. The parasite who actually acts the play is his friend Śaśa, sent to sound out Devasenā's state of mind. The scene is Ujjayinī—the same as in the other two plays ascribed to Śūdraka. It appears Mūladeva is in exile from Pāṭaliputra. The play is mostly occupied with the characters the parasite meets on his way through the city. The Prologue consists of a bare five verses on Love and Spring, at the end of which Śaśa enters abruptly but continues the discussion on Spring, which leads him naturally into an account of the affair with which he is now concerned, in order to remedy the love-sick state of Mūladeva.

1219. Śaśa meets more than a dozen characters on his way to Devasenā (in the satirical monologues of Vararuci and Īśvaradatta the parasites meet only half a dozen each), a rich and sharply contrasted collection. They include a poet, a tutor, another parasite, a grammarian, a hypocrite, an old parasite-actor, a drama student and a series of women who, though apparently all of the geisha community, exemplify several of the well recognised types of 'heroine' in love. Śaśa is especially fond of teasing everyone for their weaknesses and ridicules most of these characters. He knows everything that is going on in the geisha quarter, nothing is secret from him, and he takes care to keep up to date.

1220. The poet has chalked up a feeble verse on spring on the wall at the entrance of his house and is now playing with a yo-yo. Śaśa disturbs his trance and teases him as a cobbler of words cut out of old poems, rather than a man carried away by the goblin *piśāca* of poetry, as the poet absurdly claims to be. The parasite reads the verse, and it is indeed a flat piece of cobbling of the most conventional expressions, awkwardly tacked together without a spark of a poetic idea. However, as it says that this time (spring) gives a girl to a lover he takes it as a good omen for his errand and expresses the hope that the verse will make the poet famous and that he will not incur the envy of the Goddess of Speech (this might also carry the double meaning that he should not become conceited about his powers of expression—as if he had any to be conceited about).

1221. At this a laugh is heard: it is the tutor *piṭhamarda* [32], who remarks on the absurdity of worshipping this lord of speech with speech, like trying to make the sea wet. Śaśa calls the tutor an ignoramus, pointing out that in fact the Sun is worshipped with lamps, the Sea with water and Spring with flowers. He has displayed his tutor-nature, i.e. that his livelihood depends on the support of others (he teaches for a fee, not being rich enough to be a private gentleman, or *nāgaraka*), like the cuckoo supported by, reared by, another bird. Śaśa simply hints at this by wishing that the tutor may be like the spring, not a mere deception of 'supported by others' (cuckoo) chatter (presumably, that he might produce some spontaneous, unpaid ideas, or independent ideas having some real meaning).

1222. The grammarian Dattakalaśi, 'Offered Waterpot', is a Pāṇinīyan furious after a battle of words with some Kātantrikas, who apparently outnumbered him 'like a multitude of crows'. His language in conversation with Śaśa bristles with learned forms, extremely cacophonous in effect as well as hard to understand. Śaśa complains he is striking him with 'speech-thunderbolts'. The grammarian is a rascal fond of the geishas, and the parasite ridicules him for his harsh language, toughened in verbal disputes, sure to repel women.

1223. The hypocrite is making his way very fastidiously along the street, avoiding contact with unknown persons (for reasons of ritual purity), holding his nose and—Śaśa remarks to him—charming as a tortoise on hot ground. The parasite knows that he secretly visits a harlot and teases him for making this kind of pilgrimage. Seeing eventually that the game is up and Śaśa not only knows about his affairs but will never believe he has changed his habits, the hypocrite capitulates and asks to become the parasite's pupil. After warning him that hypocrisy is a barrier to the love of the geishas and must be discarded, Śaśa solemnly accepts him as a student-parasite.

1224. Śaśa thus reforms the hypocrite, but he can only pour ridicule and contempt on a young brahman and a Buddhist monk whom he meets in the harlots' quarter. A gardener's daughter, who had fallen in love with him, had sent a Buddhist nun as messenger to the young brahman. The nun being attractive, the brahman forcibly made love to her, instead of waiting for the properly prepared liaison to be arranged, and is now living with the nun in his house. The brahman tries to justify himself by saying that a man should not abandon a present happiness for the sake of a future one. The debauched monk is disguised in a dirty cloak as he hurries away from a harlot's house, but Śaśa sees the edge of his brown monk's robe showing underneath and accosts him. The monk then pretends he has only been to console the girl after the death of her mother, and quickly excuses himself on the ground that he must avoid having to eat at the wrong time. The parasite laughs at this concern for propriety when one of the major rules has been broken, but expresses his disgust as the monk vanishes.

1225. Śaśa makes fun of the old actor of parasite parts, nicknamed Old Ox by the geishas, who has dyed his hair and tries to look and act like a young man. The drama student escapes being teased : he comes out of the house of Devadattā and Devasenā as Śaśa approaches it and gives him the useful information that Devadattā is out. He has been sent to Devasenā by their teacher to give her her part in the fiction *Kumudvatī*

[753] and she has accepted it, though not feeling well; now she is in the garden.

1226. Among the women Śaśa meets, Vanarājikā is a young girl of the harlot's quarter, encountered as she leaves the temple of Love, whom he flatters for her fresh beauty, hinting that in due course he will introduce her to a lover. Priyaṅguyaṣṭikā also is a maiden, apparently slightly younger but already full of the consciousness of the flush of new excitement in her loins, which beguiles her as she plays ball with her girl friends. For Śaśa she unites various kinds of playful coquetry, emotions, provocative movements and 'amiability' (so highly praised by Devilaka in the Dialogue of the Rogue and the Parasite [1122]). After a flattering speech he asks her not to forget him.

1227. The *Nāṭyaśāstra* (XXIV.203 ff. Kāśī) describes eight 'heroines', actually situations of a heroine, in or after union with a lover or husband. Of these, Śūdraka seems deliberately to have illustrated at least four in this play. Tāmbūlasenā exemplifies the fortunate woman 'whose lover is dependent on her' *svādhīnapatikā* and continually at home making love to her. The parasite passing by the house stops momentarily to interrupt their bliss and teases Tāmbūlasenā when she comes to the door. She looks exhausted but is apparently ashamed of making love in the daytime as well as at night, wishing to conceal an excess evidently regarded as disgraceful, or at least as ridiculous. Seeing her wish for concealment, the parasite is not satisfied until he has given her a thorough teasing. When finally he points out that getting up in haste she has put on two left shoes, she runs in to her lover and laughs loudly. The lover calls out to Śaśa to come in, but he declines to interrupt their love feast longer and passes on.

1228. Kumudvatī is one 'whose lover has gone abroad' *proṣitapatikā* and is languishing for him during his absence. Śaśa has heard that this lover is a Maurya prince, Candrodaya, who has been sent to put down a rebellious feudatory. She is sadly offering food to a crow under the eaves of the house and asking it whether her beloved will return while she is still alive : indeed she eclipses respectable family women!

1229. Śoṇadāsī has quarrelled with her lover and is 'separated by a quarrel' *kalahāntaritā*. Śaśa finds her sitting in the courtyard of her house full of remorse, consoling herself a little with her lute. In such cases the main obstacle to reunion is pride on both sides. Śoṇadāsī tells the parasite that her pride is now conquered by love but she is afraid the lover might scorn her, particularly as she suspects he is having an affair with another girl. After some discussion Śaśa promises to effect a reconciliation.

1230. Finally Śaśa sees Magadhasundarī watching from the outer entrance to her house, keeping herself half hidden behind the opened door and singing with an impassioned voice. From her radiant appearance she confidently expects the arrival of her lover and has everything prepared for him: she is one 'who has her home ready' *vāsakaṣajjā*. The parasite jokes with her and passes on.

1231. It is immediately after this that Śaśa meets the drama student as mentioned above. Being told that Devasenā is not feeling well he suspects that what is really disturbing her is that she is in love with Mūladeva. Emboldened to complete his mission he goes to her in the garden, where she is enjoying the breeze with a confidential attendant, and gradually overcomes her reticence and shame. The *Kumudvati* part, which he takes from her and reads, helps him in this, since he is able to make her admit indirectly that her feelings are the same as those of the romantic princess. Yet she still will not speak openly. To make her speak he remarks casually that he is not really interested in other people's secrets, says goodbye, explaining that he must hurry to see Mūladeva, and starts to walk away. At this she breaks down and sobs out that she will die. He rushes back to her and insists that Mūladeva is as much in love as she is (she does not trust him and that is why she has held back). Then at last she begs him to consider what they can do. With the helpful advice of the attendant, who undertakes to manage things with Devadattā, it is decided that Devasenā shall go to Mūladeva. Thus she will be one 'who goes to meet (her lover)', another of the types of heroine in love of the *Nāṭya-śāstra* (the *abhisārikā*). Śaśa suggests she send a lotus as love-token to Mūladeva, after biting and bruising it slightly and sighing over it. She agrees and the play ends as he takes it, whence the title Lotus Gift.

1232. A number of references by the critics to the Toy Cart have been indicated above. Evidently it was picked out by them as a brilliant example of a 'fiction', showing all the recognised characteristics of the type. In addition, several commentaries were written on the play. The other two plays attributed to Śūdraka seem hardly to have been noticed by the critics. The quotations from the Vīṇā Vāsavadattā and Lotus Gift in the Anubandha to Chapter XVI of M.R. Kavi's edition of the *Abhinavabhāratī* are supplied by the editor, not by Abhinavagupta, though he claims to have followed (unidentified) old critics in giving them. The Lotus Gift is quoted by Hemacandra (+12) according to Loman in his edition of the play (p. 74), but we have not been able to find the quotation in the edition of the *Kāvyānuśāsana* used here. The Vīṇā Vāsavadattā is referred to in the *Abhijñānaśākuntalacarcā* (pp. 2 and 26). Krishnamachariar (p. 854) suggests that the *Naṭāṅkuśa* (+15) also refers to that play (the scene of Yaugandharāyaṇa's faked suicide), though he does not make it clear that the reference is specifically to this play (the Dream Vāsavadattā also has a description of a faked death of Yaugandharāyaṇa, though it is not shown on the stage). The earliest apparent quotations from the Toy Cart are in the *Pañcatantra* (+4?) [1249] (II.34 and 40 = *Mṛcchakaṭika* I.8 and 14), of verses on poverty from the Prologue and Act I.

1233. Śūdraka is praised by Daṇḍin (+7) at the beginning of his novel *Avantisundarī* (introductory verse 9), among the old *kavis* he admires. Śūdraka conquered the world twice, first with his sword and then with speech signifying his own acts. It is uncertain at present how we are to understand the last phrase. It is possible that Śūdraka wrote an autobiography not now available. The reference could hardly be merely to the brief sketch of the author in the Prologue to the Toy Cart. It may be to the acts of the character Āryaka in the Toy Cart, if Śūdraka became king himself in a similar way. Some such adventure of Śūdraka in Ujjayinī is narrated by Daṇḍin himself, in the *Avantisundarī* (pp. 200-1), but the edition is too corrupt to be clear (cf. *Sāra* IV. 184 *ff.*). In that adventure, Śūdraka had a friend Bandhudatta: Krishnamachariar (p. 578) has suggested that Cārudatta represents him in the play. It may be added that the Vīṇā Vāsavadattā also contains the adventure of an escape from Ujjayinī (by a captive king), whilst Mūladeva in Ujjayinī in the Lotus Gift was also, according to other sources [1142], a prince (an exile in this case).

1234. Vāmana (+8) refers (III.2.4, end) to Śūdraka as an exponent of 'union' *śleṣa* as a quality of meaning [243], unfortunately without quoting (for an example in Amaruka see below [1473]). With Vāmana this implies a compact style rather than double meanings. Perhaps the quotations above will sufficiently illustrate this compactness. It is not in fact incompatible with occasional significant ambiguities having dramatic effect. Vāmana quotes (IV.3.23) from the Toy Cart (prose before II.7) for an example of the figure 'distinction' *viśeṣokti* [230]:

> For gambling is indeed a kingdom for a man, without a throne.

1235. Kulaśekhara (+900) in the Prologue to his *Tapatisaṃvaraṇa* (p. 4) has an actress refer to Śūdraka as a 'great *kavi*', followed by Kālidāsa, Harṣa and Daṇḍin evidently in chronological order. His contemporary Rājaśekhara, as noted above, names Śūdraka as a famous patron, though we have no information on whom he patronised. Kalhaṇa (+12) mentions him for his heroic qualities, comparing him with Vikramāditya for his goodness and firmness (III.343).

1236. We have seen some of the discussions on Śūdraka by Dhanika, Bhoja, Sāgaranandin, Rāmacandra and Guṇacandra, Śāradātanaya and Siṅgabhūpāla, critics of the +10 to +14. Viśvanātha in the +15 (*Sāhityadarpaṇa* pp. 298-9) copies a reference from Dhanika. Bhoja probably (the edition is dislocated) gives the following from the Toy Cart as an example of play on words *vākkelī* [326], a limb of the street play (*Śṛṅgāraprakāśa* II p. 495). Cārudatta mistakes Vasantasenā, when she first slips into his house to escape from the *śakāra*, for his servant girl Radanikā (presumably a case of the 'other conjunction' 'error' [141]). He hands her a mantle, telling her to put it on his son Rohasena. Vasantasenā's speeches here are all aside, she does not reply to Cārudatta :

> VASANTASENĀ. What ? Does he take me for a servant? [*Takes the mantle and smells it..*].... It seems his youth is not indifferent. [*Secretly puts the mantle on*].
>
> CĀRUDATTA. Radanikā ! Aren't you going to take Rohasena in ?

VASANTASENĀ. I am unlucky, in you !

CĀRUDATTA. Radanikā ! Don't you even answer ? Alas :

When a man attains that state tried by fate
—oppressed by the loss of his fortune—
Then even his friends become no friends,
even people long loyal to him become disloyal.
(I.53)

(The word play here is Vasantasenā taking up Cārudatta's 'in', which in Sanskrit implies in the heart, and again in the words 'friends' and 'loyal' in his verse. The same incident occurs in Bhāsa's Impoverished Cārudatta, but with variations and a different verse.)

In his *Sarasvatīkaṇṭhābharaṇa* (p. 692) Bhoja quotes Toy Cart VIII.22 [1195] to illustrate the character *śakāra*.

1237. Namisādhu illustrating Rudraṭa VIII.1 quotes Toy Cart IV.14 for its simile on harlots—like a jasmine in a cemetery. The anthologist Vidyākara quotes (57) one verse, in *sragdharā* metre, from Śūdraka, the opening benediction of the Toy Cart:

Whose knees are encircled by the doubled twisting of
the snake whose coils form his couch,
whose breath controlled within checks his senses and
suppresses the knowledge of every (separate) thing,
Whose seeing of reality is a seeing of the world soul with
its faculties vanished in himself,
may Śiva's concentration protect you ! —which,
through seeing nothing, is fixed on *brahman* as the
dissolution of compounded things ! (I.1)

This verse recalls the benediction of Dhīranāga, also quoted by the anthologist [1139]. It perhaps represents a benedictory style, which Vidyākara enjoyed, rather than the individual style of Śūdraka. It may also illustrate the preference of the later medieval connoisseurs and critics, in poetry. Our general impression from their discussions is that Śūdraka was greatly appreciated as a dramatist but was rarely found interesting as a poet or stylist. Only Vāmana seems to have admired his relatively simple, but compact and effective, style, though perhaps Daṇḍin liked this too.

1238. Probably of the +3 is the anonymous lyric poem *Ṛtusaṃhāra*, 'Review of the Seasons', often ascribed to Kālidāsa but almost certainly not by him on stylistic grounds. The poem consists of six short cantos of detached verses, each devoted to one of the six seasons of the Indian year. The verses are simple and straightforward descriptions of the seasons, their characteristic flowers, birds and other phenomena and especially their influence on lovers. Figures of speech are rare and the whole may be regarded as 'naturalistic description' *svabhāvokti*, whilst the metrical arrangements are those of Sanskrit epics: a simpler metre (usually *vaṃśastha*) for most of the canto and something more brilliant for the concluding verses (the *mālinī* is evidently the author's favourite metre) ; the *vasantatilaka* is used for both purposes. The poet is throughout describing the seasons to his sweetheart and ends each canto with a benediction, that the season may bring her happiness.

1239. Many of the stock conventions of Indian classical poetry are found in the 'Review', particularly the natural phenomena supposed to be associated with each season, and the vocabulary similarly covers much of the standard *kāvya* stock of expressions without bringing in anything unusual or recondite. The effect is simple and elegant. The first canto describes summer, probably so as to leave spring for the climax of a poem whose aesthetic experience is the sensitive. The heat of summer brings lassitude and some respite from love in the universal quest for coolness. Animals behave strangely : those which are natural enemies mingle peacefully. The lion is too thirsty to take any notice of elephants, which in turn are not afraid of lions, being aware only of thirst. The cobra rests right under the peacock (supposed to kill snakes), whilst the frog seeks shade under the cobra's hood. Terrible forest fires break out and the animals escape to the rivers. Lovers take their pleasure at night, especially where there are fountains; the lightest clothes are worn and sandalwood paste is much used.

1240. The rains, reawakening nature, bring about the maturity of love and painful longings, tormenting those whose lovers are away (cf. the Broken Pot, end of Chapter XVIII above). Women are emboldened to go to meet their lovers under the cover of dark, cloudy nights, seeing their way in the flashes of lightning : once united with them they embrace closely, trembling at the thunder and lightning. This is the season loved by the peacocks, which sing and dance. Rainbows appear, and the red 'Indra's herdsmen' insects (cf. the old Pali lyric on the rains in Chapter XI [556, 651]). The rivers are in spate, washing away trees from their banks, their waters full of mud, and are compared (one of the very few similes in this poem) with spoiled women in their wild behaviour. The *kadambas* and white jasmine are already beginning to flower (but will continue into the next season), more characteristic of the rains are the *ketaki* (Pandanus odoratissimus), *bakula* (Mimusops elengi), *yūthikā* jasmine and *arjuna* (Terminalia arjuna).

1241. In autumn the air is clear and consequently the Moon and stars brilliant, all nature is fresh after the rains and the breezes, stirring many blossoms, especially the heavily scented white jasmine, stimulate thoughts of love. The rivers flow more slowly and become clear, *śapharī* fish can be seen glittering in them. The rice begins to ripen. Wild geese, ducks and cranes are conspicuous. Every kind of lotus and waterlily flowers, along with the *bandhūka* or *bandhujiva* (Pentapetes phoenicea) tree, the *kovidāra* and *saptacchada* (Alstonia scholaris), as well as the *kāśa* grass (Saccharum spontaneum). The red *aśoka* is also mentioned (as *kaṅkeli*), though it is generally associated with spring.

1242. In winter the cool lakes with their blue waterlilies steal men's thoughts and lovers sleep closer together. The rice is ripe and deer are seen (gleaning in the fields?) and curlews *krauñcas*. The red *lodhra* flowers (Symplocos racemosa) are characteristic of this season.

1243. The warmth of love is still more welcome in the cold season *śiśira*, when windows are closed and fires used for heating. This is the time to think of food: molasses, rice and sugar-cane, as well as liquor. Nothing is said of flowers outside, only the herons are still noticed standing in the rice fields. There are severe frosts and even snow.

1244. Spring is the season who makes new conquests for love, when all nature becomes beautiful. He uses a bow whose string is a garland of bees to shoot sharp arrows which are mango flowers into the minds of lovers : this bow and arrow is in the final verse, and generally, wielded by Love himself, so perhaps we should interpret *vasantayoddhā* in the first verse as 'who has spring as a warrior', i.e. Love (understood), instead of simply as 'the warrior spring'. The bow itself is a flowery red *kiṃśuka* tree (final verse). Besides the mango and *kiṃśuka* flowers and the bees, the chief characteristics of spring are the cuckoo, the red *aśoka* and yellow *karṇikāra* flowers, the *mallikā* and *kunda* jasmines and the amaranth *kurabaka*, but there are many other flowers in this 'flower-month'. Finally the breeze from the (Southern) Malaya Mountains, accompanying the bodiless God of Love, increases the general intoxication.

1245. Possibly of this same period is the *Śṛṅgāratilaka*, 'Ornament of the Sensitive' (*tilaka* = a decorative mark, especially on the forehead), also improbably ascribed to Kālidāsa, a collection of about thirty detached strophes (the number varies in different recensions) portraying love. The verses describe the states of mind of lovers usually through their own supposed words or thoughts, bringing in sometimes fanciful comparisons. For example the first verse contains a 'complete metaphor' in the manner of Aśvaghoṣa :

> The two arms are lotus-fibre (stalks), the face the lotus
> flower, the charm the play of the water,
> the buttocks the rocks on the beach, the eyes the
> *śapharī* fish, the braid the pond weed,
> The beloved's breasts are a pair of ruddy sheldrakes—
> Brahmā has created a delightful lake
> for those burned by the fires of Love's arrows to bathe
> in.

1246. On account of its somewhat miscellaneous nature the collection might be an anthology. Two verses recall the veiled invitations of the 'Seven Hundred', *Sattasaī*, another the first verse of Vararuci's 'Both Go to Meet'—a jealous woman affecting to send her lover off to his assumed real beloved. We have also a philosophical reflection :

Some stupid person here has defined 'release' *mokṣa*
as a state without qualities,
in which both happiness and unhappiness are unknown,
But in my opinion 'release' is the release of the knot of
the garment
of a girl with intoxicating eyes as she murmurs with
passion, pulled by a youth smiling with love.

1247. Typical of the lovers' speeches in the collection is :

If your heart has become angry, lotus eyes,
I regret that there may be another obstacle there for
you—
Give me back the strong embrace which I gave you
before
and give me back in full the kiss which I gave you !

Chapter XXI

PROSE IN THE +3 AND +4; SARVASENA AND EPIC

1248. The Vākāṭaka rulers of Mahārāṣṭra (Vidarbha and adjacent countries), who supplanted the Ābhīras and others from the middle of the +3 and built up an extensive empire in the Deccan, patronised a considerable flowering of the arts, including for example the finest paintings at Ajaṇṭā. It has been suggested above that the *vaidarbha* style, named after Vidarbha, flourished and became well known through their encouragement [190]. The founder of the Vākāṭaka Empire, Vindhyaśakti I (*c.* +250 to 280), was a brahman and he and his successors seem to have wished to further a revival of Brahmanical civilisation, including the Vedic rituals, though they were evidently tolerant of Buddhism. The *Purāṇas*, whose lists of kings end at the beginning of the +4, appear to view the Vākāṭakas in a relatively favourable light, after so many dynasties of upstart helots and vicious barbarians, and even as the main hope for the future of civilisation. It is worthy of remark that the king in the framework of the *Pañcatantra*, and his three sons who are instructed by Viṣṇuśarman, all have names ending in —*śakti*. This is not a very common ending and helps to confirm the impression that that work was written in the Vākāṭaka Empire.

1249. The *Pañcatantra* is one of the most famous works of Indian literature, both in India and throughout the world. The popularity which led to so many translations resulted also in countless 'editions' in India itself in its original Sanskrit language. Consequently we find several different recensions of the text, embodying attempts at improvement and enlargement by various editors. Much critical work has been done with a view to restoring the original *Pañcatantra* and here we may follow Edgerton's *Pañcatantra Reconstructed* as probably a close approximation to this. The authorship and date of this original remain uncertain. The narrator appearing in the text itself is called Viṣṇuśarman and no other author of the *Pañcatantra* seems anywhere to be mentioned. The date would seem to be in the region of the +4, it might be somewhat earlier. It is possible to point out similarities to Śūdraka in certain places (e.g. verses deploring poverty, including two apparently quoted from the Toy Cart[1232]), but hardly to support any chronological conclusions from them. Perhaps the author of the *Mugdhakathā*, to be considered later in this Chapter, knew the *Pañcatantra*, which would fix the date as not much later than +400. The text seems to imply that it was written in the South (Deccan), which might then mean the Vākāṭaka Empire unless the date is before +250.

1250. The *Pañcatantra* is an 'illustrating novel' *nidarśana-kathā*, the subject of which is *nīti*, 'policy', applicable in both private affairs and public politics. Its title may mean either 'Five Divisions (of the science of policy)' or 'Five Systems'. The whole is presented in the framework of the problem of educating three young princes averse to formal study. The problem is solved by the ancient sage Viṣṇuśarman, who takes up the challenge to his intelligence by instructing the princes through the medium of story telling. There follow five main narratives, the *tantras*, illustrating successively the topics of splitting an alliance (or a friendship) contrary to one's interests, forming an alliance, making war, outwitting and despoiling a fool and lastly the folly of action without reflection. These narratives contain a number of subsidiary emboxed short stories, illustrating points made by the characters. The five *tantras* are unequal in length, which perhaps encouraged later editors to add to the shorter ones. These additions were mostly of further short stories, tending to change the character of the original work to a collection of stories instead of five main narratives with an occasional incidental story. The sharpness of the satirical element in the *Pañcatantra* is enhanced by most of its narratives being beast fables. Since the sources of 'Viṣṇu-śarman' are often discussed and parallels or prototypes drawn for his stories from, for example, the Pali *Jātaka* and the *Mahābhārata*, it is well to stress that the *Pañcatantra* does not give the impression of being a kind of anthology of good stories. On the contrary it is very much of a piece and a stylistic unity, as well as a splendid model of narrative art. The incidental stories are strictly to the point and seem to have been created, or at least recreated, for the occasion.

1251. The subject being policy and political craft, in fact part of 'wealth' *artha*, ethical considerations seem to be regarded as irrelevant, except that when choosing a reliable ally his good character would be a clear asset. Human nature and political manoeuvres are shown realistically and human traits only amusingly pointed up through the interposition of animal characters. The vanity of the lion king, and the way in which he is led this way and that by his jackal minister and his scruples are suppressed, is brilliantly described. The lesson is reinforced in an ironical manner by the victim of the intrigue himself telling Damanaka a story (I No. 8) of a scrupulous lion king approving a murderous trap planned by a crow, his follower. After this cynical first *tantra* the contrasting alliance in the second of the crow, tortoise, deer and rat against a hunter is wholly delightful, though conducted with careful regard to the rules of prudence and illustrating certain dangerous weaknesses of character in its heroes. The war between the crows and the owls in the third *tantra* gives the opportunity for much display of political learning, through the characters of the ministers on both sides, until the more practical cunning of an elder minister of the crow king, insinuating himself into the confidence of the enemy, brings about the destruction of the owls. The last two books are short. The old *Jātaka* story of the monkey outwitting the crocodile shows how a fool is tricked into giving up his gains. The last *tantra* has a human hero for once, a brahman with a devoted pet mongoose which saves his child from a snake; seeing the mongoose covered with blood the brahman jumps to the conclusion that it has attacked the child and kills his benefactor.

1252. All this is narrated in a polished *kāvya* prose style, with a good many interspersed verses. Long descriptions, generally characteristic of *kāvya* prose, are almost entirely avoided here, but despite this restraint the prose is rich and fluent. Let us see how at the beginning of his story Viṣṇuśarman effects the transition from the world of men to the world of animals and launches Saṃjīvaka on his fatal adventure :

> Then as he (the caravan merchant Vardhamānaka) was going through a great forest, in a certain place one of those bulls, Saṃjīvaka, crippling a foot, which sank in he mud produced by water splashing from a waterfall

plunging from far down a mountain; through the weight of the excessive load in the cart, by the power of fate, somehow broke his yoke and collapsed. The caravan merchant Vardhamānaka saw him and was filled with utter despair. And after waiting for three days, when the bull still didn't recover his strength, he appointed guards for him and, thinking that there were many risks in the forest, in order to protect the rest of the caravan set out according to his wish for another region. But the next day the guards, thinking only of their own danger, came on and lied to him : 'Master, Saṃjīvaka is dead and we have honoured him with fire and so on'. After hearing that the caravan merchant through gratitude performed the funeral rite and went on. But Saṃjīvaka, as some of his life still remained, had his body refreshed by very cool breezes mingled with water, got up with difficulty and very slowly drew near the bank of the Yamunā. And there, eating tips of the grass which resembled emeralds, wandering at will, in a few days he became strong like Śiva's Bull, with a joyful thriving body having a full hump. And every day he kept on tearing off the tops of anthills with a toss of the tips of his horns and bellowing.

Now in that forest, not far away, a lion named Piṅgalaka, attended by all the animals in the forest, continued enjoying the happiness of the sovereignty gained by his own energy, fearlessly carrying his head high...

1253. Among the critics, Bhoja (*Śṛṅgāraprakāśa* II p. 469), followed by Hemacandra (p. 463), names the *Pañcatantra* first among examples of *nidarśanās*. In this connection he notes that a *nidarśanā* shows what ought to be done and what ought not to be done (*kārya* and *akārya*, evidently from a purely practical, not an ethical, point of view) and that it may show the actions of animals or non-animals (humans).

1254. The *Mugdhakathā*, 'Story of Simpletons', is known to us only indirectly. There exists in a Chinese translation, made in +492, the *Po Yu King* (The Hundred Comparisons) of Guṇavṛddhi, a version of a Buddhist tract by Saṃghasena apparently entitled 'Garland of Flowers' (**Puṣpamālā* or a synonym?). It contains 97 short stories of simpletons in everyday life, each of whom is compared with a seeker after enlightenment or *nirvāṇa*, such as a Buddhist monk or a student of some other philosophy, who fails to see the true state of things (i.e. understand the Buddhist doctrine or apply it properly). Somadeva's *Kathāsaritsāgara* (Lambaka X, Taraṅgas 5-8, Śaktiyaśas) has a collection of stories of simpletons under the title *Mugdhakathā* mingled with his condensation of the contrasting *Pañcatantra* as Prājñakathā, 'stories of the intelligent', suggesting an associated work also in five books. This collection contains versions of about half those found in the Chinese work, plus a few others, in Sanskrit verse. It is evidently a paraphrase of the original and probably preserves the original title. Kṣemendra's *Bṛhatkathāmañjari* (XVI 568 ff) also has versions of some of these stories, following his version of the *Pañcatantra*, introducing them as showing the comic acts of unintelligent human beings contrasting with the skill of the wise, even animals, just described. His title is *Murkhākhyāyikā*, 'History of Fools'. It is worth noting that the idea of collecting stories of foolish behaviour is anticipated at least as early as the Pali *Digha Nikāya* (No. 23, *Pāyāsi Suttanta*, Vol.II,316ff)[608], where they are framed in a Buddhist dialogue and serve a purpose similar to that of the Hundred Comparisons. The *Mugdhakathā* stories were probably emboxed in frame stories and the whole in some general framework, but it is not clear how this was done. The additional stories in the Hundred Comparisons seem to be a not very skilful supplement to the original work, drawing on other sources.

1255. We can illustrate the *Mugdhakathā* by summarising the story which appears to have stood first in it. A young man hoping to establish himself in business travelled by sea and gradually collected a quantity of fragrant aloe wood, which took him several years. He then attempted to sell it in the market, but because of the very high price no one would buy. After some days of failure he noticed a seller of wood charcoal nearby doing brisk business. Disgusted with his aloe wood he decided that the best thing would be to burn it and make saleable charcoal from it. He did so, but did not get even the price of half the quantity of ordinary charcoal for it.

1256. The last story (Book V No. 6?) seems to have been the following one. A married couple had three pancakes and decided to divide them between them. They ate one each and then, having one left, agreed that whoever spoke first should surrender it to the other. For a long time neither spoke. Then some thieves broke into the house and proceeded to loot it. Intent on their contest, the couple looked on in silence. Seeing this, the thieves proceeded to carry off the wife as well, under the eyes of her husband. He remained silent. Then the wife cried out : 'Stop thief !' and called her husband a fool for watching the thieves in silence for the sake of a pancake. But the husband clapped his hands with delight, saying that he had won the pancake and would not let her have it.

1257. It is unlikely that the style of the *Mugdhakathā* was any more elaborate than that of the *Pañcatantra*. If we are to gain an idea of the development of *kāvya* prose in the full scale novel, where its scope was unchecked, we shall have to find evidence elsewhere. No full scale novel ('standard' novel) appears to have survived intact in its original form from before the +6 (Subandhu), those of Guṇāḍhya and Pādalipta discussed above being known only through abridged paraphrases. In connection with Śūra (Chapter XVII) we considered the development of prose style in his time, contrasting his restraint with the fashion of long sentences and long compounds reflected for example in certain inscriptions [928].

1258. In order to illustrate this inflated fashion as applied in a long prose narrative of the +3 we may look at the *Gaṇḍavyūha Sūtra*, a Buddhist text of that period which, though presented as a *sūtra* (and therefore *āgama*, included in the Mahāyāna Buddhist canon), is in fact a religious novel. The *Gaṇḍavyūha* is a fictitious prose narrative of great length (in the region of 500 pages, more or less according to the edition), the story of a novice *bodhisattva*, named Sudhana, in his quest for enlightenment. It is a literary masterpiece, the most readable of all the Mahāyāna *sūtras* and organised as a work of art building up steadily to its grand climax, the meeting of Sudhana with Maitreya (who is to be the next *buddha* in our world).

1259. Sudhana was the son of a rich merchant of Dhanyākara (in Āndhra, where probably the *Gaṇḍavyūha* was written). There he hears the *bodhisattva* Mañjuśrī ('Sweet Fortune') teaching (in a preliminary scene which stamps the work as a *sūtra* the Buddha is introduced with his assembly of *bodhisattvas* in Śrāvastī, Kośala, whence Mañjuśrī sets out to teach in the

South). On account of his favourable disposition, the result of previous good actions, Sudhana is excited with the thought of attaining enlightenment and becomes a *bodhisattva*. Mañjuśrī gives him some instruction and starts him on the way of the *bodhisattvas*, advising him to be tireless in the quest for 'good friends' who will teach and guide him. He then sends him off to such a friend, a monk. The monk teaches him and then sends him on to another friend, and in the same way Sudhana's wanderings continue all over India. Altogether he meets 52 good friends, representing all classes of society (also gods and goddesses). Most follow ordinary worldly professions, i.e. are not withdrawn monks or nuns, for this is Mahāyāna Buddhism which stresses that the *bodhisattva's* way can very well be followed in society, is even most properly followed where most good can be done in the way of teaching and example. The *Gaṇḍavyūha* praises constructive worldly occupations, in fact, as forms of well doing. One good friend is a slave. Twenty are women or goddesses, surely a remarkable approximation to sexual equality in a field of high philosophical and moral endeavour, such as most societies have tended to reserve for men. Under the guidance of his successive friends Sudhana increases his knowledge and understanding and learns various forms of meditation. Thus he is taught compassion and friendliness (loving kindness, *maitri*) by a friend (the third) who lives on the sea coast of South India, contemplating the vastness of the ocean, which is like the inconceivable mind of the 'thus-gone' (Buddha). But this friend sends him on to another who can teach him more of the details of the way of a *bodhisattva*.

1260. Eventually Sudhana returns to South India, after travelling in the North, and comes to Samudrakaccha (fictitious?) on the coast, where Maitreya (friend No. 51) lives in a pavilion in a park. (In Buddhist tradition Maitreya lives among the gods, awaiting his time to be born in the life in which he will become a *buddha*; bringing him down to earth is from the Buddhist point of view fictitious as well as symbolic.) This pavilion is very elaborately conceived and the inflated prose style here rises to its highest pitch of sustained description. From the grammatical point of view these vast sentences are simple, they consist of grammatically parallel clauses continued indefinitely until the narrator has achieved what seems to be a complete enumeration of particulars. Similarly there is no definite limit to the possible length of a compound, within which of course all inflections disappear and we have a long string of juxtaposed words constituting a clause. Similes and other figures are piled up in parallel clauses giving a sense of magnificence and infinity. This pavilion of potentiality indeed embraces the whole universe. A favourite figure here is the 'contradiction' *virodha* [231] of opposed qualities or actions, demonstrating a transcending many-sidedness or the ultimate harmony below the stormy surface of phenomena. The pavilion is called the 'embryo of the ornament of the arrays of illuminations', which is one compound word in Sanskrit and a typical *Gaṇḍavyūha* expression ('embryo' implies potentiality). It is the dwelling place of those who delight in emptiness, signlessness and uncommittedness (i.e. of *bodhisattvas*). These inhabitants experience the complete interpenetration of all parts of time and space and of all principles. Their seemingly contradictory qualities include for example equanimity plus not abandoning the world of living beings, they have understood the truths of Buddhism (which should lead to abandonment of everything worldly) yet they do not leave the world (because of their compassion, the desire to help others).

1261. Maitreya is outside his pavilion with a crowd of followers. He welcomes Sudhana and then discusses the thought of attaining enlightenment with him, using many metaphors :

> For the thought of enlightenment...is the great ocean in which are gathered together the jewels of all good qualities, it is (Mount) Mahāmeru (the North Pole) for the thought of the equality of all beings [5089], it is a horizon for sheltering all the worlds, it is the Himālaya for growing the herbs of knowledge, it is (Mount) Gandhamādana for being the abode of the scents of all good qualities, it is the sky for the expansion of great qualities, it is a lotus for being undefiled by all the principles of the world, it is a thoroughbred horse for being without all unruliness, it is a charioteer for the Great Carriage to go forward without flinching, it is the medicine for curing the disease of attachment, it is the Underworld for purifying all bad

> principles, it is a thunderbolt for penetrating all principles... (p. 494—and so on for more than 60 lines of text).

Maitreya then continues with some similes :

> ...Now, son of a (good) family (*kulaputra*, this is an ordinary respectful form of address), just as there is a herb called 'fearless' through which the five fears do not exist, namely one is not burned by fire, nor affected by poison, nor wounded by a sword, nor carried away by water, nor overcome by smoke; just so, son of a family, the *bodhisattva* who holds the herb of the thought of omniscience is not burned by the fire of passion, is not affected by the poison of the sense objects, is not wounded by the sword of attachment, is not carried away by the flood of transmigration, is not overcome by the smoke of intentions (p. 496)...(and so on with many more comparisons)...just as, son of a family, there is a kind of tree called the 'coconut', which grows where the ocean rises, which, depending on its root and up to the limit of its flowers and fruits never at any time ceases to be lived upon by all beings; just so the first occurrence of the thought of omniscience of a *bodhisattva*, arising from the root of his commitment to great compassion, up to the conclusion of his being established in good principles, never ceases to be lived upon by the world including the gods; just as, son of a family, there is a kind of elixir called 'golden lustre', one ounce of which pulverises a thousand of bronze (i.e. turns it into gold), and that ounce of elixir cannot be used up or turned into bronze by the thousand ounces of bronze; just so the elixir element of a single occurrence of the thought of omniscience, including the knowledge of transformation into roots of good, uses up all the bronze of obstruction by action and attachment and makes all principles the colour of omniscience... (pp. 501-2)

Afterwards he opens the pavilion and the most fabulous description of it is given. It occupies the whole of space, but everything in it is beautiful, because of the perfect interpenetration and non-obstruction of everything. (This evidently is the way the universe appears when one is enlightened.) With Maitreya's aid Sudhana concentrates and enjoys a glimpse of enlightenment: all obstructions disappear from his mind. He understands the work of Maitreya as *bodhisattva*, seeing him engaged in good works (including the worldly arts and crafts) in countless other pavilions (=worlds) contained in the original one.

1262. This formidable stretch of prose, whose texture can be only hinted at here, powerfully suggests the inconceivable infinity of the universe and of the compassionate Buddhist thought which ideally penetrates everywhere in it. Its harmonies and antitheses, the balanced clauses and sweeping compounds, its endlessness but underlying order and grammatical simplicity, help to express the fundamental ambiguity of a universe conceived as both 'this world', as ordinarily experienced, a mass of unsatisfactory particulars, and as 'principleness' [878] *dharmatā*, perfectly harmonious, as it appears to an enlightened understanding. Such a prose style can clearly be adapted to any kind of description and to any kind of poetic or figurative device, as we see later through the works of Subandhu [1566-70] and Bāṇa. [1669, 1679].

1263. The development of prose narrative and fiction might be further illustrated from other Buddhist texts of the period lying on the periphery of *kāvya*, such as the humorous *Vimalakīrtinirdeśa* (*c.* +200?) popularising the philosophy of 'emptiness', the extensive *Avadāna* literature in Sanskrit [1276], Kumāralāta's more literary *Kalpanāmaṇḍitikā* (+3 ?)or the *Sīhalavatthu* (+3) in Pali (written in Āndhra), but perhaps enough has been said for our present purpose of indicating the trends in *kāvya* prose in about the +3 [cf. 849, 851]. [5091 ff.]

1264. Let us note here the bare names, since we seem to know no more, of four truly secular *kāvya* prose works of unknown date, all probably lost but all looked upon as classics by some of the medieval critics. Ratnaśrījñāna in his commentary (+10) on Daṇḍin's *Kāvyalakṣaṇa* (p.26) mentions the *Ratnaprabhā* as a novel in Paiśācī. In that language we must expect it to have been very ancient. Bāṇa (+7) praises Haricandra as the king of prose writers, for his brilliant, delightful and correct style (*Harṣacarita*, introductory verse 13). Since Bāṇa himself has long been admired as the greatest prose writer we may respect his judgment as to his greatest predecessor and deplore the loss of such writing. An anonymous verse in Vidyākara (1698) likewise praises Haricandra as captivating the heart.

Haricandra's date may be supposed to have been in the region of the +4 or +5. Krishnamachariar (pp. 146 and 444) suggests that he wrote a novel entitled *Mālati* but states no source for this information. Daṇḍin (+7) names a *Manovatī* (*Avantisundarī*, introductory verse 21), but the manuscripts of his work being in a fragmentary condition the name of its author is missing. From the context it may have been a novel written only shortly before his own time. The fourth work, the *Mādhavikā* (evidently the name of the heroine), is mentioned by Bhoja (+11) in his *Śṛṅgāraprakāśa* (II p. 469) as a classical example of a biography *ākhyāyikā*. As it is named before the *Harṣacarita* of Bāṇa it seems to be an earlier work, but at present we have no way of knowing how much earlier. We noted in Chapter VII the *Kāmasūtra's* reference to the performance of biographies in about the +3 [426].

1265. After the long reign of the Emperor Pravarasena I Vākāṭaka (last quarter of the +3 and first quarter of the +4), the Empire became divided. His son Sarvasena ruled the South Western part of the Empire with his capital at Vatsagulma in Vidarbha (we noted in Chapter IV that *vātsagulmī* is an alternative name for the *vaidarbhī* style). This Sarvasena is evidently the king referred to as the author of the *Harivijaya*, a classical Māhārāṣṭrī epic long famous but apparently now lost (Daṇḍin, *Avantisundarī*, introductory verse 12, calls him a king). From discussions by the critics between the +7 and +12 we see that this *Harivijaya* was an epoch making work and we learn some important things about it. The title means 'The Victory of Hari (Kṛṣṇa)' and its story was based on the episode of Kṛṣṇa's carrying off the Pārijāta tree from Indra's heaven for Satyabhāmā.

1266. Bhoja in the *Śṛṅgāraprakāśa* (especially II 474 ff; the references have been studied by Raghavan in his book on this work, pp. 824-5) gives a good deal of information about the contents of Sarvasena's epic, among other standard *kāvyas*, and it is immediately significant that, apart from the *Rāmāyaṇa* (and *Mahābhārata*, which Bhoja regards as a *kāvya* from some points of view), it seems to be the oldest epic regularly drawn upon by him in order to illustrate *kāvya* composition. It thus appears to have set a new standard or style, followed by most later writers and putting out of fashion most of the *kāvyas* which had preceded it. This at least is the view we are given by most of the critics now accessible to us. The *Rāmāyaṇa* occupied a special position, but the epics of Aśvaghoṣa's period were almost totally neglected. This almost certainly has something to do with the development of the *vaidarbhī* style [238-40, 923, 937-8], which apparently reached maturity in Sarvasena's poetry. At the same time we become aware of a parallel development in connection with *rasa*. In the drama, we have discussed the transition from Bhāsa's plays to Śūdraka's, with apparently a more conscious application of the theory of the *Nāṭyaśāstra* and in particular a more elaborate delineation of emotion, with a corresponding enlargement of scale. Preoccupation with emotion and the generation of aesthetic experience, as the essential method of literature, was extended from the drama to all kinds of *kāvya* probably in this same period, and the critics discuss the epics from the *Harivijaya* onwards from the standpoint of how their authors deal with the *rasa*. From the purely formal point of view, Sarvasena's epic inaugurates, as far as we know, the technique called *skandhakabandha* and *āśvāsabandha*.

1267. Bhoja informs us that the object of Kṛṣṇa in the *Harivijaya* is to carry off the Pārijāta and that he succeeds in this. There is a battle (in which as we know from the *itihāsa* sources, such as the *Viṣṇu Purāṇa*, Indra tried to stop Kṛṣṇa but was defeated) ending with Kṛṣṇa's victory, but his enemy is not killed, only admits Kṛṣṇa's superiority (Kṛṣṇa of course is Viṣṇu) and makes peace. According to Bhoja (*Śṛṅgāraprakāśa* II p. 474) the epic was 'marked' by the word 'energy' *ucchāha* (occurring at the end of each canto and indicating a major theme) [425, 1432]. There are several incidental descriptions, as is customary in an epic, including the hero, his mount (presumably the bird Garuḍa), a city, mountains, the season, an envoy and a drinking party *madhupāna* in a house where a 'circle' (*goṣṭhī*, of *nāgarakas*) meets (*Śṛṅgāraprakāśa* Vol. II. pp. 475-6; Bhoja regards these as examples of five different 'ornaments of a whole work' *prabandhālaṅkāras*, i.e. descriptions of places, times, characters, political activities and pleasures, the last as causes of emotion for the sensitive). According to Ānandavardhana (*Dhvanyāloka* p. 335), Sarvasena in this epic changed some of the details to suit the *rasa*, Abhinavagupta adding in his commentary that scenes were invented which were not found in the *itihāsas*. Hemacandra, however, objects that one descriptive passage in the *Harivijaya* is too long : Kṛṣṇa is engaged in placating Satyabhāmā's jealous anger but the poet inserts a superfluous description of the ocean (*Kāvyānuśāsana* p. 171). Such matters of taste were much discussed among the critics and contrary opinions upheld. In the present case of the *Harivijaya*, Bhoja reports a view that some verses in the text were not original but had been added by people who thought themselves clever (II pp. 473 f). This view, however, was advanced on the grounds of supposed changes of metre in the poem, which was supposed originally to have been in one (the *skandhaka*) metre throughout. Similar added verses could be alleged in other (later) Māhārāṣṭrī epics [1443]. Bhoja rejects the view because it depends on the definition of *skandhaka*, which could very well be understood to include all the varieties of musical metre used.

1268. This brings us to the question of the formal characteristics of the *Harivijaya* and later Māhārāṣṭrī epics. *Skandhaka-bandha* means that the whole poem is in the *skandhaka* (*khandhaā* in Māhārāṣṭrī) metre, which when used in Sanskrit has the name *āryāgīti* (this contrasts with the older *Paümacariya* [859], which is in *āryā*). From such later epics as the *Setubandha* we see that *skandhaka* here includes verses in a syncopated form of the metre, having additional 'bars' *gaṇas* and certain other variations, but avoiding the *āryā*. It may be noted that this *āryāgīti* or *skandhaka* is the prototype of the *pajjhaṭikā* metre of Apabhraṃśa poetry. The other term found here, *āśvāsabandha*, means that the sections of the epic are called not 'cantos' *sargas* but 'chapters' *āśvāsas*—though these English equivalents are rather arbitrary. It merely means that the canto organisation as found in Sanskrit epics, avoiding the musical metres altogether but with a great variety of other metres, change of metre in the concluding verses, etc., is discarded: we have continuous *skandhaka* composition cut up into chapters like prose without any corresponding metrical pattern. One other formal point of interest found in these discussions is that the supposed added verses of variant metrical structure, as well as some of the ordinary verses, had rhyme as a feature. Rhyme *yamaka* is an occasional feature of *kāvya* and regarded as a figure or ornament, but the continuous and regular use of rhyme in poetry is found (apart from *citrakāvya* such as the *Ghaṭakarpara*) only in Apabhraṃśa and the modern languages. These rhymed verses, or *galitakas*, in Māhārāṣṭrī from Sarvasena onwards may be regarded as another characteristic of poetry in transition from early Prakrit forms to Apabhraṃśa.

1269. On Sarvasena's style we have Kuntaka's authority, mentioned above in Chapter IV [288], which chooses him, along with Kālidāsa, as representative of the *sukumāra*, 'delicate', which is natural, fresh, little ornamented, dominated by emotion, its beauty springing naturally from genius. This style is Kuntaka's redefinition of the old *vaidarbhi*. The few verses quoted by critics which are identifiable as Sarvasena's seem to confirm this idea of a simple, delicate style. For example from the *Sarasvatīkaṇṭhābharaṇa* (there must be many other verses from the Harivijaya quoted in Bhoja's works but not at present clearly identifiable):

> And Satyabhāmā became angry
> when there was a failure of respect even merely equal
> to that for her friends :
> —Anger proceeds by manifesting the essence of the
> heart,
> like a reassurance of love. (p. 647, verse 263)

According to Bhoja, 'friends' here means Rukmiṇī and others.

> If you are sullied by the flowers of the gods,
> I propitiate you again simply with them :
> Then, slender one, my love,
> and not my offence, corresponds to what I have done.
> (p. 655, verse 287)

From Bhoja's comments we learn that Kṛṣṇa had given some of the divine flowers to Rukmiṇī, which enraged Satyabhāmā, and that what Kṛṣṇa means to say here is that he has given Satyabhāmā the whole tree, which is a hundred times better, showing his correspondingly greater love for her. By this she should be propitiated.

> Although it is an occasion for anger, Rukmiṇī's delight
> increases when seeing her lover,

Bringing the manifestation of a thrill,
although her lord is pale with the love of her rival.
(p. 673, verse 330)

Then Hari bestowed on Rukmiṇī the garland of flowers
of the Thirty (gods),
from which emanated the pleasure of fragrant scent,
And which he had brought himself,
—tormenting the heart of his beloved.
(p. 678, verse 351)

When her face was delightful, as she saw her lover,
anger stole her heart,
—Produced by the failure of his love—
like the mudstain of passion imprinted on the Moon.
(p. 724, verse 485)

Bhoja quotes this as an example of mixing the aesthetic experience *rasa* with a figure, where the aesthetic experience and not the figure dominates : the simile is dominated by the love. The description is of Satyabhāmā angry when she saw Hari give a cluster of the Pārijāta flowers to Rukmiṇī.

Her face has its anger a little repressed,
its delight a very little increased
And its confusion dependent on both experiences
displayed afar. (p. 727, verse 491)

This is again Satyabhāmā, according to Bhoja.

1270. These verses show that the theme of Satyabhāmā's jealousy was much developed: from the *itihāsa* we see that it was her jealousy of Kṛṣṇa's favours shown to his other wives, such as presents given to them, which led to her demand for the unique Pārijāta tree. From the probable quotations in Bhoja we gather that her main rival was Rukmiṇī. If Kṛṣṇa could succeed in wresting this wonderful possession from the King of the Gods and making it hers, she would be satisfied—but even then he blundered by giving a few flowers to her rival. This jealousy then was the 'seed' of the action.

Chapter XXII

DRAMATISTS OF THE +4 AND OTHER DEVELOPMENTS IN KĀVYA

1271. After the break up of the Kuṣāṇa Empire of Northern India the country remained divided between several states for more than a century. Prominent among these were the Śaka government of Avanti and the two Nāga dynasties, at Mathurā (Śūrasena) and Padmāvatī. Padmāvatī was between Śūrasena and Avanti and we find the Nāgas there allied to the Vākāṭakas, presumably against the Śakas, who for their part tried to control Magadha and reestablish a North Indian empire. The Nāgas, like the Vākāṭakas, appear in a favourable light in the *Purāṇas*; the Śakas, for all their patronage of *kāvya*, continued to be looked upon as barbarians. The *Purāṇas* barely mention another dynasty, among minor lines contemporary with the Vākāṭakas, as ruling in Magadha and Kośala, namely the Guptas.

1272. The origin of the Guptas is obscure (the *Vaṃśāvalīs* of Nepal seem to connect them with the Ābhīras), but they appear in Magadha after the collapse of the Śaka-Muruṇḍa government there. We find them allied to the Licchavis ruling in Vṛji and Nepal, who may have been responsible for the end of Muruṇḍa rule, whilst the Nāgas and Vākāṭakas may also have had a part in this. Candra I Gupta, probably in +320, married the Licchavi princess or queen Kumāradevī and thereby united the two realms, establishing Gupta power on a firm basis. His son Samudra Gupta, in a remarkable series of military campaigns about +350, built up a large empire across North India, including the remnant of the Kuṣāṇa domain in the North West reduced to vassalage. About +395 Samudra's son Candra II 'Vikramāditya' overthrew the Śakas at Ujjayinī and ended their rule in India. By marrying his daughter Prabhāvatī to the Vākāṭaka Rudrasena II (of the North Eastern division of the Vākāṭaka domains) he consolidated an imperial system which embraced most of India.

1273. This Gupta-Vākāṭaka system of marriage alliances and vassal kingdoms shows the full flowering of the 'feudalistic' tendencies which we noticed above under the Kuṣāṇas and Sātavāhanas (Chapter XX [1153]). As a rule, conquered kings were not dispossessed of their realms but permitted to remain as hereditary rulers if they submitted to vassal status under the conqueror, of course paying tribute or remitting taxes to him. As a result of this we find a number of the medieval dynasties persisting for long periods, sometimes more or less independent, often reduced to vassalage under the paramount ruler of the day, always clinging to their hereditary domain on the best terms they could get or enforce. At the same time the number of 'feudal' princes was steadily increased by the appointment of officers who obtained the favour of the emperor, or of members of the imperial family, to the hereditary administration of lands at the disposal of the emperor through failure of the succession or detachment from another domain or actual expropriation for some reason. Thus several medieval dynasties are found to have originated through such appointments by the Guptas (e.g. the Maitrakas in former Śaka territory, Saurāṣṭra or Gujarat). It may be added, though in our present study we perhaps need not pursue these social and political investigations in detail, that this system of vassal rulers of large territories amalgamated with the growing system of land ownership at more local levels (also noted in Chapter XX: Sātavāhana land grants) to produce a complete feudalistic hierarchy based on titles to land protected by overlords in exchange for taxes and service.

1274. Traditional stories and legends have simplified the history of the Gupta dynasty into a single ideal emperor, 'Vikramāditya'. Several of the Guptas appear to have used this name, which seems to have become almost a dynastic name like Sātavāhana, but the most famous was Candra II, on account of his conquest of the Śakas. This was truly a decisive event, establishing an empire across Northern India from the Western to the Eastern Ocean and making the conqueror a paramount ruler who could dispose of the affairs of almost all India. Whatever the *Purāṇas* may say of the early Guptas (and their record seems to stop early in the +4), later traditions, and especially the traditions of the *kavis*, eulogise Vikramāditya for his courage, generosity, justice and devotion to literature and learning. He is supposed to have maintained a brilliant assembly of scholars and *kavis* and to have been a *kavi* himself. From these traditions, with other evidence (*Mañjuśrīmūlakalpa*, Jinasena I, etc.), we have to separate out as far as we can the history of *kāvya* in the +4 and +5.

1275. We may begin with the Buddhist philosopher, grammarian and dramatist Candragomin. A long study might be devoted to the question of his date. Provisionally we may place him in the +4. He belonged to the idealist (Vijñānavāda) school of Buddhist philosophy, which developed in the +3 and +4 (*Sandhinirmocana* and *Laṅkāvatāra Sūtras*, Asaṅga). He is said by the grammarian Bhartṛhari (also +4 ?) to have brought Patañjali's *Mahābhāṣya* from the South and so restored the tradition of Pāṇinīya grammar in the North (*Vākyapadīya* II 488-9). Kalhaṇa in his *Rājataraṅgiṇī* mentions him as living in Kaśmīra, indicating a period after the Kuṣāṇas and before Mātṛgupta (and Vikramāditya), i.e. before about +400. In fact Kalhaṇa has two references (I 176 and II 16) : a Candra who brought the *Mahābhāṣya* and wrote a grammar, in the reign of Abhimanyu (I), and a Candaka who was a dramatist, in the reign of Tuñjīna (I). Both these kings fall in the period between the Kuṣāṇas and Mātṛgupta. Kalhaṇa's chronology is confused here and we cannot be certain whether there are two Candras or only one. Verse 6 of Act I of the play *Lokānanda* says that the author was a grammarian (wrote grammars). In the second reference Kalhaṇa also calls Candaka a partial reincarnation of Dvaipāyana, i.e. of the supposed author of the *Mahābhārata*. From this one might infer that the drama which the historian especially admired was one on the matter of the Great Epic, rather than the *Lokānanda*, for example the *Pāṇḍavānanda* [1583] among the classical plays now not available.

1276. The *Lokānanda*, 'Joy of the World', is now available only in a Tibetan translation, the Indian original being apparently lost. It is based on the story of Maṇicūḍa, which is found in the Sanskrit *Avadāna* literature (*Maṇicūḍāvadāna*), and is thus a *nāṭaka* (in five acts). *Avadānas* are usually stories of heroic (self-sacrificing) deeds done by Buddhist monks and nuns in their previous lives, narrated to explain their present characters. In the course of time, however, some other types of narrative were incorporated in *Avadāna* collections by some Buddhists. These collections were included in the *Tripiṭaka* in its various recensions (of the different Buddhist schools), in other words were regarded as *āgama* ('scripture'). The Maṇicūḍa story itself is one which is not properly an *avadāna*, for its hero is the Bodhisattva, i.e. a previous life of the Buddha, not of a monk, so that it is strictly speaking a *jātaka*. This confusion of *avadāna* and *jātaka* perhaps reflects ideas of Mahāyānist tendency : that all good people are really *bodhisattvas* on the way to becoming *buddhas*, consequently there is not much point in separating stories of the previous lives of one ('our', the Śākya) Buddha as a special case. The Maṇicūḍa story also seems to be relatively late, at least it is not found in the earlier Pali and Sanskrit collections of *avadānas* now available. At the same time it closely resembles an old *jātaka* story, found for example in its Pali version as the epic *Vessantara Jātaka* which we noted above in Chapter XII [579]. The name Maṇicūḍa, 'Jewel Crest', refers to an extraordinary physical feature of the hero, a jewel which had grown in the tonsure or crest of his hair as a result of good actions done in a still earlier life. This jewel had magical properties such as the power to heal diseases and neutralise poison.

1277. The action of the Maṇicūḍa story is the attainment of the 'perfection of generosity' ***dānapāramitā*** by the Bodhisattva. This is made the objective of the play. In order to be able to be generous on the grandest scale, Maṇicūda must first acquire all possible wealth. He must become a king and perform an ideal 'sacrifice' in which everything is given away. This incidentally brings us a typical example of a traditional Brahmanical ritual modified in accordance with Buddhist moral conceptions.

1278. At the commencement of the play Maṇicūḍa is a prince, son of the king of Kośala (at the capital Sāketa, often called Ayodhyā), but he is inclined to asceticism and averse to all pleasures. Though this is good from the general standpoint of Buddhist ethics and promising as regards character, it hardly opens the way towards becoming possessed of everything and thus able to exercise the perfection of generosity. As an ascetic Maṇicūḍa might renounce the throne if it were offered him, moreover it might not be offered him if he had better qualified brothers, for a king was required by tradition to have a queen : in Brahmanical law he could not perform all his ritual duties without a queen. Further, on account of the dynastic need to secure the succession as far as possible into the future, it was most desirable for a candidate for kingship to have a son. There was indeed a tradition that a king should retire from the throne when a grandson was born to him, in other words his son would succeed him on becoming the father of this grandson and perhaps a son who failed in this particular, though elder, might be passed over in favour of another who could offer the pledge of dynastic security.

1279. The source story pays no attention to these considerations, there it just happened that Maṇicūḍa became king; but Candragomin for his dramatic construction makes much of Maṇicūḍa's asceticism and the difficulty of persuading him to marry. The first three acts of the *Lokānanda* are devoted to the securing of a wife for the hero, or rather to securing the hero for a wife, and with this the possibility of accomplishing the ultimate objective. Thus the end of Act III, where Maṇicūḍa is married to Padmāvatī and hints at the sacrifice of everything, should probably be understood to cover the 'possibility of attainment' *prāptisambhava* stage of the main action [127]. The 'embryo' conjunction might be found here or in Act IV. There is a further point stressing the importance of this marriage: in Buddhist tradition the perfection of generosity includes giving away one's wife and child, as well as everything else, thus the Bodhisattva in order to attain it must first be married. As for the source story, after Maṇicūḍa becomes king a brahman suggests he ought to have a chief queen, for ritual purposes, and produces a suitable girl; the hero deferentially and undramatically agrees. Candragomin has thus invented most of his plot whilst keeping the main action of the original story as his objective.

1280. In Act I of the play Padmāvatī, daughter of an ascetic, living in a hermitage in the Himālaya, hears of Maṇicūḍa through a *vidyādharī* (female wizard) named Ratnāvalī, who shows her his portrait. She falls in love with him, which evidently is the 'seed' *bīja* of the action (leading to marriage, kingship, sacrifice and final reunion). Ratnāvalī further secures the approval of Padmāvatī's father and takes a portrait of her to Maṇicūḍa's parents, who think her suitable as a daughter-in-law. Maṇicūḍa shows no interest and continues his asceticism in a grove.

1281. In Act II Maṇicūḍa's friend Gautama, the jester *vidūṣaka* of the play, tries to persuade him to agree to the wedding, preparations for which are well advanced. But Maṇicūḍa is opposed to marriage and to the 'poison' of sense pleasures. Ratnāvalī arrives and overhears their argument, finding an opening for her purpose when Maṇicūḍa declares he is determined to strive for the welfare of all beings, being ready even to sacrifice his body to help others. Ratnāvalī demands his body for her sick friend (i.e. Padmāvatī, lovesick), because it will cure her. Maṇicūḍa gladly gives it and the wizard lady flies off with him and the terrified jester to the mountain hermitage.

1282. In Act III Ratnāvalī brings Maṇicūḍa to Padmāvatī and she recovers. Maṇicūḍa is attracted by the girl, but embarrassed by his position. Padmāvatī's father appears, everything is explained and settled and he joins the couple in marriage, but Maṇicūḍa recalls his ideal of generosity, of giving everything through compassion.

1283. Act IV : after 'more than a year' (a gesture to the proper dramatic compression of the *Nāṭyaśāstra*; it should be much more than one year) Maṇicūḍa has a son and has become king, his father having retired and become an ascetic. At last Maṇicūḍa can celebrate the sacrifice of giving away everything and is now found at the Himālayan hermitage engaged in this long operation. All kinds of gifts have been dispensed already and the rite reaches a climax as beggars throng the alms hall. But Maṇicūḍa's enemy (hereditary) the king of Kuru looks displeased at the grandeur of his rival. The Earth quakes: this is auspicious and in Buddhist tradition marks the performance of a great action. Then suddenly a demon *rākṣasa* appears in the sacrificial fire and demands a gift of flesh. A priest suggests beef, but Maṇicūḍa has prohibited animal sacrifice and refuses this, offering his own flesh instead (cf. Śivi [919] and Maitrībala [922]). The demon accepts and Maṇicūḍa cuts off pieces of his own flesh, despite the protests of all, which the demon eats. Maṇicūḍa fainting from loss of blood finally offers his whole body and then falls down unconscious. The demon then reveals himself as really the God Indra disguised and revives Maṇicūḍa: Indra has simply shown everyone that Maṇicūḍa's professions of a self-sacrificing spirit are sincere. The Goddess Earth now appears with healing herbs and restores Maṇicūḍa's body. Indra offers to take Maṇicūḍa to heaven, but the hero declines on hearing that there are no beggars there. Now an ascetic begs for Padmāvatī and her son, on behalf of the brahman sage Mārīci. Maṇicūḍa gives them to him and says he will retire to the forest. There is a touching scene here, reminiscent of one in the Toy Cart of Śūdraka (Act VI), where the boy does not understand the situation, being intent on his toys and unaware of the affairs of the adult world.

1284. In Act V we find Maṇicūḍa in the forest and not far from the hermitage of Mārīci. The faithful jester is still with him, for a brahman cannot be given away. Padmāvatī appears, pursued by two foresters intending to abduct her. Maṇicūḍa and the jester drive them off, but Padmāvatī's son has disappeared. As Maṇicūḍa is about to send Padmāvatī back to Mārīci, a brahman enters and requests the one great gift it is still possible for the hero to make: the enemy Kuru country is ravaged by a plague, so the gods have sent him to beg for Maṇicūḍa's jewel to dispel it. Maṇicūḍa tears out the jewel and gives it, but then falls down unconscious. The brahman hurries off with the jewel. Maṇicūḍa has surely now attained the perfection of generosity, but must he be left in this desolate state? Mārīci arrives at this point, looking for Padmāvatī. Then her son appears in the distance with a guard, discussing what he should do. The guard, formerly an officer at Maṇicūḍa's court, says he should suffer patiently, but the boy declares he will avenge his distressed parents. Just at that point the boy gets bitten by a snake. The guard is alarmed, but hopes to cure the bite with the jewel crest, if he can find Maṇicūḍa in time. The venom starts to work, causing swelling, and then the guard hears Padmāvatī lamenting; he hurries to her, to find her wailing over Maṇicūḍa dying, his jewel gone—so the boy too must die. Then there is a rain of flowers from heaven, which revives Maṇicūḍa. Though his son is dying, he cannot regret giving the jewel away. However, he makes an asseveration of the truth (a popular Buddhist theme) in the hope of saving the boy : if he really has no regrets and his compassion and generosity are perfect, then may the jewel reappear ! It does so and the boy recovers. Mārīci then gives Padmāvatī and the boy back to Maṇicūḍa and commands him to return to his kingdom and rule. He had begged for those two only to save them from being taken by someone else, thus looking after them until Maṇicūḍa had completed his sacrifice. Indra himself sends a chariot to take the king to Sāketa. Maṇicūḍa obeys. Universal happiness.

1285. As we have hinted above, the source story which Candragomin used for this play is rather dull and heavy in form, lacking in organisation and balance, insensitive and crude in many of the details of its content. There is no humour in it, in fact it is just a moral story hardly productive of any aesthetic experience, it is a piece of tradition apparently compiled from earlier sources in a rather pedantic manner with chunks of ethical doctrine, thus though artless it lacks simplicity. Such a moral tract needs at least a little art to present its message in palatable form and to make its descriptions of extreme actions seem less unrealistic and inhuman. Candragomin has brought to it much art—the resources of *nāṭyaśāstra* and other branches of *kāvya* technique—and has made it seem human and truly noble, though most extraordinary and heroic in its idealism. The marvellous supernatural manifestations, mostly from popular Buddhist tradition (Indra testing virtue, etc.) and retained from the source, do not clash with this humanising of the story but are subordinated to it and also made to serve the purpose of producing the marvellous aesthetic experience at appropriate points in the drama. The *Lokānanda* is thus a very fine example of the making of a work of dramatic art from raw narrative material. There is evidence that it enjoyed great and widespread success on the stage when the Indian and Buddhist theatre flourished. The Chinese traveller I-tsing reports in the +7 that it was performed and was very popular in the 'Five Indias' (five main divisions of India). It was perhaps known in Japan in the +8, whither it had been brought from Champa in South East Asia (now Vietnam : see *Hōbōgirin*, 'Bugaku'). Finally it was one of the rare dramas selected for translation into Tibetan.

1286. Following the example of Nāgārjuna and Mātṛceṭa, Candragomin wrote an epistle which became a classic. Moreover it is expressly described as a *kāvya* in its title (whether by the author himself we cannot say). This is the *Śiṣyalekha-dharmakāvya*, 'Epistle to a Pupil, *Dharmakāvya*' (where *dharma* may mean that it is about the Buddhist 'doctrine' or that its subject is 'virtue', or both). It has been preserved in Sanskrit as well as in a Tibetan translation and as printed consists of 114 verses. It is addressed to a prince named Ratnakīrti, otherwise apparently unknown and perhaps fictitious, at whose court the author is supposed to have fallen into disfavour. The prince is addicted to wealth and power and the poet remonstrates with him on the impermanence of these worldly things: as a result Ratnakīrti is said to have left the world (become a Buddhist monk). These notes are from Vairocanarakṣita's commentary (also Tāranātha). The Epistle begins by praising the Buddha, his doctrine and the Buddhist community. The unhappiness of life in the world of transmigration is then vividly described. The unpleasant effects of growing old are stressed, with regrets for what has been done and what has not been done (30). Then a man is dragged off by the messengers of Death (33 ff.). There follows a description of the miseries of ghosts, who are unable to satisfy any desire (because they have no material bodies), then various purgatories where evil actions are punished. It is difficult to be reborn as a human being, with the opportunity of learning the truth and bringing transmigration to an end. Everything is impermanent, the pleasures of life are all transient, the objects enjoyed by the senses are worse than poison. The gods too are subject to death and rebirth. Consequently Buddhist meditation is recommended, dispelling ignorance and attachment. The way to freedom is to work for the benefit of others, to be a shady tree, a raincloud, a pond for those overcome by thirst in the desert. The poem concludes with the wish that the whole world may attain enlightenment. Like Nāgārjuna's epistle, this generally follows stock Buddhist doctrine about transmigration: it perhaps does not rise to the creative level of Mātṛceṭa, though it uses a rich variety of metres and much figurative language, justifying the title of *kāvya* given to it.

1287. Candragomin also composed *stotras* (hymns),

such as the *Deśanāstava*, 'Hymn to the Teaching', in 51 verses preserved in Tibetan, and a tract (the *Udānakathā*) is attributed to him in the Tibetan *Tripiṭaka*.

1288. Before we leave the problematic personality of Candragomin we should note that there are references to a dramatist Candraka by some of the critics. It is uncertain whether this means Candragomin or another playwright, just as it is not certain whether Kalhaṇa's dramatist Candaka, said to have been very popular, was the same. According to Abhinavagupta (III p. 72) Candraka's plays (plural) served mainly the heroic and furious aesthetic experiences, consequently their language was Sanskrit (exclusively?). Although these aesthetic experiences are quite prominent in the *Lokānanda* (the furious in the scene of the demon demanding flesh), one would not expect the parts of Padmāvatī and the jester to be in Sanskrit: only by exception Candragomin might have composed them in Sanskrit, or Abhinavagupta meant only a predominance of Sanskrit if he really had this play in mind. The other references do not seem to help us much (e.g. the presumed quotation by Dhanika, discussion between VI. 34 and 35, on mixture of emotions: love, grief and anger).

1289. Several anthologists quote verses as from Candragomin or Cand(r)aka (at least fifteen verses altogether). The continuing and widespread popularity of Candragomin is attested by the fact that the Sinhalese *Gaṇṭhipada* on the *Mahābodhivaṃsa*, +12 or later, quotes verse 1 of the Epistle to a Pupil (Godakumbura, *Sinhalese Literature*, p. 34). The *Subhāṣitāvali* (3384) quotes the following (with variants), which is actually found both in the Epistle to a Pupil (verse 73) and in the *Lokānanda* (II.15):

> When pleasures, poison and sense objects are examined,
> poison is better, not sense objects whose nature is dangerous:
> Poison poisons one in one life,
> sense objects poison one in a future life too.

In the play, this is spoken by Maṇicūḍa to the jester when the latter tries to speak to him about Padmāvatī. The idea of course is that attachment to sense objects causes one to be reborn and thus undergo further unhappiness.

1290. The following verse is ascribed to Candraka in the *Sūktimuktāvali* (p. 453) and by Kṣemendra is his *Kavikaṇṭhābharaṇa* (quotation 53):

In the house where once there were many, now one
remains,
but where there was one, afterwards many, at the end
there is not even one;
In this manner throwing day and night to move them,
like the two dice,
Time (Śiva ?), with his consort (Pārvatī ?), plays
noisily with living beings as chessmen.

The imagery here is of the old Indian game of chess *caturaṅga*, where the (four?) players throw a pair of dice to determine their moves. The second line confirms that captured pieces could be put back into play by the player who takes them (a point not very clear in the manuals of the game so far printed). Jalhaṇa includes this verse in the section on renunciation *vairāgya* in his anthology. In fact most of the verses attributed to Candragomin or Candraka in the anthologies illustrate that theme, which would be consistent with their being taken from the works of the author of the *Lokānanda* and the Epistle to a Pupil. In one case (*Sūktimuktāvali* p. 202, *Subhāṣitāvali* 1629, etc.) a critic (Abhinavagupta, *Dhvanyālokalocana* p. 362) objects to the verse on the ground that the expression of love in it is spoiled by the suggestion of 'indifference' *nirveda*, i.e. disillusionment with the world, which also enters into it.

1291. Let us conclude our discussion of Candragomin with a verse from his Epistle to a Pupil, containing a 'complete' metaphor ('heat' *tāpa* in Sanskrit metaphorically means any affliction) :

Be a great tree for those distressed by the heat in the
desert of transmigration,
with discipline to spread you, energy as your trunk,
tolerance and restraint as your shoots,
Calming as your flowers, understanding as your bran-
ches, giving as your thick cover,
commitment as your crest, virtue as your shade,
offering calmness as fruit. (109)

1292. To illustrate the *kāvya* style of the +4, among the chronological uncertainties of the surviving literature, we have one long inscription, usually dated *c.* +350 (it might be a quarter of a century later), from the reign of Samudra Gupta. It was engraved at Kauśāmbī to celebrate the conquests of Samudra, the author being his minister Hariṣeṇa. This panegyric *praśasti* has eight introductory verses followed by a single enormous prose sentence (about 30 lines on a printed page), then another verse and a prose colophon saying that this *kāvya* was composed by Hariṣeṇa. The prose sentence indicates the direction of prose style from Śūra, the *Gaṇḍavyūha*, etc., towards Subandhu, Bāṇa and Daṇḍin: The emperor's achievements are presented in a series of clauses with long compounds, not unlike a description of a great king in one of the later novels. The style of the +6 and +7 is thus foreshadowed, but the complexity of figuration is not so insistent. There are not so many double meanings, although the mixture of metaphor and double meaning, so popular later, is found at least once : 'the inconceivable man who is the cause of the rise and fall of the good and the bad'—here the 'man' *puruṣa* means both the hero Samudra and the primaeval spirit *brahman* (also called 'Man' in the *Veda*), the hero of course rewards his friends and punishes his enemies, the *brahman* is the basis of the whole universe of transmigration where beings fare according to their good and bad actions; 'inconceivable' *acintya* is a word especially characteristic of the *Gaṇḍavyūha*, whose grand phrases perhaps came to Hariṣeṇa's mind as he meditated on the theme of building a universal empire. The simile in the concluding verse is worth noting as an example of the *kāvya* method: the emperor's fame is compared with the water of the River Ganges, because both pass through the Three Worlds (in heaven the Ganges is the Milky Way), purifying them, and have a series of other common epithets.

1293. Candragomin was far from being the only composer of hymns in this period. Among the Buddhists, the famous philosopher Diṅnāga (provisional date, second half of the +5), born in the South (near Kāñcī) but pursued his career in Magadha and Kaliṅga, produced as a poetic exercise a 'Mingled Hymn', *Miśrakastotra*, preserved in Tibetan, in which he has mingled his own lines with those of Mātṛceṭa's *Prasādapratibhodbhava Stotra* [890] to form a homogeneous whole.

Mātṛceṭa's ideas are thus expanded or interpreted in a poetic commentary. A fellow student of Diṅnāga, Triratnadāsa, composed the *Guṇāparyantastotra*, 'Hymn of Limitless Qualities', in a more elaborate metre (the *śikhariṇī*) than these, its subject matter being similar, with numerous references to *jātaka* stories. His much shorter *Bhagavacchākyamunistotra* is a string of epithets of the Buddha.

1294. The hymn writer Mūka (Mūkārbha Śaṅkara) brings us to a group of writers interconnected in legends and also linked with Vikramāditya. Ātmabodhendrasarasvatī's commentary (+1720) on the *Gururatnamālikā* hymn by Sadāśivabrahmendra (+16) (on verses 40 to 50, p. 53, quoted by Krishnamachariar, pp. 551f.) states that Mūka died in Śaka 359 (+437) and links him with Rāmila, Mātṛgupta and Meṇṭha, as well as with Vikramāditya. These late traditions are supported by Kalhaṇa, according to whom Vikramāditya made Mātṛgupta king of Kaśmīra (III 187) and Mātṛgupta in turn greatly appreciated Meṇṭha's epic *Hayagrīvavadha* when the poet presented it to him (III 260—2). To this group of writers we can add Somila or Saumila, on account of the latter's joint authorship of a *Śūdrakakathā* with Rāmila. A dramatist Saumilla or Saumillaka, mentioned by Kālidāsa in the prologue to his *Mālavikāgnimitra*, would appear to be the same. We do not know where Ātmabodha obtained his information and it is surprising that so late a writer should offer quotations from the works of Rāmila and Meṇṭha, now apparently lost (however, it seems manuscripts of Meṇṭha's epic were available in Kerala).

1295. As far as Mūka himself is concerned, a long *stotra*, the *Pañcaśatī*, 'Five Hundred', has been published under his name. It is a hymn to the Great Goddess as Kāmākṣī, in the form in which she is worshipped at Kāñcī, where the author evidently lived. The editors think that this hymn is not very ancient, although there is little in the text to suggest any date. The style is generally clear and smooth and the vocabulary purely classical, such as was used over a very long period. The fact that the work seems to have been hardly known until recently does not encourage us to suppose that it is really an early medieval classic. We shall probably be right in excluding it from consideration at this point. This does not help us to evaluate the tradition about an old Mūka associated with Rāmila and others. The recent Advaita Vedānta tradition is that he belonged to the line of succession of their teachers, beginning with the celebrated Śaṃkara. There are two versions : Mūka was contemporary with Śaṃkara, or was twentieth in succession from him. But Śaṃkara appears to have lived in the +7 (in the time of Kumārila and Dharmakīrti). The whole thing seems to be apocryphal, except that Ātmabodha's statements fit remarkably well with Kalhaṇa's record and the known history of the Guptas (Kalhaṇa's work was probably unknown in South India in the +18). There is thus the possibility that he depended on an authentic tradition concerning the date of Rāmila, Mātṛgupta and Meṇṭha, in association with Vikramāditya, and that the apocryphal line of Advaitin teachers was foisted onto this tradition at some time (probably long before Ātmabodha himself) to give them a semblance of historicity.

1296. Ātmabodha quotes from the prologue (announcement) of a play which he says is Rāmila's *Maṇiprabhā*, 'Jewel-Brilliance', otherwise apparently unknown. This says that Rāmila was a pupil of one Śaṅkarendra or Mūkārbha and that he and another poet, Meṇṭha, were keepers of the horses and elephants of the learned 'teacher of the world' (the emperor ?), who was proud of the poetry of his servant Mātṛgupta. Further, Vikramārka Harṣa (i.e. Vikramāditya), the Garuḍa of the Śaka Snake (destroyer of the Śaka), gave a *kāvya* which was a brahman and lord of scholars to Kaśmīra (this presumably means, following Kalhaṇa's history, that the brahman Mātṛgupta was given to Kaśmīra as king and as he was a poet it was like giving a *kāvya* to the country; otherwise a Kāvya = an Uśanas). The emperor Harṣa is also mentioned in the earlier verse about Rāmila and Śaṅkarendra (Kalhaṇa also calls Vikramāditya 'Harṣa'). All this tells us nothing about the *Maṇiprabhā* except that it was a play by Rāmila, who produced it in honour of his teacher. In one verse the name of the author is spelt Rāmilla. *Maṇiprabhā* was perhaps the name of the heroine and the play a *nāṭikā*, 'light play', but this is pure conjecture based on the usages of later dramatists in naming their plays.

1297. Little more is known of the ***Śūdrakakathā*** by Rāmila and Somila, who are praised by Rājaśekhara for its joint composition (*Sūktimuktāvalī*, Baroda, p. 43), though the title gives plenty of scope for conjecture. It is called a 'novel' yet it is on a well known, supposedly historical, hero. This may mean that it was a fictitious story about a historical hero, for which there are parallels (such as Kutūhala's novel *Līlāvaī* on Sātavāhana, mentioned in Chapter XVI above [772]). To complicate the position, another *Śūdrakakathā*, also apparently lost, is mentioned by the critics, whose author was named Pañcaśikha. One *Śūdraka* is noted as an example of a *parikathā* (cf. Chapter VII above [449]) by Bhoja (see Raghavan, who discusses what is known of these *Śūdrakas* in his *Bhoja's Śṛṅgāraprakāśa*, pp. 819 ff.). One novel seems to have been in Prakrit and to have had a heroine named Harimatī, with an old parrot serving as messenger: perhaps this was Pañcaśikha's. Then in one of them Śūdraka had a friend Bandhudatta, who aided him in winning Vinayavatī. Possibly this was in the novel of Rāmila and Somila. Daṇḍin in his *Avantisundarī* has summarised various narratives about Śūdraka, probably incorporating matter from these novels, as was his wont, and through him we may glean some idea of these *Śūdraka* fictions. Nothing more seems to be known about this Pañcaśikha. A

1298. Somila or Saumilla, like Rāmila, was a dramatist as well as a novelist, as we are told by Kālidāsa. Unless he is to be identified with Śyāmilaka (or Śyāmala or Śyāmadeva), author of the *Pādatāḍitaka*, nothing is known of his plays. Śyāmilaka seems to have lived in the second half of the +5 (see Chapter XXV below [1444]) and been a (junior ?) contemporary of Kālidāsa. Though Saumilla/Somila might have been a good deal younger than Rāmila and perhaps have completed the *Śūdraka* after Rāmila's death left it unfinished, Kālidāsa speaks of him as a dramatist not of the 'present' day, i.e. apparently as no longer living, which would seem to exclude identification with Śyāmilaka and confirm that he was a close contemporary of Rāmila.

1299. The identity of Vikramāditya, or Sāhasāṅka as he is also known [1612, 1615], is a difficult problem. Several rulers used the name. Among them, one is distinguished for overthrowing the Śakas of Avanti, as we noted at the beginning of this chapter, and may be identified with Candra II Gupta, whose reign is usually dated as *c.* +375 to +414 (it may have commenced as late as *c.* +390). Another is Skanda Gupta (+455 to 467) who met the invasion of the Hūṇas.

Samudra also perhaps used the title and according to Hariṣeṇa, in the panegyric discussed above, he was a *kavi* and a musician (on one of his coins Samudra is depicted playing a kind of *viṇā*). Attainments of this kind, however, were quite usual among Indian princes and need not be regarded as distinguishing Samudra from many other kings of his period. It is another matter when much later writers call Vikramāditya or Sāhasāṅka a *kavi*. A verse attributed to Rājaśekhara (+900) and quoted by Śārṅgadhara in his *Paddhati* anthology (+14) gives an interesting list of great writers, evidently in approximately chronological order : Bhāsa, Rāmila, Saumila, Vararuci, Sāhasāṅka, Meṇṭha, Bhāravi, Kālidāsa, Tarala, Skand(h)a, Subandhu, Daṇḍin, Bāṇa, Divākara, Gaṇapati, Ratnākara (VIII.17, also *Sūktimuktāvali* IV. 111). If we can rely on this it suggests that Candra II Gupta, patron of Mātṛgupta and destroyer of the Śaka, was the Sāhasāṅka in question. Rājaśekhara in his *Kāvyamimāṃsā* (p. 50) names Sāhasāṅka as a great patron of literature, at Ujjayinī, who favoured the Sanskrit language. The mention of Ujjayinī would exclude any earlier Gupta ruler than Candra II and the reference is surely to the celebrated patron of Mātṛgupta, Meṇṭha, etc. Probably Rājaśekhara considered these two Sāhasāṅkas to be the same person. Later in the same work (p. 55) he again mentions Sāhasāṅka as a patron, then gives a list of *kāvya* writers whose works were subjected to criticism in the 'hall' *sabhā*, a kind of academy, at Ujjayinī : Kālidāsa, Meṇṭha, Amararūpa (Amaruka?), Sūra (Śūra?), Bhāravi, Haricandra, Candra Gupta. The last would seem to be Candra II and Sāhasāṅka.

1300. King *narādhipa* Vikrama is further mentioned as an authority on dramatic theory by Sāgaranandin (3225), along with Mātṛgupta. There is a complication there, for the verse begins : *śrīharṣavikramanarādhipamātṛgupta....* Now Harṣa and Mātṛgupta are known to and quoted by Abhinavagupta and others as authorities on the drama, Vikrama is mentioned by some late writers, one of whom names a *Sāhasāṅkiya—Ṭikā* (commentary) (see Raghavan, note on p. 68 of the translation of Sāgaranandin). Perhaps we should read here (Śrī) Harṣa Vikrama as one person (Harṣa is known as the author of a *Vārttika*, or supplementing commentary, to the *Nāṭyaśāstra*). Soḍḍhala (+11) in his 'History *vaṃśa* of the *Kavis*' (*Udaya-*

sundarī 153 *f.*) gives the chronological sequence Vālmīki, Vyāsa, Guṇāḍhya, Bhartṛmeṇṭha, Kālidāsa, Bāṇa....Elsewhere (p.2) he mentions King Vikrama and his assembly, without details, and appears to connect Vikramāditya with Kālidāsa (p. 150).

1301. Jalhaṇa in his *Sūktimuktāvali* (+13) has a section in praise of *kavis,* which seems to be roughly in chronological order (Vālmīki, Vyāsa, Pāṇini, Vararuci, Bhāsa, etc., but this is quite often disturbed). He mentions Sāhasāṅka, together with Kālidāsa, Bhāravi, Māgha and Bhartṛmeṇṭha (Meṇṭha), and gives us the title of a *kāvya* of his : *Gandhamādana* (IV.57). The context here suggests that this was an epic. Nothing further seems to be known of this *Gandhamādana*. Gandhamādana is the name of a mountain in the Himālaya (or further North and more mythical in some stories), between the source of the Ganges and Kaśmīra. There are various traditions about it in Brahmanical [1440], Buddhist [1261] and Jaina literature: Buddhist monks are supposed to have introduced the valuable saffron plant from Gandhamādana into Kaśmīra, after quelling a dragon; the great *arhant* Piṇḍola Bhāradvāja is sometimes supposed to have retired there; in Brahmanical tradition it is an abode of the *apsarases*; in Jaina tradition of fairies and a favourite hunting ground of kings. In *kāvyas* Gandhamādana appears as a beautiful and romantic mountain and forest region in the Himālaya, where for example Śiva and Umā make love after their marriage (*Kumārasambhava* VIII 28 ff.) [1424] or the nymph Urvaśī goes for pleasure with Purūravas (*Vikramorvaśīya*, beginning of Act IV) and turns into a creeper after quarrelling with him [1407]. A story is told in the *Mahābhārata* (III *adhyāyas* 146 ff.) of how Bhīma (during the exile of the Pāṇḍavas) meets the monkey lord (of the *Rāmāyaṇa*) Hanumant among the Gandhamādana mountains. They defy each other, Hanumant blocking the way, until they discover that they are brothers, both sons of the Wind God. After this Bhīma is able to proceed on his way to fetch a *saugandhika* flower for Draupadī, who had desired one when the marvellous scent reached their camp, from a lake guarded by demons (these flowers are reserved for divine beings) whom he has to fight in order to take it. At the end of this episode the Pāṇḍavas receive the blessing of Kuvera, God of Wealth. Perhaps it was this very charming legend which

Sâhasāṅka expanded in his epic, but at present this is pure conjecture.

1302. A score of verses are attributed to Sāhasāṅka or Vikramâditya (mostly the latter) in anthologies. Four such lyric gems are quoted by Vidyâkara (426, 452, 1154 and 1167), but none of them seem especially to fit the context of the heroic legend of Gandhamādana : two describe young women, the last is a remarkable description of a horse, a true *jāti* miniature (see Professor Ingalls' appreciation of this verse in his translation of Vidyâkara). The first of these (426) is interesting because it is quoted (anonymously) by several critics to illustrate their theories, as well as being selected by Vidyâkara, Jalhaṇa (p. 169) and Śrīdharadâsa (494), all of whom ascribe it to 'Vikramāditya', being thus the favourite among his verses :

> For who is this (fem.) river of sensuous beauty, unlike
> others,
> where lotuses swim with the Moon
> And where the slope of an elephant's temples juts out,
> between the banana trunks and lotus-fibre stems?

Vāmana (IV.3.4) quotes this as an example of 'praise of what is not the subject' *aprastutapraśaṃsā* [219]. He points out that there is only a slight hint of the real subject, a woman, through the gender (of the pronouns 'who' and 'this'). Kuntaka also (p. 189) quotes this as praise of what is not the subject. Namisādhu (pp. 11f.) on the other hand introduces the verse when discussing qualities of the sentence, i.e. as exemplifying the power of language itself rather than a figure of speech. He explains in detail that by 'Moon' the poet means 'face', by 'lotuses' the two 'eyes', by 'elephant's temples' the 'breasts', by 'banana trunks' the 'thighs' and by 'lotus-fibre stems' the 'arms'. Yet the words themselves do not actually express these things, there is not even the illusion of a metaphor here. It is the quality of the sentence, taken as a whole, to express what the poet intended. For Ānandavardhana (p. 459) the verse has 'subordinate implied meaning' (the girl) [250]. Śāradātanaya (p. 308) quotes the verse for *alaṅkāradhvani* since the standards of comparison imply the parts of the girl [251-2].

1303. The following verse is attributed to 'Sāhasāṅka'

by Śrīdharadâsa (2073) and describes a female ruddy sheldrake at sunset, the point depending on the poetic convention that these birds suffer the unhappiness of having to separate from their mates at night :

> She lifts up a wing, she falls down on the earth, she scratches her breast with her claws,
> she thinks of her companion and looks again with a tear-filled eye,
> The sheldrake's mate at the time when the day is ending does this and that, perplexed,
> because the Sun, through pity, though his orb is reddish, doesn't set.

1304. For Mâtṛgupta's quality as a poet it is enough to have Kuntaka's testimony, noted above in Chapter IV [290], which puts him first among the masters of the 'intermediate' *madhyama* style combining the natural and cultivated beauties of the other two. Brief references have been made above [95, 166, 336] to Mâtṛgupta's contributions to dramatic theory (on the nature of the aesthetic experience, etc.). After being made king of Kaśmīra by Vikramâditya of Ujjayinī (Kalhaṇa III 125; probably *c.* +410: the country was presumably detached from what had been Kuṣāṇa territory and a loyal vassal installed), Mâtṛgupta exercised his powers as patron and critic by rewarding Meṇṭha for an epic poem. Kalhaṇa's story (III 261) is that as Meṇṭha was tying up his manuscript, after reading it, Mâtṛgupta showed his appreciation by putting a gold vessel under it, fearing that the beauty *lāvaṇya* might be lost.

1305. Mâtṛgupta reigned less than five years : when Vikramâditya died (*c.* +414) he abdicated in favour of Prince Pravarasena, a claimant to the throne, and went to Vārāṇasī to live as an ascetic in retirement, though liberally supported by Pravarasena. He lived another ten years. According to Kalhaṇa, Mâtṛgupta had attended various courts before approaching Vikramâditya, but was still living in poverty, a poet whose merit had not received much recognition. The historian gives very favourable pictures of the characters of all these three, Vikramâditya, Mâtṛgupta and Pravarasena, as rivals in magnanimity, and values their story for its purifying ethical content.

This does not explain Mātṛgupta's career as a writer, though Kalhaṇa cites certain verses as the poet's own words. One verse improvised by him for Vikramāditya expresses poetically his loyalty, the privations of poverty and his hope for an appointment (III 181, also *Subhāṣitāvali* 3181); another is sent from Kaśmīra to thank his master, praising him for his gifts given without ostentation, like a tree giving fruit or a cloud silently raining (III 252). [5820]

1306. Some verses are cited as Mātṛgupta's by the critics. It is curious that Kṣemendra (+11) quotes one in order to point out what he considers an impropriety in it. Mātṛgupta writes with metaphors and using the figure 'concealment' *apahnuti* [229]:

> This is not the Moon, that flamingo on the lotus face
> of night,
> whose body is lovely as the cheek of a Kāśmīrī lady;
> My lord, this flood of light which shines in the sky,
> a mass of foam of the ocean of milk, is your fame.

Kṣemendra's objection to this is that it restricts the 'fame' to the singular number and compresses it into the disc of the Moon, when the plural would have been better to describe its limitless expansion (*Aucityavicāracarcā* illustrative verse 69 and comment).

1307. Vidyākara quotes one verse in his section on indifference *nirveda*, i.e. revulsion against the ways of the world and the meanness of everyday people, especially wealthy people hardened by enmity in a competitive society. The verse expresses this powerfully:

> Those who through their compassionate attitude do
> not deal for their own advantage, who, regarding
> the advantage of others,
> give help to the distressed even with their lives, those
> good people are far away:
> The person who is present is harsh, through pursuing
> enmities he has not acquired pity—
> O eye! Curb the impulse to tears, before whom will
> you now weep? (1499)

1308. In view of Mātṛgupta's known interest in the drama it is quite likely that he wrote plays and that some of the verses quoted by critics may have been drawn from them, but at present we seem to have no information on the question. The critics discuss a number of plays not now available to us, without naming their authors; among these one might seek works of Mātṛgupta if any clues could be pointed out suggesting his authorship.

1309. For example we have some information on a play about Kuvalayāśva and Madālasā, entitled *Māyāmadālasa*, the 'Deceit Madālasā' or 'Illusion Madālasā', since Sāgaranandin (472 ff.) gives a complete summary of it according to the structural theory of Mātṛgupta (cf. Chapter III [166-7]). This might indicate that the play is not too far removed in time from Mātṛgupta or even that he was also the author of it. The play was very neatly constructed in that the author made five acts of his story, arranging them so that each act contained one of the five conjunctions *sandhis*. Further, each conjunction contains a 'triad' of elements (see Chapter III above [166-7]).

1310. The main source in Tradition as we now know it, for this story, is the *Mārkaṇḍeya Purāṇa* (*adhyāyas* XXff. Bibliotheca Indica; XVIIIff. Veṅkaṭeśvara edition; cf. *Viṣṇu Purāṇa* IV *adhyāya* 8). It is set in or just before the time of Arjuna Kārtavīrya [527], who appears about a generation junior to Kuvalayāśva. In the time of Kuvalayāśva's father King Śatrujit (of Kāśi ?—this is not stated in this *Purāṇa*), the sage Gālava (XX.42) complains of a demon (*daitya* or *dānava*) assuming many (animal) forms and plaguing his hermitage. The sage brings the King a marvellous horse, named Kuvalaya because he can 'Circle the Earth'. This horse had fallen from the sky in response to the sage's sigh when he was worried by the demon. The sage explains that the horse can go anywhere, even in the sky or the Underworld (Pātāla), and that the King should use it to kill the demon: the King's son Ṛtadhvaja will become famous through this horse. Śatrujit sends his son with the horse and Gālava. Afterwards Ṛtadhvaja came to be called 'Kuvalayāśva', 'Having the Horse who Circles the Earth'.

1311. Defending Gālava's hermitage (XXI), Kuvalayāśva wounds the demon and chases it away, falling through a chasm in the Earth into the Underworld. He loses sight of the demon, but finds a deserted city, Purandarapura. He sees a woman and follows her into a palace, where he finds Madālasā, daughter of the King of the Gandharvas (celestial musicians). Kuvalayāśva and Madālasā fall in love at first sight. Madālasā has been abducted and kept in the Underworld by the demon Pātālaketu, who turns out to be the one Kuvalayāśva was chasing. Her companion is the widow of a victim of another demon. Kuvalayāśva lights a fire and marries Madālasā in due form, then takes her and fights his way out, finishing off Pātālaketu and killing many other demons, returning to his father's city (Vārāṇasī ?—not named here and the other sources have not been fully clarified: at some stage they were ejected from Vārāṇasī and established themselves on the Gomatī or in Vatsa or both).

1312. Tālaketu, brother of Pātālaketu, deceives Kuvalayāśva by taking the form of a sage and asking him to protect his hermitage on the Yamunā, then going to the city and reporting that he has been killed fighting demons (XXII). Madālasā dies of grief. When Kuvalayāśva returns (XXIII) he declines relationships henceforth with all women, because he will not love any but Madālasā. He now devotes himself to literature, the theatre, warlike exercises, etc., with other young men, and at this time two young dragons, taking the forms of brahmans, join him in these diversions (XX.1ff.).

1313. These two tell their father, the Dragon King Aśvatara, the tragic story of Kuvalayāśva and he resolves to intervene (XXIII). He engages in asceticism at the source of the River Sarasvatī in the Himālaya (Plakṣāvataraṇa) and invokes the Goddess Sarasvatī, daughter of Brahmā, with a hymn. She grants him a boon and he asks for his elder brother Kambala back and knowledge of all the art of music. Then the two dragons propitiate Śiva on Kailāsa and the Himālaya, with music, and he grants the boon that Madālasā shall be restored. She shall be born as Aśvatara's daughter, springing from his hood exactly as she was before she died. Aśvatara guards her in his citadel and sends his sons to fetch Kuvalayāśva. They invite him; then, as they cross the Gomatī they draw him into the Underworld and he sees they are dragons. Kuvalayāśva feasts and drinks with Aśvatara.

1314. Preparing the way by offering gifts, which Kuvalayāśva declines, and then promising an illusion of Madālasā when his sons point out what is the hero's real wish, Aśvatara gently reunites the lovers and sends them home (XXIV). Kuvalayāśva afterwards becomes king when his father dies. Madālasā bears him four sons, Vikrānta, Subāhu, Śatrumardana and Alarka (XXV ff.).

1315. The rest of this source story is taken up almost entirely with religious instruction, but after a long reign Kuvalayāśva and Madālasā retire to the forest to end their days in seclusion.

1316. The Illusion Madālasā either followed a very different recension of this story in Tradition or else handled it with extreme freedom. The *Mārkaṇḍeya* version itself is a work of art in the old Epic manner; it would thus seem difficult to improve it: either the dramatist must stage it faithfully according to the source, assuming this was the source, or he must construct a new plot. Perhaps also the dramatist might have found some difficulty if he wanted to follow the principles of dramatic construction and the stage very strictly. To have Madālasā actually die might not be tolerated in the classical theatre, therefore it might be better to continue the abduction theme instead, but that will eliminate Aśvatara.

1317. In Act I of the *Māyāmadālasa* Kuvalayāśva, who is already king, meets the sage Gālava. The sage wishes for the slaying of Tālaketu, the son of a demoness, who is ruling in a city at the foot of the Eastern Mountain (where the Sun rises) and has abducted Madālasā, the daughter of the God of Fire and the nymph Menakā (who was also the mother of Śakuntalā), and is hindering the rites of the sages. The King's impatience for an object, namely to visit the hermitage, coalesces with this 'wish' of Gālava. The 'commencement stage' consists of the ensuing dialogue between Gālava and Kuvalayāśva, in which the sage says that he himself could check the enemy but that it is the King's duty to do so, as king. The King reflects that he will as king acquire the sixth part of the results of the rites if he thus contributes to their successful performance: this is his 'thinking of the cause (or means)'. The 'seed', hinting at the final objective of the action, is the mention of Madālasā in the same Act and of her abduction by Tālaketu, who used 'deceit' or 'illusion' to effect this, implying the objective to be accomplished, of rescuing her. The conjunction of the above 'wish', 'commencement' and 'seed' constitutes the 'opening'.

1318. In Act II we learn that Kuvalayāśva has killed Tālaketu and married Madālasā, his marriage being the 'acquisition of the means' (to final success, i.e. bringing her back). The arrow which killed Tālaketu is also brought back to him, as it will be necessary to free her from a new threat. At this point the action is extended by the appearance of Pātālaketu, brother of Tālaketu, who stops Madālasā from leaving because she has been responsible for his brother's death ; thus a new enemy appears. The 'continuity' is the resulting repetition of the abduction motif, when Madālasā cries out for help as Pātālaketu stops her. The conjunction of the 'acquisition', 'extension' and 'continuity' constitutes the 're-opening'.

1319. In Act III after the battle with the demons Kuvalayāśva asks Madālasā to embrace him to remove his fatigue, this indicates 'enjoyment' and also 'capability'. But Madālasā's right eye throbs, an omen of something undesirable, namely separation: this is the 'germination'. Kuvalayāśva tries to counteract it by 'seeing success', saying that it has throbbed for something good. Following this Kuṭilaka (presumably another demon) tries to kill Madālasā, who as a result of his deceit or illusion (the *māyā* theme again, which gives the play its name) falls into a fire in grief (this is not explained; possibly he induced her to commit suicide by producing an illusion of Kuvalayāśva's death). But she is not burned (Fire is of course her father in this play), this being the 'success of a friend', namely of the Fire God, who thus shows himself as Kuvalayāśva's friend. The conjunction of 'enjoyment', 'germination' and the 'success of a friend' constitutes the 'embryo'.

1320. In Act IV we have the 'loss' of Madālasā, which is Kuvalayāśva's separation from his primary means (of success). Probably he believes she is dead (cf. *Sāhityamimāṃsā* p. 98 : compassionate). But the sage Bṛhadaśva meets him and tells him of the results of his father's asceticism, implying 'something better' for him despite the obstacle. The 'acquisition of the seed' here is indicated by the fact that Tālaketu and other enemies have been killed (presumably suggesting that things will continue to work out well in the end). The conjunction of 'loss', 'something better' and 'acquisition of the seed' constitutes the 'pause'.

1321. In Act V we have the 'accomplishment of the desired object' when Subāhu, having killed the enemy, returns with Madālasā. 'Success' is the accomplishing of what was to be accomplished, namely that Queen Madālasā was not burned in the fire and Subāhu has been able to destroy the enemies of the gods. The finishing of everything which had been commenced is the carrying out of what had been undertaken. These constitute the 'conclusion'.

1322. Though this analysis appears somewhat artificial at first sight, it will repay a little reflection, comparing it with the less precise indications of the *Nāṭyaśāstra* theory and with the structure of other plays of about the same period. The basic idea of the 'seed' growing to the objective is the same, but the converging 'wish' and 'impatience' leading in to the commencement suggests a more rigid structure unless interpreted freely rather than literally. The continuity of a motif and a plot even with change of characters is an interesting possibility, providing here for three successive enemies. Obviously their characters will be less fully developed than if they were one, but in this case the author presumably had no sympathy with the demoniac nature he portrays in them. It is not clear whether there is understood to be any kind of sub-plot. Apparently not, though Mātṛgupta's theory provides for the possibility of one in the third conjunction, in the 'success of a friend'. It hardly seems, however, that the activities of the Fire God here could have been worked out to such an extent. It appears that Subāhu is a son of Kuvalayāśva and Madālasā, as in the Purāṇic source : in which case long intervals must elapse between the acts of the play and the separation of the heroine from the hero must have been long, though it is not clear what Madālasā's situation was during it. Perhaps the Fire God protected his daughter but could not return her to her husband until the demons had been destroyed. Possibly after entering the fire she had to await her resurrection through Aśvatara.

1323. On account of its large mythological component, this play invites comparison with those of Kālidāsa on similar stories (Valour Urvaśī [1402], Token Śakuntalā [1418]). Illusion Madālasā is better as a drama than Kālidāsa's, on account of its coherent plot and sufficiency of action. The mythological component is much better blended in with the human, instead of standing out against it as something improbable which makes nonsense of all human effort. The hero is a strong and active character who, according to Sāgaranandin (276), dominates the whole play, appearing in every act. Of the details of the characterisation, and particularly of Madālasā, we can hardly speak further unless we have the good fortune to recover the text of the play.

1324. Among the verses quoted by Sāgaranandin from this play, the following is spoken by Kuvalayāśva to Madālasā during the battle in Act II (evidently with Pātālaketu):

> The bow in my hand has obtained consecration for the ceremony of the loss of all the enemies of the gods,
> —pretty thighs! Be done with fear!
> See! Quickly among the sharp-tips (arrows) the quarters
> have offerings made of necklaces of cut off heads of demons! (503-6)

In style this and the other verses are perhaps not inconsistent with the verses attributed to Mātṛgupta. A moderate use of alliteration can be seen in all of them and long compounds are avoided except where specially appropriate, as in this battle verse.

1325. One other play, known now from a very few identified fragments, which might be considered here, is the *Rāmānanda*, 'Joy of Rāma'. The fragments have been collected by Raghavan (*Some Old Lost Rāma Plays*, pp. 82-7). The title of the play is mentioned by Kuntaka (p. 243). The style of the fragments resembles that of the verses attributed to Mātṛgupta. Śāradātanaya (p. 235) mentions the play to illustrate Mātṛgupta's statement that a *nāṭaka*, though based on former events, may be to some extent invented in its subject matter. Thus in the *Rāmānanda* Vibhīṣaṇa [1029-30] is introduced before the abduction of Sītā. The play was based on the main action of the *Rāmāyaṇa* from some point before the abduction (probably the first embroilment with the demons during the exile) up to Rāma's triumph.

1326. The author begins modestly, or perhaps ironically with the critics in mind (this presumably is from the Prologue):

> No good quality at all is found in my composing of
> speech,
> even though searched for with great effort;
> Yet good people lovingly appreciate
> this arrangement of the Rāma story.
> (Śiṅgabhūpāla p. 269)

1327. The following verse describing the beginning of the rains probably belongs after the abduction, setting the scene for the intensification of Rāma's grief at Sītā's loss (such a description is found in this part of the *Rāmāyaṇa* itself and in many *kāvyas* based on it):

> The sky wears a blanket of cloud dark with the necks of
> sparrows;
> the tribe of frogs, mad with its clamourings, is as if
> reaching the end of discussion;
> The burned up ground through the rain gives off a scent
> fragrant with doused fried grain;
> the lord of radiance, though hard to see, is discovered
> by the laughter of the lotus pools.
> (*Sarasvatikaṇṭhābharaṇa* p. 712)

Bhoja quotes this to exemplify mixture of figures of speech and Śiṅgabhūpāla (p. 248) gives it as an example of 'ornamentation' (the first 'characteristic' [186]), because it has the qualities 'union', 'clarity', 'concentration', 'evenness', etc., as well as the figures simile, metaphor, fancy and 'cause' *hetu*. Rājaśekhara (*Kāvyamīmāṃsā* p. 109) quotes it for the description of the rainy season. The 'lord of radiance' is of course the Sun, whilst laughter is conventionally white because the teeth are shown. Perhaps the 'Rains Act' *Prāvṛḍaṅka*, to which Raghavan has found three references in Sāgaranandin, with a quoted verse, belongs to this play and the above verse also is from it (*Some Old Lost Rāma Plays*, pp. 99-100).

Chapter XXIII

MEṆṬHA; FICTIONS OF ABOUT THE +5

1328. Meṇṭha or Bhartṛmeṇṭha is a *kavi* whose reputation once stood far higher than Mātṛgupta's among the critics and other *kavis*. Rājaśekhara (*Bālarāmāyaṇa* Act I, verse 16) says that the *kavi* who formerly was Vālmīki later attained the state of being Bhartṛmeṇṭha, then he became Bhavabhūti and now (he flatters himself) he is Rājaśekhara. In other words Meṇṭha belongs among the greatest poets and dramatists, between the author of the *Rāmāyaṇa* itself and Bhavabhūti (early +8), the latter still the favourite of many connoisseurs of Sanskrit poetry and drama. Somadeva (I, | 10, *Yaśastilaka* II 113) names him in his list of great *kavis*. Padmagupta (*c.* +1000; *Navasāhasāṅkacarita* I 5 and 6) places Bhartṛmeṇṭha first among the old *kavis*, who 'touched reality' and cultivated the *vaidarbha* style which is like the blade of a sword. Ruyyaka (?....on Mahiman p. 214) quotes an anonymous verse which similarly names Bhartṛmeṇṭha as the first of artists able to extract *rasa*. The epic poets Śivasvāmin (+9) and Maṅkha (+12) name him as a model. The former (*Kapphiṇābhyudaya* XX 47) claims he has imitated Kālidāsa and practiced the style of Meṇṭha, whilst beating Daṇḍin (these three writers are all regarded as champions of the *vaidarbha* style). The latter (*Śrikaṇṭhacarita* II 53) says that the Goddess of Speech (i.e. Sarasvatī) is in despair at the loss of Meṇṭha, Subandhu, Bhāravi and Bāṇa, but he will try to reconcile her. Of these four only Meṇṭha and Bhāravi are known to have written epics (Subandhu and Bāṇa are famous in prose writing) and Bhāravi's *Kirātārjuniya* is surely the finest Sanskrit epic now available. Soḍḍhala (*Udayasundarī* p. 154) has this allusive verse :

Bhartṛmeṇṭha, whose name is famous in the world,
  is a painter in poetry
Whose brilliance of colours flashes at his pleasure,
  even in the flood of aesthetic experience.

Here 'colours' *varṇas* means also 'phonemes'. 'Aesthetic experience' *rasa* may mean 'water' and the 'flood' no doubt alludes to the description of the great Flood by Meṇṭha.

1329. In support of these tributes we find that Meṇṭha is quoted or referred to by almost all the critics and anthologists, even if the number of his verses cited is relatively small (at least 25) compared with some other *kavis* (no doubt it would be much increased if we had the means to identify verses quoted anonymously). It appears that he was not primarily a lyric poet and did not offer many lyric gems to the anthologists, but his sword-edged epic verses provided some brilliant examples of figurative speech (especially *paryāyokta*, 'circumlocution', and *utprekṣā*, 'fancy'). Dhanapāla has a verse (quoted by Jalhaṇa in the *Sūktimuktāvalī* IV 61) praising Bhartṛmeṇṭha for his 'figurative expression' *vakrokti*, which taken with other pieces of evidence seems to indicate that Meṇṭha was an exponent, in the highest degree, of Bhāmaha's ideal type of *kāvya* (the notes to the *Kāvyamīmāṃsā* attribute this verse to Rājaśekhara --p. 207). Ratnaśrījñāna (+10) in his commentary on Daṇḍin's *Kāvyalakṣaṇa* (p. 15), comparing the theories of Bhāmaha and Daṇḍin, appears to take Daṇḍin's *kārikā* I.22 as referring to Meṇṭha's epic *Hayagrīvavadha*, where by praising the nobility, heroism and learning even of the enemy the poet reflects still greater honour on the hero who overcomes him, thus delighting the reader. Rāmacandra and Guṇacandra (p. 155) support this appreciation of Meṇṭha's epic, rejecting Hemacandra's criticism (*Kāvyānuśāsana* p. 171) and calling the description of the enemy a special ornament because the aesthetic experience is the heroic. This indirect praise is clearly a kind of figurative expression, which Ratnaśrījñāna then declares to be the chief thing in *kāvya* (*kāvyaṃ hi vakroktipradhānam*), adding that this procedure is the very nature *svabhāva* of *vakrokti*. He afterwards mentions '*Hayagrīvavadha*, etc.' as illustrating this procedure, implying that Meṇṭha's epic was an outstanding example of it and confirming Dhanapāla's statement. On the *Hayagrīvavadha* we have Bhoja's opinion (*Śṛṅgāraprakāśa* II 470), where he gives '*Hayagrīvavadha*, etc.' to exemplify epic poems, indicating that he considered Meṇṭha's work preeminent among them: this supports the opinions of Maṅkha and Śivasvāmin noted above. Bhoja also quotes Daṇḍin I.22

for the second of his two 'ways' followed by *kavis*, which constitute his last kind of 'ornament of a whole work'. The first is the straightforward and naturally beautiful way, as in the *Rāmāyaṇa*, where a good hero overcomes his enemies (Daṇḍin I. 21). The second is this figurative way of enhancing the hero by praising the enemy and thus delighting us. Surely Bhoja thought of Meṇṭha's epic here.

1330. Most of what is known about the life and date of Meṇṭha has been noted above in connection with Rāmila, Vikramāditya and Mātṛgupta. The prefix Bhartṛ- often appearing with his name is an honorific or title meaning 'Master'. The name Meṇṭha means 'elephant keeper' and may be the sole basis of the idea that he was Vikramāditya's elephant keeper, in Rāmila's verse. In the anthologies the name Hastipaka, which means 'elephant driver', appears as an author of verses; this approximate synonym evidently refers to Meṇṭha, since *Saduktikarṇāmṛta* 1852, 'Bhartṛmeṇṭha', – *Subhāṣitāvali* 640, 'Hastipaka'. If there is any truth in the traditions we have recorded, Meṇṭha would seem to have worked first at Vikramāditya's court in Ujjayinī and then gone to Kaśmīra following Mātṛgupta. There he completed his epic, *Hayagrīvavadha*, and on the basis of our tentative chronology we arrive at a rather precise date for this completion, since the new work was submitted to Mātṛgupta during the latter's short reign: the poem was finished *c.* +412 and hardly more than a year before or after that date. Like Rāmila, Meṇṭha was a pupil of a certain Śaṅkara or Mūka according to Ātmabodha in the passage discussed above. Ātmabodha there quotes a verse as from the *Hayagrīvavadha*, which states that Meṇṭha was taught by Śaṅkarendra.

1331. The *Hayagrīvavadha*, 'Slaying of Hayagrīva', appears to have been based on suggestions found scattered in the *Mahābhārata* and *Purāṇas* (especially *Agni Purāṇa* I, *Padma Purāṇa* CCLVIII, *Bhāgavata Purāṇa* VIII. 24, but the last is so late it is very likely based on Meṇṭha's epic). The extant *Purāṇa* texts offer a variety of myths concerning the wars of the gods and demons and the 'incarnations' or 'introductions' *avatāras* of Viṣṇu in different forms as champion of the gods. These texts are generally late and not yet critically edited, but some of the legends in them may have been current in other forms earlier than the time of Meṇṭha. At present we cannot say what the poet's primary source was for the incarnations of Viṣṇu or whether he himself imagined much of his matter. Meṇṭha's epic took up the story of one of the incarnations, in which Viṣṇu as the great Fish (Matsya) slew the demon Hayagrīva after the Flood in the time of Manu Vaivasvata (cf. Chapters IX and X above on this story in *Veda* and *Itihāsa*, there is a version of it in the Third Book of the *Mahābhārata*). The story goes that at the end of the cycle of history which began with the sixth Manu (Cākṣuṣa), when the world was growing corrupt, Hayagrīva stole the *Vedas* from the mouth of Brahmā as the latter was falling asleep (the sleep or night of Brahmā marks the end of a cycle, which is a mere 'day' in his life, though there are some variations and complications in this doctrine which need not detain us here). Meanwhile Viṣṇu had become incarnate as a small fish, which the seventh Manu (Vaivasvata), who was to inaugurate the next cycle, caught when washing. Manu spared the fish and looked after it until it grew large, when he put it in the sea. Before disappearing, the fish warned Manu of the impending Flood, which would sweep away the corrupt society at the end of the cycle, and instructed him to build a ship in order to escape. He must embark with the Seven Sages (*ṛṣis*, Seers), taking all kinds of seeds to restart the world after the Flood. Terrible storms followed and the Earth was deluged with rain, whilst the sea rose and flooded over it. Manu completed his preparations and embarked in the ship, whereupon the great Fish appeared: Manu made his ship fast to a horn on its head and the Fish towed it safely through the stormy waves. After a long time the sea began to subside and the Fish towed the ship to the Himālaya mountains (in Kaśmīra according to some versions) as they reappeared from the water. Manu landed and in due course inaugurated the new cycle of society, producing a daughter by means of a Vedic rite. From Manu and his daughter all the ancient dynasties of kings of our present cycle traced their descent. Hayagrīva during this time of chaos, as well as stealing the *Vedas* had conquered Heaven from the gods, defeating Indra, their king. At last Brahmā awoke, to begin his new 'day', and the gods found a champion in Viṣṇu to liberate them from the oppression of Hayagrīva. The great Fish killed Hayagrīva with a blow of his horn in the demon's chest, recovered the *Vedas* and restored them to Brahmā.

1332. This remarkable myth provides plenty of scope for imaginative treatment and it appears that Meṇṭha did full justice to it, though all we now possess of his epic is perhaps twenty known (and no doubt others not identified) verses quoted by the critics, together with some discussion by them of its contents. (According to the *Catalogue of the Sanskrit Manuscripts in the Panjab University Library,* Vol II, 1941, p. 271, that library, in Lahore, possessed a manuscript of the *Hayagrivavadha* in Malayalam script, but incomplete. Nārāyaṇa's *Campū Matsyāvatāra* (+17) appears to summarise Meṇṭha's epic, since it agrees closely with the story as we have reconstructed it here. A thorough search should be made in Kerala for manuscripts of this epic.) Meṇṭha began with a description of Hayagrīva, the first verse being :

> There was a Daitya (Demon), Hayagrīva,
> in the dwellings of whose friends
> Fortunes (or beauties) proclaimed the strength of
> his arms,
> with smiles like white parasols.

This incidentally is an example of beginning an epic by plunging straight into the story (*vastunirdeśa, Śṛṅgāraprakāśa* II 472 as the 'ornament of a whole work' *prabandhālankāra* 'commencement with a salutation, etc.'). Even though there is no invocation (another way of beginning an epic), this beginning is auspicious because the word 'Fortunes' *śriyaḥ* occurs in the first verse. With this verse we are already in Meṇṭha's world of *vakrokti* or figurative expression : the fact that Hayagrīva's friends (or allies or vassals) had Fortunes (Goddesses of Fortune) indicates that he was a great conqueror who had bestowed lands and gifts on his companions. The white parasols are emblems of royalty, just as the possession of a Fortune implies kingship (which is not incompatible with the status of being a feudatory of a great emperor). The word *śriyaḥ* may also mean simply beautiful women at the prosperous courts of Hayagrīva's vassals. Smiles are white because the teeth are shown. The 'demons', it may be remembered, are not different in kind from the gods but in

Tradition are found to be mixed up with them in the genealogies : only their behaviour is generally regarded as improper, instead of keeping to their allotted place in the universe they try to overthrow the divine hierarchy. **Kṣemendra** in his treatise on metres (*Suvṛttatilaka* after III.16) quotes this verse as a model opening of an epic in *anuṣṭubh* (*vaktra*), a metre especially appropriate for this purpose.

1333. A number of other verses, perhaps also from the first or second canto, describe the defeat of the gods and the conquest of Heaven by Hayagrīva, the poem apparently opening with this episode. Mammaṭa quotes (end of Chapter I) this 'fancy', though saying it lacks implied meaning, is only literal:

> "That pride-destroyer has gone out from his mansion"
> —hearing of him just by chance,
> Amarāvatī (Indra's city) closed her eyes as if in fear
> —her bolt shut quickly by agitated Indra.

One verse quoted several times describes by 'circumlocution' (Tilaka on Udbhaṭa IV.6) how Indra and his war elephant Airāvata lost their courage when Hayagrīva appeared (presumably as he routed the army of the gods):

> Having seen whom (Hayagrīva),
> the arrogance in Airāvata's face and the pride in
> Indra's heart
> Lost their affection for their homes,
> though they had lived there for a long time.

(Raghavan has collected this and some other verses by Meṇṭha in his *Bhoja's Śṛṅgāraprakāśa*, see p. 788). A verse quoted by Ruyyaka suggests the conquest of Heaven by Hayagrīva, again by circumlocution, by expressing its effects :

> Whose soldiers touched contemptuously
> the clusters of flowers on the Pārijāta tree
> In the Nandana Gardens (of Indra's Heaven), which
> had been caressed
> by the contact of Śacī's hair.

Śacī is Indra's consort, who was particularly fond of the Pārijāta : here Meṇṭha stresses the humiliation of the King and Queen of Heaven, unable to protect their most cherished possessions. A

1334. The following verse, apparently addressed to Hayagrīva by one of his companions or ministers, perhaps belongs later in the epic, since it foreshadows the fight with Viṣṇu by suggesting Hayagrīva has nothing to fear from him :

> Before, when your Moon-like face was born,
> which enjoyed the love of (flirtatious) frowns,
> The tribe of Vasudeva
> became a mere name.

(Raghavan p. 786, from Bhoja; Vasudeva was the father of the Kṛṣṇa incarnation of Viṣṇu, so strictly speaking this is an anachronism.) We are told by Bhoja (*Śṛṅgāraprakāśa* II 475) that the *Hayagrivavadha* contained as ornament of a whole work a famous 'counsel' *mantra* episode, in which such a verse as this might have occurred, but a more likely place for a counsel in this story would be where the defeated gods consider plans for a counterattack [1267]. Here is another verse on Hayagrīva:

> This arm of the Lord of the Dānavas (Demons)
> —does it not repeatedly
> Make a companion of Destiny (or Death),
> in successes intending ruin?
>
> (*Kāvyamimāṃsā* p. 89)

This may be taken as another circumlocution for Hayagrīva's victories which humbled the gods.

1335. We have mentioned already the discussions among the critics as to the propriety of this long and fulsome description of the enemy of the real hero (Viṣṇu) of this epic, and seen how the criticism was met with the argument of figurative expression reflecting greater glory on the hero. Ānandavardhana (p. 265), Mahiman (p. 494) and Ruyyaka (*Alaṃkārasarvasva* p. 148) argue over the figures and implied meaning in:

He could state all
the qualities which dwelt in Hayagrīva
who could find out the ocean's measure
in waterpots.

The description of Hayagrīva was not limited to a single canto, or to his nobility, heroism and learning (the latter acquired by the theft of the *Vedas* ?). We learn from Viśvanātha (+15: *Sāhityadarpaṇa* p. 193) that the epic contained a description of Hayagrīva's water sports (probably in Heaven after his victory, or in the great Flood itself). This type of description belongs to a branch of lovemaking and thus to the production of the sensitive aesthetic experience, for which a place should be found in any good epic, according to the theory, even when the story was a myth which seemed to allow no scope for love. Here again some critics seem to have found fault with the idea of describing the lovemaking of the enemy. The presence of this episode suggests that Meṇṭha took care to include in his epic a proper range of descriptions, as well as aiming to produce all the varieties of aesthetic experience (cf. Chapter VI above [405]).

1336. The terrible Flood would offer scope for vivid description, though there is little evidence but Soḍḍhala's tribute to show how Meṇṭha handled this part of the story of his hero. According to Bhoja (*Śṛṅgāraprakāśa* II 475) the *Hayagrīvavadha* contained as an ornament of the whole work a noteworthy description of night [1267]. Its story offered opportunity for the description of no ordinary night, but of that of Brahmā himself at the end of the cycle and the dissolution of the world. This ought to coincide with the Flood as part of the final horror which engulfed mankind. A

1337. We find some verses on the heroism of Viṣṇu quoted as Meṇṭha's, which probably belong to the *Hayagrīvavadha*. Ānandavardhana (*Dhvanyāloka* p. 225) quotes a verse, which Ruyyaka identifies in Mahiman's critique and corrects (commentary on *Vyaktiviveka* p. 272, new edition p. 315: see also Indurāja, p. 86):

Who (Viṣṇu), with just the forceful command to strike
once,
created for the brides of Rāhu

A rite of lovemaking in which only kissing remained,
a fruitless play for (their) unrestrained embraces.

This refers to the myth of the churning of the Ocean, after which, in the struggle for possession of the ambrosia, the demon Rāhu's head was cut off (by Viṣṇu's discus at his command) [331, 592]. Since Rāhu had already tasted the drink of immortality his head remained alive, but being severed from the body offered severely limited possibilities for lovemaking, as Meṇṭha wittily points out. This verse is again an example of the figure circumlocution, for which Kuntaka quotes it (p. 191). A verse given by Vidyākara (1558) seems to belong to this epic, describing Viṣṇu's unshakable confidence as the army (presumably of demons just before the final battle) approaches:

Hari (Viṣṇu), his eyes languid,
having looked proudly at the army went to sleep again;
But his beloved, her fear ended by discovering her
lord's valour,
did not even look.

1338. A few more verses can be traced to the *Hayagrīvavadha,* such as one quoted by Rājaśekhara (*Kāvyamimāṃsā* p. 83), evidently from the narrative of the final battle:

Hayagrīva's body became blackened
with the cuts dug in it by the sword resplendent with
flashes of light:
As if stained by the wickedness of his intention,
sprung from his sudden anger, to destroy the family of
Viṣṇu.

1339. The verses from the *Hayagrīvavadha* show in a very high degree the qualities and methods of the classical *kāvya* epic which are known to us in a somewhat earlier form in the epics of Aśvaghoṣa. They evidently belong to chains of discontinuous stanzas, independent except for the minimal support of a context which would tell us to whom a relative pronoun refers. Possibly Meṇṭha linked these chains as Aśvaghoṣa does, with a series of such relative pronouns, or by using the same figure, such as his favourite 'circumlocution', through a chain. Nevertheless the content of each verse is concentrated on its moment of vision, which yet suggests indirectly entire phases of the action which it typifies. Thus several of the verses given above, whilst each offers its own vivid picture of a moment of time, as when Hayagrīva's soldiers rough-handle the treasured Pārijāta tree, suggest the action of Hayagrīva in defeating the gods. At the same time there are more general statements among these particular ones, such as the description of Hayagrīva's arm dealing death. Taken as a whole, the epic suggests an optimistic view of the ultimate triumph of good over evil, of the renewal of the cycle of life even after the terrible dissolution of the Earth at the end of the old cycle and the temporary ascendancy of the demons in Heaven. This is suggested at different points by reference to other periods of history, when the eternal hero Viṣṇu, in different incarnations or simply as a god, battled against demons and overcame them: the names used to refer to him and his family tend to suggest Kṛṣṇa in particular, whilst we noted the allusion to the decapitating of Rāhu.

1340. These verses have the true *kāvya* epic compactness, richness of meaning and feeling of a sustained narrative force telling a great story. We have noted that the epic seems to have covered a rich range of descriptions and to have produced all the recognised aesthetic experiences. The main experience, evidently, is the heroic, as pointed out by Rāmacandra and Guṇacandra (*Nāṭyadarpaṇa* p. 155). These are tantalising glimpses of what we have good reason to believe was an epic unsurpassed by any other poet; let us hope that somewhere a manuscript of a work long so greatly and widely appreciated still survives.

1341. We are less certain whether some other verses preserved in the anthologies belong to the *Hayagrīvavadha*. The following may belong to the celebrated description of night, though hardly of the dreadful night of Brahmā :

The Sun, fallen upon by the floods of darknesses, was
stepping on the Earth,
his thoughts not stupified despite the danger :
He stayed in each house in the guise of a lamp,
as if he had broken his body in many pieces.

(Raghavan p. 789 : *Subhāṣitāvali* 1903).

Then there is this verse on the quality of true heroes:

For wise men say that this is the sign of great ones,
the indicator of the distinction of greatness,
—That when happiness or unhappiness arise
their mind does not fall into the power of joy or despair.
(Raghavan p. 789 : *Subhāṣitāvali* 268)

Next to this in the *Subhāṣitāvali* (267) stands the following, which is perhaps a little too simple for its attribution there to Meṇṭha (it is also found in Bhartṛhari's *Triśati*, 14):

Firmness in misfortune, then forbearance in success,
cleverness in speech in the assembly (but) valour in battle,
Pleasure in good reputation, addiction to learning,
—for this is accomplished in the nature of noble persons.

1342. Very different again, though in the same style as the verses of Meṇṭha, is this :

By discharging the bow with five sharp arrows (one for each of the five senses)
and wishing to conquer even a person never conquered before,
By preparing with love with excessive violence,
you are certainly the (bow-) string here (in this world) which is called "woman".
(Raghavan p. 789 : *Subhāṣitāvali* 1462)

Perhaps the following verse, in the same *puṣpitāgrā* metre, belongs to the same context (canto ?) as the last :

And wine with a blossoming lotus as ear-ornament, lotus,
and the whitewashed (palace) roof covered with moonbeam-sprays,
And the beloved woman who has the confusion engendered by love,—

this is the (real) fruit for the wealthy; other things
are (mere) aggrandisements (or 'ashes'—a pun).
(Raghavan p. 788 : *Subhāṣitāvali* 2233)

1343. The next, on the other hand, can be compared and contrasted with the verse on true heroes quoted above (both are in the *vaṃśastha* metre) :

He who carries out his affairs after having had them
examined several times
by reliable friends and after having considered the
dangers
With his own understanding,—he indeed is intelligent,
only he is a fit person for Fortune and fame.
(Raghavan p. 789 : *Sūktimuktāvali* p. 404)

There are a number of other such verses on policy *nīti*, a subject very proper to epic poetry, attributed to Meṇṭha, e.g. *Sūktimuktāvali* p. 404 :

Affection for chance successes,
disdain for honouring elders,
—These two illnesses of Fortune on the earth
are known as incurable.

1344. The anthologies contain some more descriptive verses on women which are ascribed to Meṇṭha. They would not appear to fit into the *Hayagrivavadha* (would Hayagrīva have found village women or women of Andhra in Heaven or would such women have followed his army ?) and may therefore have belonged to some other work. The following are given by Krishnamachariar (p. 133; the first two also by Raghavan, p. 789):

Speeches raining with sweetness,
navels with loosened garments,
Glances with trembling brows,
—these are the ornaments of the women of Andhra.
(*Saduktikarṇāmṛta* 564)

Yet the face of the charming village woman
has a shoot (-like) lower lip
With natural and boisterous laughter
—it deserves a whole kingdom !

(*Saduktikarṇāmṛta* 576)

Not so do the coquetries
of city women delight us
As the naturally innocent
actions of village women.
(Aufrecht, ZDMG 36 p. 369—conjecturally by Meṇṭha?)

1345. The anthologies also contain some verses describing elephants which are ascribed to Meṇṭha or 'Hastipaka' (the first of those given here is ascribed to 'Meṇṭha' by Śrīdharadāsa, 1852, to 'Hastipaka' by Vallabhadeva, 640, which seems to confirm that the two names refer to the same author):

Take a mouthful of hay ! O young elephant, give up the bond of love for the female elephant !
Now you must continually anoint your wounds, caused by the knots of the snare, with mud !
You have been separated from those feet of the Vindhya (Mountains), grey with the pollen of flowers fallen near the banks of the Revā,
where are seen the wanderings through playfulness of the excellent brides of the Śabaras (mountain tribesmen of the Vindhyas) !

The Vindhya Mountain, your father, has been abandoned, and the Lady Revā River, who is like your mother,
and the other elephants, your contemporaries, whichever had their minds bowed in the bond of affection;
Isn't it through your own greed, O female elephant, that you yourself have surrendered your body to imprisonment,
that you live far away and the hard goads roll on the cushion of your head ?

(Śrīdharadāsa 1853; these two verses are given by Raghavan, p. 789, and Krishnamachariar, p. 132.) Vāmana (II.2.17) quotes the second phrase of the first line of the first verse in order to justify the expression 'young elephant' *karikalabha*.

> At midnight the elephants in the (toddy-) palm
> groves hear the clamour of the shower,
> the water of the downpouring clouds;
> The flapping of their ears quieted, their eyes half closed,
> their trunks resting on the points of their tusks.
> (Vidyākara 1161)

This last description of elephants in its realism recalls the description of a horse which Vidyākara seems to have taken from Vikramāditya, as we noted above [1302]. If we are right in accepting the tradition that the two poets were contemporaries it may be no accident that this kind of sharp observation of animals is found in both verses.

1346. It has been suggested that it was these verses about elephants which gave rise to Meṇṭha's names or nicknames and to the story that he was Vikramāditya's elephant keeper. The verse of Dhanapāla which we have already referred to [1329], as praising Meṇṭha for his figurative expression, alludes to this idea about the poet, by saying his *vakrokti* was like a goad pricking the *kavi*-elephants, making them shake their heads (in India this is a gesture of admiration).

1347. Among these verses of Meṇṭha we may look for the recognised characteristics of the *vaidarbha* style. The leading theoretical protagonist of that style in works now accessible to us is Daṇḍin [240], who perhaps was an admirer of Meṇṭha, as we suggested when discussing Ratnaśrījñāna's remarks on *Kāvyalakṣaṇa* I. 22. There is a certain simplicity in Meṇṭha's style, for all his 'figurative expression', in which we may identify Daṇḍin's qualities of 'clarity', the meaning not too far-fetched, and 'lucidity of meaning', where no extra words have to be understood and the meaning is fully expressed. The vocabulary also is relatively simple, the words used not being rare or of extraordinary formation though they are 'poetic' in the sense of being largely words favoured in *kāvya*. 'Union' or 'tautness' (well-knittedness) is observed, though not at the expense of fulness of expression, and some of the verses are tightly packed with meaning. Balancing the simplicity of expression we find 'concentration' (ambiguity) in the use of words in secondary senses or metaphorically, an important ingredient in figurative expression. Thus the word 'Fortunes' *śriyaḥ* in the first verse of the *Hayagrīvavadha* is pregnant with suggested meanings. If 'exaltation' means elevated content it is certainly present in the *Hayagrivavadha*. 'Evenness', 'sweetness' and 'softness' have to do with the sounds of the language rather than with meaning and are easily felt in these Sanskrit verses, which have a natural delicacy and pleasing texture produced by touches of alliteration baıely felt and rarely obvious. 'Strength', meaning the use of compounds, according to Daṇḍin, is in the *vaidarbha* generally avoided in verse Meṇṭha is in fact very sparing of compounds but may be described as using a sufficient stiffening of two and three word compounds to give consistency to his verses (thus in *Hayagrivavadha* I. 1 'frienddwellings' in the first half of the verse and 'whiteparasolsmiles' in the second). The verses on elephants, as befits their longer metres and more lyric nature, contain compounds of four and even six words (e.g. 'Revābanksnearfallenflowerpollengrey'). If 'graciousness' is that beauty of expression which is unspoiled by the crudeness of exaggeration, Meṇṭha deserves the fullest praise for it. Instead of exaggeration we find here precise and realistic description, the *bhāvikatva* (realism) of Bhāmaha where everything is as if present before our eyes [198].

1348. If Meṇṭha was supposed to be a reincarnation of Vālmīki he presumably retold the story of Rāma in some way, as did Bhavabhūti and Rājaśekhara later. Though we do not at present know of any Rāma *kāvya* ascribed to Meṇṭha, we do know of a number of masterpieces based on his story now apparently lost, whose authors are nowhere mentioned, among which we might seek Meṇṭha's missing work (or works). These Rāma *kāvyas* known to us only in fragments, through the writings of critics, are all plays; no Rāma epic seems to be heard of which might be Meṇṭha's. By way of pure conjecture we may here look at what is known of two old plays, which have characteristics perhaps not alien to Meṇṭha, the *Kṛtyārāvaṇa* and *Chalitarāma*. Their vigorous but subtle styles and their humour might be Meṇṭha's and the special attention to the enemy *pratināyaka*, in this case Rāvaṇa, recalls the description of Hayagrīva which disturbed some critics. Rāma in these plays pays very heavily for his eventual success and some critics remarked that in the *Kṛtyārāvaṇa* he is portrayed in too many grievous situations (Rāmacandra and Guṇacandra, p. 155). In both plays the story was handled with great freedom.

1349. The *Kṛtyārāvaṇa*, 'Rāvaṇa and the Witch' (i.e. play about Rāvaṇa in which the special feature is the appearance of a witch—Kuntaka p. 243 notes that the title is especially significant), was a *nāṭaka* in seven acts covering the story of the *Rāmāyaṇa* from the abduction of Sītā up to her rescue following Rāma's victory. Raghavan has put together the available fragments of it, which are quite considerable since it was popular with the critics (*Some Old Lost Rāma Plays*, pp. 26-49). The aesthetic experience produced by this play seems to have been a matter of controversy: the main experience was perhaps the furious, produced by the anger and violent actions of Rāvaṇa, with a very strong accompaniment of the compassionate in relation to Rāma and his sufferings. But on the other hand the compassionate might presumably be taken as the main *rasa*, if Rāma is the real hero. Rāmacandra and Guṇacandra (p. 155) took the compassionate to be in fact the subordinate aesthetic experience and then criticised the play for having the subordinate *rasa* overdeveloped.

1350. In Act I the demon Mārīca is sent by Rāvaṇa to take the form of a golden deer in the Pañcavaṭī forest and entice the exiled Rāma away from Sītā so that she can be abducted. Rāvaṇa's sister Śūrpaṇakhā separates Sītā from Lakṣmaṇa (example of 'outwitting' *adhibala* as a limb of the street play, *Śṛṅgāraprakāśa* II p. 493, *Nāṭyadarpaṇa* pp. 119-20 [326]) while he carries her off (which eventually takes place in Act II). It is in Act III that Rāma returns from hunting the deer and discovers his loss, also finding the dying Jaṭāyus who vainly tried to oppose Rāvaṇa: here the scenes of Rāma's extreme grief begin. In Act IV his grief due to separation from Sītā is further developed, whilst in this and the following act the story is taken through the acquisition of the monkey allies and search for Sītā up to Rāma's arrival on the coast opposite Laṅkā.

1351. In Act VI we have the monkey Aṅgada as emissary in Laṅkā, taunting Rāvaṇa, which leads into the battle episode.

Early in the battle, Lakṣmaṇa is seriously wounded (*Nāṭyadarpaṇa* p. 155), causing extreme grief to Rāma (Lakṣmaṇa's life is saved and the tide of battle turns in Rāma's favour afterwards, but we have no details at present as to how this was handled in the play). Probably at the end of Act VI, otherwise at the beginning of Act VII, Rāvaṇa becomes desperate in his anger (presumably as his army begins to be defeated, especially when his son is killed) and orders a demoness, Dāruṇikā (perhaps it is she who is the 'Witch', but that is not clear), to kill Sītā. Dāruṇikā is unwilling to commit such a murder and escapes from the dilemma, between that and disobeying Rāvaṇa's order, through the device of Sītā being shown an illusion of a severed head which looks like Rāma's. Seeing this brought in and believing her husband has been killed in the battle, Sītā wishes to die by immolating herself in fire (*Nāṭyadarpaṇa* p. 89 has an extract from this episode, but without letting us see clearly whether Dāruṇikā was responsible for the illusion). A

1352. In the first part of Act VII, Rāma is reported to have felled Rāvaṇa in the battle. This is the limb 'ability' *śakti* of the obstacle conjunction (*Nāṭyadarpaṇa* p. 88 [149]). Though Rāvaṇa is dead, the objective of the play is not yet attained, because here in Act VII the report of Sītā's suicide is brought to Rāma's followers. Here we have the limb 'contradiction' *virodha* of the obstacle conjunction, which 'contradicts' the objective [149]. This makes it clear that the recovery of Sītā is the objective of the play (*Nāṭyadarpaṇa* p. 86, passage missed by Raghavan):

CHAMBERLAIN [*to Lakṣmaṇa and Vibhīṣaṇa*] Prince ! It—

BOTH. What ?

CHAMBERLAIN. Nay ! This—

BOTH. Sir ! Speak ! Speak !

CHAMBERLAIN. What can I do? Listen. The Lady Sītā saw an illusory head of the Master (Rāma), brought by a servant at Rāvaṇa's command, and, although reassured by her companions, renounced her purpose, saying : "I won't torment myself" and—

ALL. What did she do ?

CHAMBERLAIN. What it is not possible to say:

Like the digit of the Moon at the close of day,
like a female wild goose impatient in a thicket of lotuses,
The Princess, experiencing the death of her husband,
entered a fire with quivering terrific flames.

This Chamberlain is presumably the one in charge of Rāvaṇa's palace and the scene is the victors' entry. Whether Sītā was actually seen as if entering the fire and thus reported dead, or was only rumoured to have done so, is not clear. It appears, however, that the dramatist here may have had the brilliant idea of amalgamating with this attempted suicide the well known fire ordeal of Sītā, through which she proved her chastity whilst a captive [1032].

1353. In any case at the end of the play we find that the Fire God has protected Sītā and brought her to Rāma. The *Nāṭyadarpaṇa* (p. 100) quotes the 'consummation of the *kāvya*' *kāvyasaṃhāra* [150]:

FIRE. My dear! Tell me what further joy I can add for you.

RĀMA. My lord! Is there a joy beyond this?

After this the actor of Rāma's part speaks the 'panegyric' *praśasti* [150] or final benediction (*Nāṭyadarpaṇa* p. 101):

RĀMA. Nevertheless, may this be:

As my desire, the object of my anxiety,
is complete,
So let the stage free itself
from all the evils which have come to it.

And also:

May the people be without calamities,
may the good be long lived,
May writers become famous through literature,
may mothers be completely happy!

The 'evils' which had come to the stage were bad plays, with too many words and too little action, which our author criticises through his Producer in the Prologue, to which we shall turn below.

1354. As Abhinavagupta says (II 410), there is evidently no scope for the 'tender' *kaiśikī* mode of acting in Rāvaṇa and the Witch, an exception to the rule for *nāṭakas* [181]. Instead it is full of 'violent' *ārabhaṭi* scenes, to some of which Abhinavagupta refers (III 104) to illustrate the violent mode. Kuntaka has said that the title of this play is significant, consequently we have to understand that Rāvaṇa's use of witchcraft is essential to the main action: this may refer both to the tricks through which Sītā is abducted and to the final unsuccessful attempts to destroy both Rāma and Sītā.

1355. A quotation is preserved (in the *Nāṭyadarpaṇa*, p. 132) from the prologue of the *Kṛtyārāvaṇa*, in which the Producer humorously leads in to the appearance of Mārīca. The Producer announces to an actress that he is utterly disgusted with acting and intends to resign from his job and give up this bad way of life; instead he will think of his future in the other world. His reason for disgust is that acting is nothing but diffuse verbiage, the action being insipid and small. This no doubt intends a criticism of certain trends in the drama of that day; we may suppose of a tendency to fill the large scale form, which seems to have begun with Śūdraka, with long winded descriptions instead of with action. We may conclude from this criticism that the author of the *Kṛtyārāvaṇa* did his best to cultivate an opposite trend with plenty of action and no unnecessary words, in effect in the 'violent' mode (in which action and the use of gestures predominates). On the actual leading in here, Raghavan has suggested that the disgust of the Producer introduces the disgust of Mārīca, the first character presumed to appear, who though feeling bitter against Rāma, as a result of past events, is nevertheless disgusted at the part Rāvaṇa has ordered him to play in bringing about the abduction of Sītā. This would be an instance of 'parallelism' *avalagita* [139] between the actions of the Producer and the character, one of the rhetorical devices for leading in from the prologue to the play (in the event it seems neither of them resigns his job as yet: the play goes on and Mārīca carries out his commission).

1356. From the fragments we get the impression that the dramatist really avoided verbiage and kept his language taut and concentrated. When Rāvaṇa proposes to Sītā, before abducting her, that they make a good match and she should (voluntarily) join him he says simply but pointedly (Act II:)

> The world has been conquered by me with valour
> and by you with beauty:
> Therefore you should love me
> as a fellow student who loves you.
>
> (Raghavan p. 37 : *Nāṭyadarpaṇa* p. 70)

But Sītā replies with equal point that he has not yet conquered himself, let alone the world. This is an example of 'thunderbolt' *vajra*, a limb of the re-opening [147].

1357. In Act III Rāma sees a great bird fallen in the forest and gradually realises it is Jaṭāyus:

> This is a mountain whose wings have been cut off by
> the King of the Gods today,
> or it is Garuḍa cut down by the Lord of the Demons
> after making an enemy of him;
> Or else I think it is my father's dear friend here—
> Alas! Is it not Jaṭāyus whose life is departing?
>
> (Raghavan p. 40)

This incident is an 'intervention' *prakari*—Abhinavagupta III p. 15 [122]—through which Rāma gains the information that it is Rāvaṇa who has abducted Sītā. The *Nāṭyadarpaṇa* (p. 73) quotes it for the limb 'appearance' *rūpa* of the embryo [148].

1358. In Act IV Lakṣmaṇa expresses the fatigue *kheda* (a limb of the 'obstacle' conjunction [149]: *Nāṭyadarpaṇa* p. 86) of the search for Sītā:

> The ways passed over are thorny, their sand is hot and
> dust blows up from them;
> the places trodden on have huge rocks, exceedingly
> rough, from the mountains;
> There are also elephants confused by the terror engendered by the proud lord of the lions;
> and water has been drunk, pungent through being
> sullied and mingled with the streams of rut of
> the elephants.
>
> (Raghavan p. 41)

1359. The following verse relating to the sub-plot *patākā* [122] (says Abhinavagupta, III 17, quoting Lollaṭa) is thought by Raghavan to belong to Act V and to be spoken by Sugrīva, Rāma's ally. The point is that the action of the sub-plot decisively promotes the main action :

Fortunate are those who are successful,
praiseworthy is the event of their birth,
Who by abandoning their own affairs
accomplish their prosperity.

(Raghavan p. 42)

—the word 'accomplish' *pra-sādh* may also mean 'embellish': thus they abandon their own affairs to help a friend, but his success is to their advantage too, which may be considered embellished by being brought about in this unselfish manner. According to Lollaṭa this sub-plot exhibits five sub-conjunctions *anusandhis* in its action, of which the 'opening' is found in this verse. The re-opening is found in a verse referring to Vālin, not given in full here. The embryo is when herbs are brought to heal Lakṣmaṇa, struck down by Rāvaṇa's *śakti* weapon, by Hanumant. The obstacle is in the scene described in our next paragraph, with Aṅgada as envoy and the spurning of Mandodarī. The conclusion is in a speech reproaching a male character, as powerless, and checking a female character, very likely Rāvaṇa and the Witch respectively in the scene where Sītā's murder is shown. It would thus appear that it is Sugrīva who foils Rāvaṇa's attempts to kill Sītā. Perhaps the text is corrupt and the Aṅgada scene should be the embryo, followed by the *śakti* episode as obstacle. The style of the verses in this play is not dissimilar to that of the *Hayagrīvavadha*.

1360. For the 'violent' *ārabhaṭi* mode of stage business we may refer to a scene from the beginning of Act VI, preserved in part by the critics (e.g. Abhinavagupta III 104), where the emissary Aṅgada taunts Rāvaṇa by rough-handling his queen, Mandodarī. Aṅgada's mocking speech to Mandodarī exemplifies 'derision' *dyuti* in the obstacle (*Nāṭyadarpaṇa* p. 85) [149]. Rāvaṇa is disturbed, apparently when engaged in his witchcraft, by the cries of his queen. It is reported that the commotion in the palace is caused by a monkey. When Rāvaṇa reaches the scene and exchanges words with Aṅgada we have a fine mixture of Mandodarī frightened, Aṅgada heroic and playful, mocking Rāvaṇa, and Rāvaṇa angry. The 'limb' here is identified as the 'panic' *vidrava* in the embryo conjunction [148] by Śaṅkuka (quoted by Abhinavagupta, III 52), which might seem to conflict with the analysis of the play in the *Nāṭyadarpaṇa* finding a limb of the obstacle as early as Act IV (see above). But perhaps there has been a confusion here with 'desperation' *drava* in the obstacle [149]. The possibility of such widely different analyses by early critics is a point worth noting: it may mean in fact that the illustrations are adduced just as scenes which happen to show the kind of action under discussion, not as relating to the action of the play quoted when taken in its development. On the other hand it may exemplify the overlapping of limbs and conjunctions which Abhinavagupta approves (III 62) [152].

1361. Śāradātanaya (p. 238) names Rāvaṇa and the Witch as his example of the 'full' *pūrṇa nāṭaka*, which has the regular five conjunctions of the *Nāṭyaśāstra* theory. He is here expounding Subandhu's doctrine of five kinds of *nāṭaka*, adding comments also from Drauhini, where three of the other kinds have conjunctions other than the regular ones [165]. We have been concerned above with two of those other kinds of *nāṭaka* (by Subandhu [653] and Bhāsa [984]). Śāradātanaya does not analyse the *Kṛtyārāvaṇa* for us, but we have found enough indications of its structure elsewhere to be able to outline its 'full' and regular form according to the *Nāṭyaśāstra* method. The 'opening' appears to coincide with Act I, though here we have few details. The main business of that Act is that Mārīca prepares the abduction of Sītā. There should be somewhere some indication of the 'seed' hinting at her recovery as the ultimate objective. A limb of the re-opening, namely the 'thunderbolt', has been pointed out above in Act II: Sītā's reply to Rāvaṇa when he approaches her. In this Act the preparations have been followed up by the beginning of the main action. The 'embryo' is indicated by its limb 'appearance' in Act III, in the scene where Rāma learns from Jaṭāyus what has happened to Sītā. The main plot is now set, with Rāma making progress in his quest thanks to this 'intervention' *prakarī*. The 'obstacle' embraces the main action from Act IV (the 'fatigue' of Lakṣmaṇa) to the first part of Act VII ('contradiction'—Sītā reported dead). Here the sub-plot *patākā* intervenes (Sugrīva in Act V) and Rāma is decisively helped by his allies ('derision' of Aṅgada in Act VI, etc.). The 'conclusion' is of course the last part of Act VII, ending with the 'consummation of the *kāvya*'. That this play was an established classic of the stage down to the +14 is attested by almost all the drama critics of the period known to us.

1362. The *Chalitarāma*, 'Rāma Deceived', dramatises the story of Rāma's return to Ayodhyā, after his victory and recovery of Sītā, and the apocryphal last book of the *Rāmāyaṇa* (cf. the *Kundamālā*, Chapter XIX above). In this version of the story Rāma is misled by his surviving enemies, the demon Lavaṇa leading them, into suspecting Sītā's virtue while a captive. The play gets its title from this theme. Rāma banishes Sītā when she becomes pregnant and her twin sons, Kuśa and Lava, are born in exile. After they grow up it happens that Rāma decides to perform the horse sacrifice traditional for a universal emperor. The sacrificial horse is released according to the Vedic rite and wanders, watched over by Lakṣmaṇa with a detachment of troops. Lava seizes the horse but is attacked and taken prisoner by Lakṣmaṇa. Taken before Rāma, Lava sees at the court a golden statue of his mother (for the Queen must be present at the rite and Rāma, not having taken another queen, substitutes a statue for the banished Sītā). This recognition leads to explanations and at the end Rāma and Sītā are reunited, Rāma being convinced that Lava is his own son. The objective is the discovery that Sītā is still living (*Nāṭyadarpaṇa* p. 92). Raghavan has collected the fragments of this play (*Some Old Lost Rāma Plays*, pp. 50-9). It was a *nāṭaka* in six acts (or doubtfully more: there seems to be no information available about the precise way the play ended). Bhoja indicates that the story was handled very freely in this play, especially in that it is Lavaṇa who is responsible for Rāma's deception and not Kaikeyī and her confidante. According to him this change eliminated a 'fault' which would detract from the aesthetic experience of the play (*Śṛṅgāraprakāśa* II p. 460). Since the horse sacrifice is the decisive event, Abhinavagupta says (I 39) that in this play *dharma* ('virtue' or religion, the duties laid down by the *Veda*) predominates.

1363. The *Nāṭyadarpaṇa* (p. 132) quotes from the *Chalitarāma* as well as from the *Kṛtyārāvaṇa* in its discussion on 'parallelism' *avalagita* for leading in from the prologue to the play. Here we learn that the Rāma Deceived began with Rāma's arrival at Ayodhyā and meeting Bharata, including his respectful entry into the city on foot, but we do not discover how this was actually paralleled in the prologue. It is noteworthy that the two plays used the same technique for leading in, though it seems there was a controversy even on that point. In Act I, after Rāma's consecration we learn of the enmity with Lavaṇa: Rāma commissions his youngest brother, Śatrughna, against Lavaṇa, whilst the latter sends two demons to insinuate themselves into Rāma's confidence and then poison his mind against Sītā. Sītā is pregnant and on the occasion (in Act II ?) of her *puṃsavana* ceremony (after conception, to ensure the birth of a son) the two demons impersonate Kaikeyī and her confidante and make disparaging remarks about Sītā having been so long with Rāvaṇa (this is the limb 'thunderbolt' in the re-opening—Sāgaranandin 697-9). The ruse succeeds and Sītā is banished.

1364. Following this we have an act (perhaps the third) in which Rāma shows his remorse at having banished her (Sāgaranandin 1824; cf. 974-6 and Śāradātanaya p. 250). We hear also that Sītā has borne twin sons. In a later act (the fourth ?), when the boys have grown up, Vālmīki proposes to take them to attend the horse sacrifice, presumably planning a reunion if opportunity can be found. There is a touching scene where Sītā tells her son Lava how to behave before Rāma, not telling him that he is his father and covering a slip of the tongue *avasyandita* (a limb of the street play [326]) by describing Rāma figuratively as father of the whole earth (as emperor he is a father to all) (Dhanika p. 68). Matters are then precipitated when the sacrificial horse wanders into the hermitage, where Sītā is living, and Lava seizes it, but is afterwards taken prisoner by Lakṣmaṇa (this perhaps is in Act V). The binding of Lava exemplifies a limb of the obstacle according to Dhanañjaya and Dhanika (p. 22), which they call 'panic' *vidrava* and which in their discussion replaces the *Nāṭyaśāstra's* 'fatigue' [149]. In Act VI the prisoner is taken before Rāma and the scene occurs in which Lava unknowingly reveals that Sītā is still living (evidently Rāma did not know where she was, or rather we gather he believed she was dead, *Nāṭyadarpaṇa* p. 92, and despite his remorse could do nothing to bring her back). Lava recognises the statue of his mother (the characteristic 'similarity' *sārūpya* [186], Raghavan p. 53 from Bhoja). When Rāma asks Lava if this (statue) is his mother, he says yes but this 'mother' is flamboyant with ornaments.... This and the ensuing discussion show 'investigating' *virodha* (or *nirodha*, *Nāṭyadarpaṇa* p. 92) as a limb of the conclusion, connecting with the objective which had seemed lost — Sītā is alive.

1365. That is as far as the fragments take us, but clearly Vālmīki has gained his opportunity and will soon bring Sītā to Rāma. Probably by his bravery in opposing Lakṣmaṇa, moreover, Lava has convinced everyone that he is truly the son of the great hero Rāma. We have fewer quotations from this play than from Rāvaṇa and the Witch, but its construction is generally clear. The style seems similar to the other play; the two fit together exactly to cover the whole story of the abduction of Sītā and its aftermath. We see that Rāma Deceived was another classic familiar to the medieval drama critics.

1366. Whilst we are on the subject of famous plays of about the +4 or +5 which are not now available, we should consider two fictions once prominent in the Indian repertory, written by Brahmayaśas and Śuktivāsa. Their dates are conjectural (the former was perhaps known to Daṇḍin in the +7 —see below) and they do not seem to be known except for one play each, though for all we now know they may have been the authors of other dramas, discussed anonymously by the critics. Raghavan has discussed these two plays briefly in his article 'The Social Play in Sanskrit'. Since they are fictions it is more difficult to reconstruct their stories from the available fragments than in the case of *nāṭakas*.

1367. The *Puṣpadūṣitaka* of Brahmayaśas is a story of merchant class life, the action arising from an unjust suspicion of a wife's behaviour by her father-in-law (Abhinavagupta II 432). Some circumstances in the story, however, are not clear to us at present. It appears that Samudradatta has married Nandayantī secretly. Now Daṇḍin in his *Avantisundarī* (pp. 186 ff.), as pointed out by Raghavan, has incorporated the synopsis of a story of a Samudradatta, a merchant of Ujjayinī in the -2, first a friend then an enemy of the notorious Mūladeva (cf. Chapter XIX, end). Mūladeva swears that if Samudradatta marries he will abduct his wife. Consequently Samudradatta secretly marries Suvratā, the daughter of a poor merchant, with the agreement of her father, so that he can produce a son to continue his family. Mūladeva eventually finds out about this marriage and succeeds in his design at least to the extent of compromising Suvratā, entering her house through a tunnel. Daṇḍin perhaps based this story, which we need not follow further, on the *Puṣpadūṣitaka*, just as he has worked a number of other stories from old plays and novels into his own novel. On the other hand both Brahmayaśas and Daṇḍin may have utilised some other, older, story of Samudradatta. At any rate it is possible that the secrecy of Samudradatta's marriage to Nandayantī in the play, despite the difference of the wife's name, was due to fear of a dangerous enemy, whether Prince Mūladeva or another. Someśvara's *Kāvyādarśa* (p. 214) appears to suggest that a fiction, i.e. the *Puṣpadūṣitaka*, took its story from an earlier *kāvya*, the *Mūladevacarita* [1142], itself drawn from the *Bṛhatkathā* (cf. Abhinavagupta II 430).

1368. At the beginning of Brahmayaśas' play, in the opening conjunction, Samudradatta's father, Sāgaradatta, hears a rumour and suspects the virtue of his daughter-in-law, while her husband is absent abroad (at the coast) and longing to return to her (Kuntaka p. 236). In Act II (re-opening) Samudradatta returns and pays a secret visit to his wife in the garden at night. To gain admission to the garden he bribes a guard, Kuvalaya, with a ring (Kuntaka pp. 226 and 236). No doubt having heard a report of a visit to his daughter-in-law by an unknown stranger, Sāgaradatta then in Act III drives the pregnant Nandayantī out and she goes to live in the forest under the protection of a Śabara general. In Act IV Kuvalaya, who has been away in Mathurā, returns and shows Sāgaradatta the ring, which proves that the nocturnal visitor was Samudradatta, filling Sāgaradatta with remorse (Kuntaka p. 226: the invention of these incidents of the ring in Acts II and IV exemplifies a kind of contextual figurativeness, where the parts of a *kāvya* beautifully support the construction of the main plot and are supported by it [281]).

1369. In Act V a certain Lāmakāyana brings Nandayantī, in the forest, news of Samudradatta. We have a quotation from the same Act, presumably showing the heroine in the forest offering a meal to brahmans as an act of religious virtue to secure her own welfare (example of the 'sensitive' in relation to virtue — Sāgaranandin 2822-6 and Sarvānanda on Amara), illustrating the limb 'reproach' *apavāda* [149] of the obstacle (*Nāṭyadarpaṇa* p. 83):

> BRAHMAN. But 'cleaned-up' (*mārjitā* — a rich dish of yogurt with spices, etc.), sweet in the mouth of a brahman, is the snare of Fate! For:
>
> My son was killed, my brother was killed,
> my father was killed by 'cleaned-up';
> Yet I drink this
> destroyer of my clan, like blame!

(This is supposed to hint a reproach at Nandayantī as a destroyer of her family.)

It is evident, however, that Samudradatta has heard rumours and is not yet certain of the conduct of his wife. She has given birth to a son in the forest: is the boy his? A scene is quoted from Act VI of the play, where Samudradatta is near Nandayantī in the forest but does not reveal his presence, instead meditating suicide (*Nāṭyadarpaṇa* pp. 90-1 for another limb of the obstacle). He thinks she would not even recognise him in his miserable state, still less could he ask her who was the father of her child. His miserable state perhaps indicates that he is in serious trouble and even a fugitive, which could be due to his enemy's machinations. Afterwards, however, Samudradatta questions the Śabara General concerning the date of the child's birth and is gradually satisfied that he himself is the father, as a result of his secret visit in the garden, calculating the dates from the position of the Moon among the stars, which he and Nandayantī had noted on that fateful night. Here we have the limb 'decision' [150] of the conclusion (*Nāṭyadarpaṇa* p. 93), where Samudradatta remembers his astronomy (or has just consulted an astronomer — Ālambāyana mentioned below?) and works out the dates. Then he again has doubts and goes on arguing with the General in a remarkable dialogue quoted by Rāmacandra and Guṇacandra (pp. 97-8). In this short passage they find nine limbs of the conclusion, namely 'conjunction' *sandhi*, 'investigating' *virodha*, 'knotting' *grathana*, 'censure' *paribhāṣaṇa*, 'derision' *dyuti*, 'grace' *prasāda*, 'delight' *ānanda*, 'agreement' *samaya* and 'marvelling' *upagūhana* (or *pari-*) :

SAMUDRADATTA. Is this a dream?
GENERAL. No !
SAMUDRADATTA. Is it mental derangement? (conjunction)
GENERAL. Don't say such a thing !
SAMUDRADATTA. Then who is she, here? (investigating)
GENERAL. Your wife ! (knotting)
SAMUDRADATTA. How then does she have a young baby in her lap? (censure)
GENERAL. That is your son !
SAMUDRADATTA. It is false ! (derision)
GENERAL. Ālambāyana here surely knows the connection of what has happened. (grace)
SAMUDRADATTA. By whom has this been clumsily effected? (delight)
GENERAL. By Fate ! (agreement)
SAMUDRADATTA. Everything is fitted together ! (marvelling)

Now these thirteen speeches form a single verse in the *śārdūlavikrīḍita* metre:

Is this a dream? No ! Is it mental derangement?
Don't say such a thing ! Then who is she, here?
Your wife ! How then does she have a young baby
in her lap? That is your son ! It is false !
Ālambāyana here surely knows the connection of
what has happened.
By whom has this been clumsily effected? By Fate !
Everything is fitted together !

The husband and wife are then reunited and the play ends with Act VI (Kuntaka pp. 236-7, contextual figurativeness where the six acts are the 'contexts' invented in relation to the five conjunctions and producing aesthetic experience [281]). The exact conclusion is not quite clear : perhaps the establishment of the fact that the boy is Samudradatta's son makes it possible to make the marriage public, since his enemy's presumed plan to prevent him from having a legitimate son has been successfully frustrated.

1370. The *Puṣpadūṣitaka* evidently stood in the first rank of classical fictions, alongside such masterpieces as the Toy Cart, and was greatly admired by such critics as Abhinavagupta and Kuntaka, as well as made extensive use of as a standard classic by Sāgaranandin and the authors of the *Nāṭyadarpaṇa*. The style of the quoted fragments is simple and dramatically effective : a play of action, situation and dialogue rather than of lyrics and elaborate language, a play for the theatre but not for the anthologist.

1371. It is difficult to guess the significance of the title 'Spoiled by Flowers' (or perhaps 'Spoiled like a Flower'), since the critics do not explain it to us. Sāgaranandin (3164-8) illustrates two limbs of the *bhāṇikā* [382] from Act II, where Nandayantī first complains of her misfortune and thinks of suicide (this is 'resignation' *vinyāsa*) and then compares her husband's heart with a *karṇikāra* tree in the garden (this is 'proposal' *upanyāsa*). The idea behind the comparison, again a complaint, is that the flower of the *karṇikāra* is beautiful but has no scent. Without a context, we can only conjecture that the complaint is of Samudradatta's absence, at the beginning of Act II before his sudden secret arrival. Perhaps later on, when things go so badly for Nandayantī, she recalls this comparison and complains again of his heart, unsatisfactory like the scentless flower because he has apparently deserted her. What we do not know is, why was he away and why all the secrecy ? Kuntaka lists this play among titles indicating the main feature of the plot, along with the Rāvaṇa and the Witch and Rāma Deceived, so perhaps it has to do with the critical garden scene and the exposure of Nandayantī to suspicion, but at present we lack evidence to establish the exact point. According to Abhinavagupta (III 6), Samudradatta in this play has his desire accomplished by fate *daiva*, but Rāmacandra and Guṇacandra as we have seen [1210] qualify this by saying there is sufficient human activity here to develop the interest of the audience.

1372. A verse is quoted as by Brahmayaśas or Yaśaḥsvāmin in the anthologies *Śārṅgadharapaddhati* (3464) and *Subhāṣitāvali* (1335), which might be from this play or from another work of the author. The critics Ānandavardhana (pp. 305 and 417) and Kuntaka (p. 33) also quote the verse, the latter for 'lexical figurativeness' in the last line [274] :

> Her face bowed through shame in the presence of the elders,
> holding in her anger, bound by her two agitated breast-pitchers,
> How was it possible she did not say 'Stay !', as, shedding a tear,
> her third of an eye, captivating like a frightened doe's, was fixed on me ?

This verse might well have been spoken by Samudradatta about Nandayantī, but at present we seem to have no evidence for it. The *Subhāṣitāvali* attributes two other verses (715 and 1403) to the same author. Thus Brahmayaśas had some standing as a poet as well as fame as a dramatist.

1373. Śuktivāsa's *Anaṅgasenāharinandin* is less prominent among the critics, but something of its plot is reported by Rāmacandra and Guṇacandra. The title 'Anaṅgasenā and Harinandin' is composed of the names of the heroine and hero. The play seems to have had ten acts. Among the other characters is another heroine, Mādhavī, and a Prince Candraketu, also a brahman Puṣpalaka and his mother. In the *Nāṭyadarpaṇa* (p. 84) the limb called 'forbearance' *chādana* in the obstacle conjunction [149] is illustrated by explaining part of the action of this play. Prince Candraketu gives a pair of earrings to Mādhavī, but she sends them to Harinandin. Harinandin gives them to Puṣpalaka's mother to be used to free Puṣpalaka from jail (Puṣpalaka, friend of Harinandin, is perhaps the jester in this play). This attempt miscarries, however, because the earrings are recognised as having come from the palace and it is assumed that Puṣpalaka had stolen them: instead of being freed he is at once sentenced to death as a thief and marched out for execution. When in Act IX Harinandin hears of this from Puṣpalaka's mother he intervenes and takes on himself the dishonour of being blamed for the theft in order to save the brahman. This is his 'forbearance' according to one interpretation of that limb. For the sake of the main objective something normally unendurable is endured. The rest of the plot is at present a matter of conjecture for us, but what we know suggests some similarity to the Toy Cart: false accusations and a dangerous royal rival. Anaṅgasenā was probably a geisha girl.

1374. Of some other early fictions now apparently lost still less is known and their dates are quite uncertain. We may mention three titles here, their authors being unknown, to give some further idea of the range of such plays. Of a *Taraṅgadatta* (name of the hero) it is remarked that the main heroine is a geisha girl (in contrast, therefore, to the *Puṣpadūṣitaka*) and the play is several times mentioned as a standard fiction of that type (Śāradātanaya p. 243, Bahurūpamiśra on *Daśarūpaka* III. 39f., etc.).

1375. The *Padmāvatipariṇaya*, 'Marriage of Padmāvatī', contained an intrigue in which Vilāsavatī, jealous of Padmāvatī, tried to prevent her marriage (Sāgaranandin 2783, 2789, 2876). In the last reference, Sāgaranandin finds an example of the limb *pracchedaka* of the *lāsya* [363], as defined by Rāhula, in Vilāsavatī's outburst of jealous rage after seeing her rival with the man she loves. The hero was a brahman (Śāradātanaya p. 243) and a minister (Bahurūpamiśra on *Daśarūpaka* III. 39).

1376. The *Prayogābhyudaya*, 'Success of the Scheme', is quoted for a humorous incident between the jester and a maid, who alternately tease and (insincerely) flatter one another (*Nāṭyadarpaṇa* p. 123, *prapañca* as limb of the street play [326]).

CHAPTER XXIV

KĀLIDĀSA

1377. Kālidāsa is traditionally associated with 'Vikramāditya'. Abhinanda (+9), in a verse appended to canto XXXII (or prefixed to canto XXXIII) of his *Rāmacarita*, associates the poet with 'Śakārāti', suggesting Candra II Gupta. Soḍḍhala (+11) appears to connect the poet with Vikramāditya (*Udayasundarī* p. 150). Bhoja (+11) reproduces a tradition (see Raghavan, *Bhoja's Śṛṅgāraprakāśa*, pp. 779 ff.), of a supposed embassy of Kālidāsa from Vikramāditya to a king of Kuntala (which might mean one of the Vākāṭakas, of the South Western branch, or a minor feudal ruler in that region). A poem *Kuntaleśvaradautya* on this theme, now apparently lost, is sometimes said to have been composed by Kālidāsa himself (e.g. by Kṣemendra, *Aucityavicāracarcā* before verse 64). The commentary *Rāmasetu*, on the epic poem *Setubandha* written by the Vākāṭaka emperor Pravarasena II (*c*.+410 to 440), says that Kālidāsa assisted the emperor by revising his poem (Raghavan p. 782). If there is some historical truth behind these traditions we may look for a patron of Kālidāsa in the +5, in the Guptas Candra II 'Vikramāditya' (*c*.+375 to 414) or perhaps Skanda 'Vikramāditya' (*c*.+455 to 467), keeping in mind also Kumāra 'Mahendrāditya' (*c*. +414 to 455) who comes between them. There is, further, circumstantial evidence in his works that Kālidāsa lived in Ujjayinī, which was conquered from the Śakas by Candra II in about +395. It has been suggested, moreover, that the titles of two of Kālidāsa's *kāvyas*, *Vikramorvaśīya* and *Kumārasambhava*, were intended to have flattering reference to Vikramāditya and Kumāra (Gupta), or even to Skanda Gupta (since the god Kumāra of the *kāvya* is also called Skanda). Skanda Gupta saved India from the critical invasion of the Huns, just as the god Skanda saved Heaven from the demons led by Tāraka, thus the mythological epic might please the emperor by its significant parallelism to his historical achievement. This is conjectural, but such topical allusiveness in *kāvyas* is not at all unlikely and can be clearly exemplified in later centuries.

There is some further rather tenuous evidence bearing on the date of Kālidāsa, namely his apparent relative chronological position among *kavis* praised by later writers. We have already mentioned [1298] Kālidāsa's own reference to Saumillaka, who seems to have flourished in the early part of the +5, as a formidable predecessor whose works held the stage. Later eulogies of *kavis*, where chronological, seem generally to place Kālidāsa immediately after Meṇṭha and before (sometimes after) Bhāravi (Bhāravi lived about the middle of the +6 [1491]). Some of these eulogies have been noted above [1299-1301, 1328]. Here we might add from Soḍḍhala's (+11) *vaṃśa* ('succession', 'history') of the *kavis* (*Udayasundarī*, p. 154) the sequence Bhartṛmeṇṭha — Kālidāsa — Bāṇa, noting that Soḍḍhala's historical sequence is correct in its other parts. Unfortunately Soḍḍhala gives no other writers between Meṇṭha and Bāṇa. Tentatively we can do no better than place Kālidāsa in the middle of the +5 (his *floruit* say *c.* +430 to 470).

1378. Kālidāsa has attained great and lasting popularity almost everywhere where Sanskrit has been studied. Consequently six of his *kāvyas* are extant (many other works are sometimes attributed to him, but it would seem to be falsely in every case, whilst at least one later writer had the same name). They may be listed as follows in highly conjectural chronological order: *Mālavikāgnimitra*, *Raghuvaṃśa*, *Vikramorvaśīya*, *Meghasandeśa*, *Abhijñānaśākuntala* and *Kumārasambhava*.

1379. Kālidāsa is essentially a lyric poet and owes his popularity to the beautiful lyrics found scattered in his works, whether in the actual lyric poem *Meghasandeśa* (his most admired work among the connoisseurs) or in dramas or epics. In addition, his epics are enlivened in places by a strong vein of humour, whilst his descriptions of love, the theme which dominates all his works, have claimed careful study by the pandits. His *kāvyas* may be said to exemplify a trend in the art, whilst it must be insisted, contrary to widespread popular opinion, that this is only one trend and by no means typical of *kāvya* generally. This trend is of course the lyrical one, which carries to an extreme the possibilities suggested by the independence of the stanzas in an epic, together with an assumed implication of the theory that it is the emotions which constitute the essential content of a work of art. We have traced above the rôle of lyric poetry in the development of the *kāvya* medium and seen how its techniques pervaded epic poetry, drama and prose composition. We are also familiar with the originally dramatic theory of the presentation of emotions, producing the aesthetic experience. The trend which Kālidāsa represents would reduce all *kāvya* to lyric poetry, eliminating the narrative element necessary to the epic form, and would concentrate on depicting emotion whilst neglecting the action which constitutes the matter of drama and the real basis of emotional experiences.

1380. Kālidāsa's style is universally recognised as exemplifying the *vaidarbha*, following in the wake of Śūra, Sarvasena and Meṇṭha among its greatest exponents and with them eclipsing such pioneers as the poet of the *Aśmakavaṃśa*. Ratnaśrījñāna (p. 34) brackets Kālidāsa with Śūra as 'Southern', i.e. *vaidarbha* style, writers. At the same time his verses are less simple than Meṇṭha's and he is more inclined to be far-fetched, no doubt through seeking originality. His wild fancies are often successful, sometimes too strained. He uses compounds, rare words and difficult constructions more frequently than Meṇṭha and seems careless of word order, so that his verses as a rule do not have the same clarity and lucidity of meaning as Meṇṭha's. This difference can very well be understood if he is a later poet than Meṇṭha, trying to produce new effects and do new things with the language. It can also be understood in part as reflecting his lyric spirit, contrasting with Meṇṭha's epic genius. Here we should remember Kuntaka's judgment [288], which makes Kālidāsa and Sarvasena representative of his *sukumāra* or 'delicate' style: this has the simplicity of the old *vaidarbha*, but its being dominated by emotion and its name 'delicate' suggest the lyric trend, very different from Meṇṭha's *vaidarbha*. The waywardness of Kālidāsa's ideas was evidently appreciated by Kuntaka as the spontaneous play of genius. Kālidāsa is also appreciated for his power of suggestion (Ānandavardhana names him among the few 'great' *kavis* in his sense of exponents of the poetry of implied meanings, p. 93, after I.6). Both Bāṇa (*Harṣacarita*, introductory verse 17) and Daṇḍin (*Avantisundarī*, introductory verse 15) refer to the quality of sweetness *mādhurya* as characteristic of Kālidāsa, the latter adding that he 'purified' the *vaidarbha* way with his speech having this quality, presumably in contrast to his predecessors in the style. Soḍḍhala also calls his speech 'sweet as ambrosia' (p. 154).

1381. Though so popular with the critics, it is interesting to find that Kālidāsa was also criticised unfavourably by some of them, and perhaps owes some of his renown to a certain notoriety for having ventured on some dangerous, in fact blasphemous, descriptions and other offences against good taste. Mammaṭa (late +11), who might be called the taste-setter of the majority of recent pandits, on account of the extraordinary popularity of his *Kāvyaprakāśa*, rejects as in bad taste the eighth canto of the *Kumārasambhava*, where Kālidāsa describes the love-making of Śiva and Pārvatī: love-making should not be described in the case of the highest deities and in the case of the 'Parents' (of the world) is absolutely improper (p. 256, Sivaprasad's edition). Mammaṭa is here opposing the view of Ānandavardhana, who had defended Kālidāsa from the same criticism on the ground that the impropriety is concealed by the genius of the poet (*Dhvanyāloka* p. 317). Evidently this controversy had gone on for several centuries and may have begun even in Kālidāsa's time. There were always some religious people who found the artistic depiction of the gods as having human emotions offensive, but the 'great poet' was surely true to the spirit of *kāvya*. Mammaṭa also criticises Kālidāsa for the fault of redundancy on account of too much repetition in the lament of Rati in the fourth canto of the same *Kumārasambhava* (p. 255), which is quite a different matter, being purely aesthetic criticism. The same critic objects to a number of individual verses taken from Kālidāsa's works, on a wide variety of grounds from harshness of sound and obscurity of sense to clash of aesthetic experiences. Such criticisms are largely subjective, whilst it was standard practice among the critics to illustrate 'faults' from well known literature, perhaps taking some pride in a connoisseurship fine enough to detect slight blemishes in the classics. At the same time it does not seem entirely uncharacteristic of Kālidāsa that Mammaṭa should find him so useful for illustrating faults. Such a poet, who allowed free play to his natural genius (Kuntaka), may be expected to be a little careless of technique and theory in his pursuit of pure fancy. We may hope to appreciate Kālidāsa the better for understanding his true characteristics.

1382. Before we discuss Kālidāsa's works it will be useful to add some general points gleaned from a study of Indian literary criticism, for which we can follow Dr. Hari Chand in his *Kālidāsa et l'art poétique de l'Inde*, the fundamental work for the appreciation of Kālidāsa. By collecting and studying the quotations from Kālidāsa in the critical works available to him, Dr. Chand has shown clearly the number and extent of the authentic works of Kālidāsa now extant and also the degree of esteem in which each of them has been held. The results are striking and clear. The critics ignore the apocryphal works, such as the *Ṛtusaṃhāra* (probably a much earlier poem, see our Chapter XX above [1238]), and the apocryphal cantos added to the *Kumārasambhava*. Kālidāsa's most admired work is the *Meghasandeśa*, followed in popularity by the *Kumārasambhava* (despite all criticism), *Abhijñānaśākuntala*, *Raghuvaṃśa*, *Vikramorvaśīya* and *Mālavikāgnimitra* (allowing for the varying extents of the works, naturally). It might be a reasonable conjecture that this is the reverse of the order in which the *kāvyas* were written, the poet's art gradually maturing, but we may hesitate to suppose that it took him so long to discover the lyric form which perfectly suited his genius. Again, the dramas are not strictly commensurable with the epics, offering relatively few verses to illustrate points of poetics but having instead other points of interest (Dr. Chand has not considered prose quotations in works on dramatic theory, most of which in any case remained unprinted when he wrote). It is therefore possible to think of the *Raghuvaṃśa* as an early venture (whose popularity has been enhanced by its subject matter, the favourite Solar dynasty of Rāma including a synopsis of the *Rāmāyaṇa* itself). These highly speculative considerations lead us to the order we prefer here.

1383. The *Mālavikāgnimitra*, 'Mālavikā and Agnimitra', is a *nāṭaka* in five acts, whose hero is the Śuṅga emperor Agnimitra (of Magadha, ruled –151 to –143). The story has some reference to history, but its substance is an intrigue at court through which Agnimitra adds a beautiful and mysterious girl, who in the end turns out to be a princess, to his collection of queens. He is opposed by two of his existing queens, the older and 'chief' Queen Dhāriṇī, who reacts with firmness and dignity, and the younger Irāvatī, evidently the most recent favourite, who lacks self-control, drinks heavily (Act III) and reacts with violent jealousy. It is not clear how far the adventures of the princess Mālavikā are historical, whilst the plot of this play strongly resembles those of the later 'little plays' *nāṭikās* [339]. In Kālidāsa's play Agnimitra is not yet emperor, but governor at Vidiśā (presumably of the province of Avanti) during the reign of his father Puṣyamitra (–180 to –151), the rebel general who founded the Śuṅga dynasty, whilst Agnimitra's son Vasumitra is accompanying the 'general' on a campaign against the Greeks with a view to accomplishing a horse sacrifice. We can thus date the action in about the period –160 to –155. Meanwhile Agnimitra is involved in war with the ruler of Vidarbha, Yajñasena, who is connected with the old Maurya dynasty of Magadha which Puṣyamitra had overthrown. Yajñasena's cousin Mādhavasena had wanted to come to terms with the Śuṅgas by entering into a matrimonial alliance with them, but Yajñasena opposes this and imprisons his cousin, whose sister Mālavikā, however, is sent away for safety but disappears when pursued by Yajñasena's men. In fact Mālavikā is found by Agnimitra's frontier commander Vīrasena, brother of Queen Dhāriṇī, who, not knowing who the girl is but seeing she is educated, sends her to his sister to serve as a lady in waiting. At the beginning of the play Vīrasena is ordered by Agnimitra to attack Yajñasena and free Mādhavasena. (This story of the struggle between the Mauryas and Śuṅgas may be compared with the traditions about Mūladeva, see towards the end of Chapter XIX above [1142].)

1384. Kālidāsa restricts his action to the intrigue at court: Mālavikā appears as an unknown but beautiful and talented (in dancing) girl in the train of the Queen; Agnimitra sees her and falls in love with her and, with the aid of his clever jester, is able to develop the intrigue despite the precautions and later the drastic measures taken by Irāvatī and Dhāriṇī. Agnimitra appears somewhat afraid of his queens, or at least his instincts of chivalry and propriety cause him to try to avoid unpleasant scenes or forceful measures. He does his best to conciliate all the ladies, even when the poor offending Mālavikā is thrown into a vault by the queens, and relies on the resourcefulness and presence of mind of his jester to overcome every obstacle. The jester manages to obtain Dhāriṇī's signet ring, by showing which he can claim her authority to release Mālavikā. In Act V Agnimitra receives news of the victory of Vīrasena in Vidarbha and the release of Mādhavasena by him. Gifts are sent from the conquered country, including two girl artists. When these are presented at court they recognise Princess Mālavikā and reveal her true identity as Mādhavasena's sister. Apologies follow for her having been treated like a slave. Agnimitra in a spirit of magnanimity, but also with some political astuteness, orders that Vidarbha be divided between Yajñasena and Mādhavasena, both of whom will be his vassals. Now Agnimitra receives a letter from his father reporting a victory over the Greeks by Vasumitra. This good news is especially good for Queen Dhāriṇī, because Vasumitra is her son and the honours he collects are reflected on her, enhancing her prestige. She had already relented towards Mālavikā and in this moment of joy and renewed strength she formally presents the Princess to Agnimitra as a new bride and a new queen, having also persuaded Irāvatī to agree to this. Thus all ends happily and Agnimitra enjoys the favours of all his queens, whilst his father, son, ministers and generals subdue the empire.

1385. At this distance in time it is difficult to be sure of Kālidāsa's intention in this play. Is he ironically presenting Agnimitra as a trifler, amusing himself with love intrigues whilst others attend to the serious business of life and the state, dependent even in his amorous undertakings on a resourceful jester; is this a criticism of unworthy kingship ? Or are we rather to admire the policy of Agnimitra in securing such a life for himself? Perhaps the latter should be regarded as only a surface appearance, sufficient for a frivolous audience, whilst the criticism is the meaning intended by Kālidāsa's recognised power of suggestion, which the true connoisseur may appreciate. As for the aesthetic experiences, the sensitive seems to predominate, but if the critical implications suggested are accepted as the real meaning we may think rather that the comic is most developed. Here much would depend on the producer of the play, who could make the most of the comic scenes, such as that where Mālavikā reproaches Agnimitra for being afraid of the Queen (in Act IV, preceding verse 14), bringing out the ironical effect, or could preserve the dignity of the hero by stressing the chivalrous side of his character (Agnimitra replies that he must be courteous to the Queen because that is the custom in his family, but his life really depends on Mālavikā—i.e. he is really afraid only of her—verse 14: after which he tries to embrace her, but she resists vigorously). Bhoja (*Śṛṅgāraprakāśa* Chapter XXXVI, see Miss Munshi's edition of the *Śṛṅgāramañjarī*, p. 102) gives Agnimitra's love for his queens as an example of 'mud' *kardama* passion, the kind most easily washed out for something new.

1386. As a drama, Mālavikā and Agnimitra may be considered Kālidāsa's best. This judgment directly opposes that of the critics in the field of poetics, as we have seen, for in fact the play contains far fewer lyric gems than Kālidāsa's other two. Śiṅgabhūpāla, the dramatic critic, on the other hand, refers to the play several times. This play shows the least development of what we may call Kālidāsa's new lyrical trend in literature and offers the most drama. In what, then, consisted the modernity which Kālidāsa claimed for this play in his prologue, contrasting with Bhāsa, Saumillaka and others? Perhaps just in this critical presentation of a prince, or perhaps in the presentation in the theatre of the new Gupta-Vākāṭaka politics of marriage alliances and vassal kingdoms, though in the guise of ancient history. As we have briefly seen, there are various points of interest in this love intrigue at court, very different from the deeper loves of Bhāsa's heroes and perhaps from any others we have met so far in the Indian dramas available to us.

1387. The *Raghuvaṃśa*, 'Line of Raghu', is a kind of historical epic on the Solar Emperor Raghu and his descendants, especially Rāma. It was probably modelled on the lost *Aśmakavaṃśa* (Line of Aśmaka, or Dynasty or History of Aśmaka), these and other similar epics being regarded by the critic Bhoja as constituting a special kind of epic which he calls a *saṃhitā*, 'collection', meaning that they include stories of a series of heroes (a line of kings) instead of one hero (*Śṛṅgāraprakāśa* II 470, Bhoja's examples are a *Yaduvaṃśa* and a *Dilīpavaṃśa*, neither of which seems to be available at present). Inevitably a poem of this kind lacks unity, except for the idea that all its heroes belong to the same dynasty, and consists of a series of episodes. It does not observe the requirements for an epic usually given by the theorists, that it should have a single hero and unity of action, the story being developed with the five conjunctions (see Chapter VI above

[405]). The *vaṃśa* form of epic *kāvya*, however, seems to have been well established in the literature, which is presumably why Bhoja thought it desirable to give it a separate status. Clearly it arose on the basis of actual histories (belonging to the *itihāsa* branch of literature, not to *kāvya*), both in the ancient *Purāṇas* and separate dynastic histories and other historical narratives, the poets selecting portions of them for retelling in artistic form. The fact that the 'history' retold in the *Raghuvaṃśa* is of a legendary and even mythical character does not affect these considerations. Kālidāsa's sources seem to have been a *Purāṇa*, not quite the same as the present *Viṣṇupurāṇa*, and the *Rāmāyaṇa*.

1388. The Line of Raghu consists of 19 cantos. After an invocation [407] to Śiva and Pārvatī and an apology, the poem starts with the Emperor Dilīpa, the father of Raghu, in order to introduce the birth of Raghu, then gives some account of the reigns of the successive emperors Raghu, Aja, Daśaratha, Rāma, Kuśa and Atithi, with a general characterisation and characteristic episodes for each of them and a fairly comprehensive summary of the whole story of Rāma. Then the eighteenth canto reviews rapidly the reigns of the next twenty-one rulers. The last canto describes the reign of the dissolute Agnivarṇa, who wrecked his health and died prematurely through his depraved habits, leaving only an unborn child to succeed him: the ministers enthrone his pregnant queen as regent. Here the epic ends.

1389. Some have supposed that the poem is incomplete, a conclusion more appropriate for such a distinguished line of rulers being either unwritten or lost. On account of the episodic nature of the work, which seemingly might be extended indefinitely, it is difficult to prove or disprove such a supposition. We may do well, however, to treat the Line of Raghu provisionally as a complete poem, in order to see if we can understand the poet's conception on that assumption. If the results of such an approach seem unsatisfactory, then the field will remain open for conjectures about the supposed incompleteness of the poem (such as that critics found fault with the canto on Agnivarṇa, so that Kālidāsa abandoned the work, adding nothing further). We may remark at once that it was not Kālidāsa's plan to cover the whole Solar Dynasty or the greater part of it. The *Purāṇas* give nearly a hundred generations of kings from Manu Vaivasvata down to the time of the Bhārata Battle, then thirty more

Solar rulers of the same (Ikṣvāku) dynasty down to Sumitra, when the line became extinct. Dilīpa belonged to the sixtieth generation: Kālidāsa omitted all earlier rulers in order to introduce at once the immediate predecessors of Rāma, who is the greatest and central hero of the poem (his life fills cantos X to XV). After Rāma the dynasty went into decline: unless the poem ended with Rāma himself it would be hard to avoid an anticlimax except by completely abandoning all pretence of following the well known Tradition. The seventh king after Agnivarṇa was killed by Abhimanyu in the Bhārata Battle: would there be any point in pursuing the Line of Raghu as far as this inglorious episode in the Great Epic ? Rather we should expect a limited number of kings to be described following Rāma, somehow balancing those described before him, and then an ending which could be regarded as auspicious, perhaps as suggesting that the dynasty would continue for a long time rather than suggesting its end. Soḍḍhala (p. 154) evidently regarded the work as complete, saying that Kālidāsa's fame, disguised as speech, "attained the other side" of the river of the fierce solar clan. Let us now examine the content of this epic.

1390. According to Bhāmaha (cf. Chapter VI above [406]) an epic poem should be instructive in all the ends of humanity: virtue, wealth, pleasure and release (but especially wealth). Kālidāsa seems to have had this conception very much in mind in composing the Line of Raghu. His own outlook appears to be that of a strictly orthodox brahman (unlike Bhāmaha's) and he is inclined to stress virtue *dharma* especially and to dwell on the details of Brahmanical rituals. Dilīpa is described at the outset of the Line of Raghu as a rigorously Brahmanical ruler, so much so that for him wealth and pleasure were merely part of virtue, he pursued them not because he liked them but because it was part of his Brahmanical duty to do so: he must carry on the government (this is the basis of 'wealth') for the sake of stability, he must marry for the sake of children (to continue his line and with it the Brahmanical tradition) — I.25. He exploited his empire ('milked the Earth') for the sake of sacrifice (I.26), i.e. in order to expend the revenue in ritual undertakings. This perfectionist, however, is somewhat ironically shown as having committed a small breach in his ritualistic virtue, by omitting to circumambulate the sacred cow Surabhi one day when he was in a hurry to perform his ritual duty in the marriage bed (I.76). As a result he remained childless until he and his queen had expiated their fault by a period of humble attendance on another cow, Surabhi's daughter. A celebrated simile (II.20) describes the cow on its way, in between the king and queen, like twilight between day and night. Thus the sin was expiated and Raghu was conceived.

1391. Raghu on the other hand may be regarded as the exponent of wealth, acquired by the emperor through the conquest of other kings, reduced to vassalage and payment of tribute. He shows his mettle in his youth, protecting his father's sacrificial horse by fighting Indra himself, for these semi-mythical ancient rulers live in close association with the gods. Then on becoming emperor himself Raghu engages in a career of conquest in all four directions (Canto IV). However, he follows his father's example in that he expends his wealth in sacrifice, culminating (IV.86) in the *viśvajit* rite in which his whole property is given away. This leaves him in a difficulty when a student asks him for some money to help pay his teacher's absurdly high fee, demanded in a fit of anger. It is inconceivable that a proud king should send away a deserving suppliant empty handed, yet Raghu has no money. His vanity thus stung and quick action being necessary, Raghu determines to make war on some rich ruler. Since he has already plundered the wealth of all human kings, however, he prepares to invade the domain of Kubera, the God of Wealth (V. 26). Kubera's capital is at the top of the Himālaya, on Mount Kailāsa, but Raghu's chariot can cross the sky, let alone mountains, therefore he expects to reduce the god to vassalage (V. 27-8). Kubera does not wait to be attacked, but showers a vast quantity of gold from the sky into Raghu's treasury. Thus Raghu's majesty is so inconceivable that he can milk Heaven as well as Earth (V.33).

1392. Aja, coming next in succession, is an exponent of pleasure. In appearance he resembled Love (Kāma, 'Pleasure') himself (VI.2). The Sixth Canto gives a vivid and delightful description of the marriage by 'self-choice' *svayaṃvara* of Indumatī, sister of the king of Vidarbha, in which she chooses Aja among a great assembly of royal suitors. We may note in passing the special affection which Kālidāsa shows for the country of Vidarbha, indulging it repeatedly in his works. In his time it was the homeland of the Vākāṭaka Empire, bound by marriage alliance to the Gupta, thus when he picks out a classical theme of marriage to a princess of Vidarbha the poet surely offers a pleasing precedent for the imperial union of his own days. The following canto describes the wedding celebrations of Aja and Indumatī and the fight of Aja with disappointed rival suitors on the way home from Vidarbha to Ayodhyā afterwards. In Canto VIII Aja has to lament the mysterious premature death of Indumatī, who was really a heavenly nymph only temporarily condemned to take on human form as the result of the curse of a sage whose asceticism she disturbed at the command of Indra (VIII.79-82). Aja does not want to live longer and rules, inconsolable, only until his son Daśaratha is old enough to relieve him of the throne, then fasts to death and is reunited with his beloved in Indra's Heaven, in the Nandana Gardens (end of Canto VIII).

1393. Daśaratha, it seems, though at first described as a virtuous ruler (especially IX.7), falls into unvirtuous ways and thus provides a lesson of contrast with the preceding emperors. He goes hunting, which his ministers unfortunately approve (IX.49), becomes addicted to it and does what is in any case forbidden even to kings, namely attempts to shoot an elephant (IX.74). But the noise he heard among the bamboos on the river bank was made not by an elephant but by a boy ascetic: he has killed him with his arrow and the boy's embittered father curses Daśaratha to die of grief on account of his own son (this of course foretells Rāma's exile and Daśaratha dying heartbroken afterwards, as in the *Rāmāyaṇa*, which from here until the end of Canto XV is Kālidāsa's source). Following this sin (*pātaka*, IX.82) Daśaratha, already described as enjoying the company of playful women (IX.48), goes on to grant the boons he had previously promised Kaikeyī, exiles Rāma and declares Bharata his successor (XII.5-6). Then he abandons his life in grief (XII.10).

1394. For the story of Rāma Kālidāsa generally follows the *Rāmāyaṇa* but adds some points not belonging to the original (some of which may have been borrowed from other *kāvyas* on the story, such as those we have mentioned above). Thus Rāma is introduced (Canto X) as an incarnation of Viṣṇu, begged by the gods to free them from the oppression of the demon Rāvaṇa.

His brothers also are partial incarnations of Viṣṇu, so that together they look like an *avatāra* of virtue, wealth, pleasure and release (X.84). Rāma is thus virtue, though later (XIV.21), when finally installed as emperor, he is said to deal equally between virtue, wealth and pleasure (his virtue is perfect and he now possesses the Empire, i.e. wealth, and is united with Sītā). Kālidāsa describes the actions of Rāma's youth, which reveal his character already, in detail (Canto XI), then condenses the exile, abduction of Sītā and victory over Rāvaṇa into Canto XII. Ruben (*Kālidāsa*, p. 45) has pointed out a remarkable feature here: when Rāvaṇa's sister Śūrpaṇakhā sees the handsome Rāma in exile in the forest, seeks his love and is rejected, Sītā laughs scornfully at her (XII.36). Śūrpaṇakhā is infuriated by this insult and vows vengeance. Ruben suggests that in this way Kālidāsa makes Sītā herself responsible for all her sufferings, when Rāvaṇa abducts her to avenge his sister. One would certainly have expected more dignified behaviour from an educated lady. Though for a time Rāma may have dealt equally with the three ends of humanity, he soon sacrificed pleasure to virtue, or at least to honour *yaśas* (XIV.35), by abandoning Sītā when criticised by the citizens of Ayodhyā for taking her back from the demon, though he knows she is faultless (XIV.40). Kālidāsa spreads this part of the story over two cantos, generally conforming to the apocryphal part of the Rāmāyaṇa but perhaps expressing disapproval of Rāma's action (as Ruben suggests, p. 46), especially when he makes Vālmīki say he is angry with Rāma for his tainted *kaluṣa* procedure, despite all his good qualities (XIV.73). Sītā does not forgive Rāma at the end but returns to the Earth whence she originally came (XV.81-4).

1395. The rights of pleasure are reasserted by Rāma's son Kuśa, who enjoys water sports with the young ladies of his court and then marries the dragon girl Kumudvatī, who tries to steal a precious ornament of his which he loses in the water. When he dies, she follows him to Heaven (XVII.6-7).

1396. Atithi observes a balance between virtue, wealth and pleasure (XVII.57), but in his system of government, which is described in detail, seems to be chiefly an exponent of wealth, as the principal end, and of policy *nīti* and heroism *śaurya* (XVII.47), as the means to attain it. One may wonder whether, when Atithi is compared with Kumāra under the name Ṣaṇmukhavikrama (XVII.67), Kālidāsa is suggesting a reference to Skanda Gupta (Vikramāditya).

1397. After Atithi we have a series of twenty conventional kings variously praised for their good points but briefly dismissed, followed by a somewhat longer description of Sudarśana, who becomes king when a boy of six. The picture of a small boy on the grand throne is charming. The Goddess Fortune finds his chest too small for her abode and, while waiting for him to grow up, as if feeling ashamed of her situation, disguises herself as the shade of his royal sunshade in order to embrace him without being seen (XVIII.47). Sudarśana easily acquires the sciences which are the basis of the three ends (XVIII.50), as if he remembered studying them thoroughly in a former life, then finally, after consecrating his son Agnivarṇa on the throne, becomes an ascetic aiming not at any result (but at absolute release, *mokṣa*, though Kālidāsa does not use this word) (XIX.1-2). He seems to be the only one of his line to aim at the fourth end, thus in a way completing Kālidāsa's survey of kings in relation to the ends of humanity.

1398. There remains, however, the dissolute reign of Agnivarṇa, in which pleasure is supreme. This is not the devoted love of Aja, who follows his beloved to Heaven, nor the weakness of Daśaratha, who suffers terrible remorse for his bad actions and dies of grief, but a rout of pleasure which sacrifices virtue, wealth and soon health and life itself to shallow flirtations and entertainments. Surely this completes the survey with a warning against neglect of the proper cultivation of the ends. Kālidāsa says that Agnivarṇa was protected by his majesty from being conquered by other kings (XIX.48), adding that instead he was carried off by consumption (suggesting that this rapid decease perhaps forestalled the other kings and saved his kingdom). The ministers meanwhile conceal the truth from the people, presumably to maintain order and to avoid inviting invasion by news of weakness. The 'counter example' in this system of instruction in all the ends is clear enough, but the crisis is for the time being survived and Kālidāsa ends on an optimistic note. It had been feared that Agnivarṇa would die childless, extinguishing the dynasty, but his queen is found to be pregnant and thus obtains the royal Fortune (XIX.55). Being consecrated, she rules in accordance with the injunctions (of Brahmanical tradition) whilst awaiting the birth of her child, guided by the elder ministers (XIX.57). The future of the dynasty is felt to be secured. We may feel that Kālidāsa has completed his epic, whilst conforming reasonably closely to the historical record. He has given us a study of the pursuit of the ends of humanity and he has portrayed a famous line of kings. The theme of the ends may be taken as giving some unity to the epic, despite its episodic construction. It does not seem desirable to add more, which would tend to be just repetition of a character already described.

1399. Kālidāsa has introduced a number of the standard subjects for description recognised as suitable for an epic [1267]. There are several battles and expeditions. Among the seasons we find autumn, the best time in India to begin a war, heralding Raghu's campaign of conquest. Daśaratha enjoys women and hunting in the spring and Kuśa enjoys his water sports (another standard subject) in the summer. Lovemaking has been sufficiently referred to above, culminating in the frivolities of Agnivarṇa. The ocean is described in the first part of Canto XIII, when Rāma passes over it in a flying chariot with Sītā on the way from Laṅkā to Ayodhyā and points out interesting sights to her. Afterwards they pass over a number of places visited before in their wanderings, mostly hermitages but briefly noticing several rivers. Kālidāsa finds some scope for his lyric genius, but not enough to deploy it fully because his chronicle must soon move on.

1400. Let us, however, pick out an example or two of Kālidāsa's imagery. On the birth of a son:

> As the king was drinking in the dear face of his son,
> his eye motionless as a lotus in the calm;
> His intense delight could not be contained within himself,
> like the high tide of the great ocean after seeing the Moon.
>
> (III.17: the Moon is a son of the Ocean, extracted by the gods and demons at the Churning.)

Śiṅgabhūpāla (p. 130) quotes this for 'joy' as a 'transient emotion' [56].

At the self-choice:

> She who was appointed to hold the staff (as usher)
> led the princess to another prince,
> — As a line of waves raised by the wind
> (led) a female flamingo to another lotus.
>
> (VI. 26)

1401. Despite his famed *vaidarbha* style, Kālidāsa in this poem shows himself very fond of alliteration and other verbal effects and surprisingly often reminds us of Aśvaghoṣa. In fact there are so many parallelisms of phrase and imagery that we must suppose Kālidāsa made a thorough study of the epics of the great Buddhist poet, which tended to be reflected in the Line of Raghu in spite of his lyricism and cultivation of a newer style. These two contrasted poets are linked especially by a certain playfulness and sense of humour.

1402. The *Vikramorvaśīya*, 'Valour Urvaśī' (i.e. the play on Urvaśī in which the special feature is that she is won by valour), is based on the very ancient story of Purūravas and the nymph Urvaśī, which is found in one of the ballad-dialogues of the *Veda* (*Ṛgvedasaṃhitā* X 95 [510]), as a prose story elsewhere in the *Veda* (*Śatapathabrāhmaṇa* of the *Yajurveda*, XI.5.1 [515]), in the *Harivaṃśa* (I.26) and in several *Purāṇas*. In the earliest versions it is not explained how the nymph came to love a man, but only that after a time she deserted him. He goes in search of her and eventually comes upon a flock of water birds in the lotus lake Anyataḥplakṣā, which in fact are Urvaśī and other nymphs (the *āti* is presumably some kind of duck; there were no swans in India, though translators have often used 'swan' as a suitable conceptual equivalent to this and other birds, such as the *haṃsa* which is a kind of wild goose). They reveal themselves and Purūravas begs Urvaśī to return to him, but she is cruel and refuses, telling him that there is no friendship with women, so he should not take it to heart but return home. In the prose version she eventually relents a little and secures for him the opportunity to become a divine being like herself, or rather a celestial musician *gandharva*, these being the natural companions of the nymphs. The 'problem' in this story, therefore, is how to win the heart of Urvaśī. We may remember, from Īśvaradatta's Dialogue of the Rogue and the Parasite, Devilaka's warning against the ancient (though they possess eternal youth) nymphs, who are false, arrogant, quarrelsome, etc. But Urvaśī in the earliest version of her story warns Purūravas against women in general, using strong language (on the meaning of which Vedic scholars are not agreed). Kālidāsa, true to the spirit of *kāvya*, presents Urvaśī as a woman, just as his gods are only men with special privileges and facilities. The *Purāṇas* in their different versions of the story explain Urvaśī's living on the Earth as due to a curse, a popular device, and sometimes introduce Indra to play a major part, since the nymphs have come to be represented as attached to his court. Plays on Urvaśī had perhaps been composed at least as early as Patañjali's time (– 2), as we noted in Chapter XIII.

1403. Kālidāsa's drama is generally regarded as a 'musical play' (*toṭaka*, Sāgaranandin 2774, Śāradātanaya p. 238; sometimes spelt *troṭaka* [343]) and is in five acts. The commentators Raṅganātha and Koṇeśvara and some manuscripts (in the prologue) call it a musical play, but other manuscripts call it simply a *nāṭaka*. Of course, a *toṭaka* is in effect a kind of *nāṭaka*, in which divine and human characters meet and in which, we have supposed, music with dances and songs plays a prominent part. Thus the two descriptions are not contradictory. There is a further point here, namely that a substantial number of the dances with songs in the fourth act (*carcaris* [359], *dvipadikās* [370], etc. [371]) are present in some manuscripts but not others; thus there are two recensions, one of which appears to be a special 'musical' version and might be called a *toṭaka*, whilst the other might perhaps be regarded as a *nāṭaka*, though the characteristic mingling of the divine Urvaśī and the human Purūravas remains. It is noteworthy that none of these songs are quoted by the critics, a rather strong indication that they are not original. They may therefore have been added by some late producer of the play who wished to create a definitely musical version, developing further the emotional content of the most popular act. So far we have no adequate critical edition of the play which would clarify the status of these songs. They do not affect the plot. The Valour Urvaśī is further referred to by Śāradātanaya in connection with Subandhu's theory of the 'playful' *lalita* as one of his five classes of *nāṭaka* [165]. It is not quite clear that

Śāradātanaya (pp. 240-1) takes this play as a whole as a 'playful' *nāṭaka*, or whether it simply illustrates certain of the special features of that class, though the former would seem appropriate enough. The critic mentions Urvaśī as an example of 'frustration', in the sensitive experience which alone occurs in the playful class. He quotes from Indra's message to the hero at the conclusion of the play for the explicit 'mention of the consummation of the matter' as the last conjunction characteristic of this class. The mode of stage business is naturally the 'tender'.

1404. The play opens with the appearance of a crowd of frightened nymphs crying for help. Purūravas drives to the scene in his chariot (this grandson of Manu Vaivasvata and of the Moon, like Raghu and other ancient emperors, has a flying chariot) and finds that two nymphs, Urvaśī and Citralekhā, have been carried off by a demon as they were on their way back from Kubera's palace. He dashes off in pursuit and soon returns with the two terrified nymphs in his chariot, having defeated the demon. As they drive back and Urvaśī revives from her fright, she falls in love with her brave rescuer — thus it is his valour which wins her love. He too, finding this most beautiful of nymphs at his side, falls in love with her. Abhinavagupta quotes (III p. 38) a verse (I.10) here for the limb 'beguiling' *vilobhana* of the opening [146]:

> At the rite of her creation was the Moon the Creator,
> giving his charm?
> Was it Pleasure himself, with the sensitive as the one
> aesthetic experience? Was it the Month who is
> the source of flowers?
> — For how could an ancient sage, dull through studying
> the *Veda*, his interest averted from sense objects,
> create this delightful appearance?

Bahurūpamiśra on the other hand (on I. 25 ff.) quotes the King's speech, concluding with this verse, for the limb 'surprise' *paribhāvanā* of the opening [146]. This might also be regarded as an example of 'doubt' *vitarka* as a transient emotion [56] (cf. Bhoja, *Sarasvatikaṇṭhābharaṇa* p. 370, who makes a figure of this). Dhanika (p. 77) quotes this impression of Urvaśī to illustrate a 'cause of emotion' *vibhāva* [54]. The verse is a favourite with the critics and anthologists (e.g. Vidyākara 456), for example Kuntaka quotes it and discusses it in detail (pp. 140-2, 146 and 219) for its 'imposed' subject matter [280] and for the mixture of figures to be found in it [234], including 'fancy' [213], in the first half, 'contrast' [209], in the second half, hyperbole [196] and 'having doubt' [233], besides the 'having *rasa*' recognised by some critics [215, 276]. Thus the 'seed' *bīja* is produced [123]. As the chariot shakes, coming down to Earth, the shoulders of Urvaśī and the King touch. Through various hints they understand each other, but after rejoining the other nymphs they part, Citraratha, the chief of the celestial musicians, having arrived to conduct the nymphs back to Indra and Purūravas modestly declining the honour of being presented as a hero to the king of the gods. But he expresses the hope to see her again as she takes her leave. In a 'playful' *nāṭaka* the 'opening' is replaced by the 'play' *vilāsa* conjunction, identifiable in this Act.

1405. In Act II the jester meets one of the maids of Queen Auśīnarī, who cleverly extracts from him the secret of the King's new love. Then as Purūravas walks with his jester in a park, discussing what can be done, Urvaśī arrives with Citralekhā and conceals herself near them, hoping to hear how strong his feelings are towards her. She is satisfied by what she hears: Purūravas passes this test. Urvaśī is unable to reveal herself, overcome by shame, but quickly writes a love letter in the form of a poem and throws it near him: she returns his love and now even the breeze in the Nandana Gardens seems unbearably hot to her (this suggests that she would like to escape from Indra's court, but how?). The jester sees the letter and gives it to the king, who reads it to him and then gives it to him for safe keeping. Urvaśī is still too timid to reveal herself, but after hearing Purūravas' reply asks Citralekhā to go and greet him for her. She does so and finally Urvaśī follows her, very shyly, but the king is able to find suitable words, takes her hand and makes her sit down. At this moment a messenger arrives from Heaven: Urvaśī must return at once because Indra wishes to see a performance of a play in which she is one of the actresses (at the beginning of Act III we learn that the play is the *Lakṣmīsvayaṃvara* composed by the Goddess Sarasvatī: it was perhaps Kālidāsa who invented this, though it has got into two *Purāṇas* also and the critics later note it as an ancient *nāṭaka*, cf. the end of Chapter

XIX above [1146]). Purūravas lets her go, simply asking her to remember him. After her departure, the jester wants to comfort the King with her letter, but he has lost it. Then the Queen arrives with her maid and finds the letter, which has been blown in her path by the wind. She confronts Purūravas with it. He makes a feeble attempt to cover the matter but she turns away scornfully, so he begs her to forgive him, saying he is her slave. She goes off without a word. In this class of play the 're-opening' is replaced by the 'frustration' *vipralambha* conjunction (*Śāradātanaya* p. 240), which seems exemplified here, whilst five limbs of the standard re-opening are necessary (p. 241), namely 'check', 'explanation' (?), 'apology', 'flowery speech' and 'thunderbolt', which may be seen here.

1406. In the supporting scene [126] of Act III we learn from two divine drama students that Urvaśī, acting her part as Lakṣmī in Sarasvatī's play, has, because of her love for him, said 'Purūravas' instead of 'Puruṣottama' (Viṣṇu). This is a case of the 'other conjunction' 'blunder in names' [141] (*Śṛṅgāraprakāśa* II p. 500). For this she has been cursed by Bharata, the producer, to fall from Heaven, but Indra, knowing the true state of affairs and being kindly disposed towards his comrade-in-arms (against demons) Purūravas, rules that the curse be modified: Urvaśī may attend on (love) Purūravas as long as she likes until Purūravas sees his offspring (then she must return to Heaven). Thus Urvaśī's love wins her her freedom, for a time at least, and the rest of the action will depend on her: her character and the relationship between her and Purūravas can be fully developed, though there is still the question of Queen Auśīnarī. In Act III Urvaśī arrives again with Citralekhā at Purūravas' palace, at night, dressed in dark blue as befits one 'who goes to meet' (her lover). Again they watch the King with his jester, as he goes to join the Queen in a ritual at her request (the nymphs are invisible, either because they are deities or because they are hidden in the sky by their blue robes). Purūravas is saying what Urvaśī wants to hear and she is about to reveal herself, but the Queen appears. Urvaśī admires the Queen's majestic bearing. Citralekhā approves this rejection of jealousy. As the rite proceeds, the maid explains to Purūravas that the Queen's object in performing it is that she should be reconciled to him. The King speaks courteous and affectionate words to Auśīnarī, making

Urvaśī feel embarrassed, but Citralekhā reassures her with the observation that gentlemen whose love has been transferred to others are more courteous to their wives. Then the Queen solemnly declares her consent to the King's new love. She desires his happiness. She retires immediately and Urvaśī reveals herself to Purūravas.

1407. It is in Act IV that we find Purūravas separated from Urvaśī as a result of her own action, as in the earliest versions of the story. The third conjunction in a 'playful' play should be 'separation' *viprayoga*, perhaps to be identified here. In the introductory scene Citralekhā tells another nymph that Urvaśī took Purūravas for a holiday or honeymoon on Mount Gandhamādana. There they saw a wizard girl named Udayavatī, whom Purūravas contemplated rather long. Urvaśī became angry with him for this — the other nymph remarks that she is intolerant, also very much in love, and that destiny is strong — and left him despite his entreaties. But in her delusion she strayed into Kumāra's Forest, where women are not allowed, and was immediately changed into a creeper. Now the distracted Purūravas, not knowing what has happened to her, is searching everywhere in the forest for Urvaśī. The nymphs decide there is no remedy for this separation except the Jewel of Union which was created out of the cosmetic paint on Pārvatī's feet, and hurry away to find it. (Some manuscripts do not mention this jewel here, but only that the nymphs go to look for a remedy.) There follows the long and pathetic scene of Purūravas, driven mad by the disappearance of Urvaśī, rushing about in the forest: he fancies he sees a demon carrying her off, but it is a cloud with lightning in it (this scene is acted as an *uttamottamaka* limb of the *lāsya* [363], Abhinavagupta III p. 75); he cannot understand what has happened, for he knows she loves him and that her anger cannot last long, whilst no one would dare to carry her off. He thinks he sees some traces of her cosmetics marking the way and follows, asking a peacock if he has seen a woman in the forest, but he gets no reply. Then he asks a cuckoo, mistakes the cry of a flamingo for the tinkling of anklets, and so continues, asking various birds, a bee, an elephant, a mountain — but hears only an echo. Everywhere he seems to see her as if metamorphosed into the beauties of nature. How can she have abandoned him when he loves her? Then he finds the jewel (which the nymphs have evidently thrown in his way) and a voice from off stage tells him what it is (the characteristic 'encouragement' *protsāhana*, cf. Sāgaranandin 1774). At last he sees the creeper, which somehow resembles Urvaśī, looking forlorn without any flowers, and embraces it ('coincidence' [227]—Vāmana p. 67). Urvaśī at once appears. She asks him to forgive her. In her mind she has been aware of everything that Purūravas was doing. Either here or at the beginning of the next act (or both) we might look for the fourth conjunction in a 'playful' play, namely 'clearing' or 'purifying' *viśodhana*.

1408. In the last act a vulture flies off with the Jewel of Union, to the great consternation of the King. After some time it is brought back to him with an arrow marked with the name of the person who shot the bird : 'Prince Āyus, son of Urvaśī, grandson of Ilā....' (Ilā is Purūravas' mother). Thus he learns that he has a son, when he believed he was childless. The boy is brought before him. Purūravas sends for Urvaśī and treats her with honour as the mother of his heir. She explains why she sent the boy away, concealing even his existence in order to postpone the operation of Indra's commands concerning her return to Heaven. Purūravas had known nothing of all this. Now he is in despair because he must lose her. He decides to abdicate, but Indra knows what has happened and sends his messenger the sage Nārada with his commands. He still needs Purūravas' aid against the demons, so the King must continue to rule, but he consents to Urvaśī remaining with Purūravas as long as he lives (quoted by Śāradātanaya, p. 241). In conclusion Nārada consecrates Āyus as heir-apparent and Urvaśī tells him to go and pay his respects to his 'eldest mother', i.e. Queen Auśīnarī: Purūravas says they should all go to her and the play concludes with an exchange of courteous speeches between the King and Nārada.

1409. In this play Kālidāsa has made considerable use of the opportunities afforded for the introduction of lyric verses delineating the emotions of the characters, especially in Act IV. This is in marked contrast with Mālavikā and Agnimitra. The main interest of the play is the character study of Urvaśī, though it is a sketch, if a brilliant sketch, beside Bhāsa's rich portrayal of Vāsavadattā. Purūravas, it seems, has to demonstrate to her the reality and strength of his love, and much of this is expressed through the lyric verses which Kālidāsa gives to him. The possibly apocryphal dance-songs in Māhārāṣṭrī and Apabhraṃśa in Act IV greatly prolong these lyric effects and give the act the character of a ballet, where the actor representing Purūravas, or a dancer representing him, dances and mimes his emotion of love to produce the sensitive in frustration.

1410. The *Meghasandeśa*, 'Cloud-Message' (message sent by cloud), is Kālidāsa's most perfect and most characteristic work. Nearly a third of its verses have been quoted by the old critics, showing that it has been more popular with them than any of his other compositions. This lyric or 'short *kāvya*' has externally the form of a 'hundred' *śataka* [418], containing a little over a hundred verses (a critical edition would produce 110, but it is possible some of these are not original; 20 more were added later by imitators), but they all belong to the same incident and constitute a single poem. The first five verses are the poet's introduction, the rest are put in the mouth of his character, a certain *yakṣa*. The *yakṣas* or 'sprites' are in this period the spirits who guard the treasures of Kubera, the God of Wealth, on Mount Kailāsa. This one, who is not named, has been deprived of his power and banished for a year by Kubera for neglect of his duties. Now he is living in the South at Rāmagiri ('Rāma's Peak'), one of the places where Rāma had lived in exile (its exact position is uncertain). At the beginning of the rains, when he has already been away for eight months, he finds his separation from his beloved especially painful. Seeing a cloud butting against the peak on its way North (as the South West monsoon brings the rains from the Indian Ocean), in his state of distraction due to eagerness to send her a message he imagines it possible to ask the cloud to take one for him. After the introduction explaining this, verses six to the end of the poem consist of the *yakṣa's* address to the cloud: his request to it, attractive description of the route to be followed, directions how to find the house and the lady, the actual message to be given her and a final benediction on the cloud for doing such a favour.

1411. It is worth noting in connection with this story that the critic Bhāmaha, whose date is not far removed from Kālidāsa's (it may be late +5, immediately after Diṅnāga [1293], in the course of his advocacy of realism in literature attacks the introduction by poets of incongruous messengers such as clouds, the wind, the Moon, bees and birds (I.42). He allows, however, that sometimes a person as if mad from eagerness (*utkaṇṭhā*, also translatable as 'longing') may be made to speak in this way (I. 44). Kālidāsa has taken care in his Cloud-Message (verse 5) to justify himself by saying:

> A cloud is just a conglomeration of mist, radiance, water and wind,
> whilst the meanings of messages must be retained by living beings having sharp senses;
> Through eagerness the *yakṣa* asked him, not considering this,
> for those afflicted by love are miserable in their entreaties to both sentient and insentient beings.

Thus he seems to be aware of the kind of discussion recorded by Bhāmaha and anxious to parry possible criticism by invoking the 'eagerness' (Kālidāsa's word is *autsukya*) clause. He presents the situation poetically with a 'corroboration' *arthāntaranyāsa* [208] in which, according to the commentator Mallinātha, the figure 'incongruity' (*viṣama*, first found defined in Rudraṭa only, however [260]) has been incorporated (the last line of the verse is the corroboration, the first two explain the incongruity). We may infer from all this that message poems of this type were popular in Kālidāsa's time, though no examples seem to have survived from that period except his, which successfully withstood criticism but which above all was prized for the beauty of its poetic expression.

1412. The poem is throughout in a single metre, the *mandākrāntā*, a long drawn out, nostalgic rhythm of 17 syllables to the line, perfectly suited to the emotion expressed by the *yakṣa* in his isolation. Each line begins with four long syllables, followed by five shorts leading into three successive syncopations. The first four syllables (which are followed by a caesura) suggest the feeling of longing or yearning, the series of shorts intensify this by suggesting an outward rush of anxious feeling and the syncopations heighten it further with their uncertainty ending in suspense. Kālidāsa has skilfully blended the musical notes of his Sanskrit expressions with this rhythm, to portray a passion enhanced by separation.

1413. The *yakṣa* describes to the cloud in detail the route which he should follow to reach Kailāsa. In this beautiful description all nature is personified, for the cloud (masculine) is assumed to be the lover of the rivers (feminine) and he will also flirt with the women and female birds he meets on the way. Thus the cloud is recommended to enjoy himself — it will be a pleasure for him to take the message, the *yakṣa* hopes to convince him. A detour must be made to Ujjayinī, however, though it is out of the way, because the cloud will have lived in vain if he does not enjoy the quivering glances of the women of that city, whilst on the way there he will meet the delightful Nirvindhyā River who needs him to replenish her thin stream, emaciated through separation. Kālidāsa dwells through several verses on the heavenly Ujjayinī. Afterwards the cloud will refresh himself by drinking up water from the Gambhīrā River. He will rest on the way on the summits of mountains and also on the roofs of the whitewashed palaces of Ujjayinī. After passing over Mount Kailāsa and escaping from the young goddesses who use him as a shower bath, by threatening them with thunder, the cloud will enter Kubera's city of Alakā and finally come to rest on the rock garden (miniature mountain) of the *yakṣa's* house. There the cloud should gently introduce himself and deliver the message, including as token of authenticity a reminder of a dream his lady had once told the *yakṣa*.

1414. In this poem consideration for delicate sound-effects appears to take precedence over the supposed simplicity of the *vaidarbha* style. There are long compounds, appropriate enough for the metre used, the word order is generally disregarded, so that the verse does not readily reveal its meaning, and in place of straightforward expressions words are often used in unusual transferred senses [267]. These last are frequently most effective in building up the emotionally charged atmosphere. Naturally it is rarely possible to reproduce such effects in a translation and we can give only a simple, literal statement of the meaning to exemplify the imaginative power of the Cloud-Message:

Where (in Ujjayinī) the breeze from the Śiprā (River) at
daybreak, fragrant through the friendship of the
scent of the opening waterlilies,

prolonging the shrill cry of the cranes, sweet with
passion;
Being agreeable to the body, takes away women's tiredness caused by lovemaking,
coaxing affectionately like a lover. (31)

Ānandavardhana (pp. 511-2) quotes this for the word 'friendship', the literal meaning of which is not intended at all (*dhvani* with *avivakṣitavācya* [250]), here mixed with figures of speech (fancy, etc.).

1415. In the *yakṣa's* garden:

There is a pool in it, approached by steps formed of
emerald stones,
sewn with golden waterlily buds having stems of soft
lapis lazuli:
In whose water the wild geese, making their dwelling,
will not think of (Lake) Mānasa, though it is
nearby,
even when they have seen you, because their grief will
have vanished.
(73; Pūrṇasarasvatī 72)

(Wild geese are supposed to migrate to Mānasa when the rains begin, because the water of other lakes and pools becomes muddy; but this wonderful pool remains clear, so that the grief of the birds on seeing the cloud approach will soon vanish [1081.)

1416. On arrival outside her window:

At that time, O cloud, if my beloved should be asleep,
be patient for a watch, attending on her without
thundering;
When with difficulty she may have found me, her lover,
in a dream,
let not her close embrace suddenly have the knot of its
creeper-like arms fall from my neck.
(94; Pūrṇasarasvatī 93)

1417. Part of the message:

Limb with limb, hot body with intensely hot body,
falling tear with tear, unceasing eagerness with eagerness,
Hot sigh with deeper sighing: the one who is far away
unites with you in intention when his way is obstructed by hostile fate.

(99; Pūrṇasarasvatī 98)

Bhoja quotes this for 'anxiety' *cintā* [56] (*Śṛṅgāraprakāśa* II p. 582) and again in discussing 'being abroad' as a situation of the sensitive in frustration (Chapters XXII-XXIV, pp. 34, 63, 93 in Yadugiriyati's edition).

1418. The *Abhijñānaśākuntala*, 'Recognition Śakuntalā' or 'Token Śakuntalā', is often looked upon as Kālidāsa's best play, because its lyrics are much more often quoted than those in Mālavikā and Agnimitra or Valour Urvaśī. Here lyricism is carried to an extreme which disregards story and plot and is interested only in highly emotional, preferably pathetic, situations. The hero, Duṣyanta, is shown as doing nothing, though capable of a certain amount of feeling and anxiety. Things happen to him through fate, a curse, or divine intervention. His character remains a blank and we cannot believe in the depth of his feelings. The heroine, Śakuntalā, is more real but still the helpless plaything of supernatural powers. She can be seen as a thoughtless girl whose love is tested and matured by a long and harsh separation. The curse she brings on her love is due to her own negligence resulting from a real passion.

1419. The story is taken from the *Mahābhārata* history of the Lunar (Paurava) emperor Duṣyanta, his marriage to Śakuntalā and the birth of Bharata. There Duṣyanta meets Śakuntalā, daughter of the nymph Menakā and the (or a) warrior-priest Viśvamitra, at a hermitage, and they marry by the aristocratic rite of simple mutual consent. But Duṣyanta returns to his palace and Śakuntalā remains at the hermitage, where a son is born to her. When he is six years old she takes him to the emperor, but he disowns them. Finally a voice in the air confirms that the boy is Duṣyanta's son. (*Mahābhārata* I *adhyāyas* 62ff. contains the history of Duḥṣanta or Duṣyanta.) Kālidāsa in his play, a *nāṭaka* in seven acts, has varied this story chiefly by introducing the curse of a sage angered by the negligence of Śakuntalā in love, which causes Duṣyanta genuinely to forget Śakuntalā and not to recognise her when she comes to his palace (Bhoja notes this avoidance of a 'fault' in the original story which spoils the *rasa* : *Śṛṅgāraprakāśa* II p. 460). He had given her a ring as a token, and the curse was supposed to terminate when he saw it, but Śakuntalā lost it in the River Ganges on the way and nothing else could recall her to his memory. She becomes angry and criticises him ('altercation' [149]) but he is not conscious of any fault. As she leaves him, Menakā carries her off into the sky ('ability' [149]) and leaves her on Mount Hemakūṭa in the Himālaya, to be looked after by Aditi, the mother of the gods. A fisherman finds the emperor's ring in the belly of a fish and thus it is restored to him: he remembers Śakuntalā now but can do nothing about her. Like his ancestor Purūravas, however, Duṣyanta is employed by Indra in his wars against the demons, thus an opportunity is provided ('resumption' [149]) for him to fly over the Himālaya in Indra's own chariot, whose charioteer takes him near Hemakūṭa and instigates a visit to this sacred place. Thus Duṣyanta and Śakuntalā are reunited by the gods. First Duṣyanta recognises his son, then Śakuntalā appears. It is explained to her that Duṣyanta is blameless; she has only herself to blame. Abhinavagupta indicates (III p. 13) that the emperor's obtaining a son is the objective of the play, as of the source story.

1420. Such a play might be made effective, in producing aesthetic experience, if presented from the point of view of the suffering heroine, as Bhāsa presented Vāsavadattā. Unfortunately Kālidāsa has not done this but has the king dominate the stage throughout. What is his emotion when, due to the curse, he has completely forgotten his love ? How can we imagine such a thing, which is completely outside our experience ? What *rasa* can we have from it ? In short the play does not deal with human experience. It is a fairy story, which perhaps has religious or philosophical significance.

1421. The king expresses a fatalistic mood at the outset:

This hermitage is a place of tranquility
—my arm trembles (a portent), what could happen
here as a result of that ?

— But rather there are entrances everywhere
to the inevitable. (I.14)

The commentator Rāghavabhaṭṭa notes that here we have the limb 'extension' of the opening [146]. Whilst engaged in his new love affair in the hermitage the king knows that ascetics are dangerous if provoked:

In ascetics, though they are generally calm,
there is a hidden energy which can burn:
As the 'sunstones', though agreeable to the touch,
may discharge, overcoming the energy of others.
(II.7)

When he has forgotten Śakuntalā because of the ascetic's curse he nevertheless sometimes has a vague feeling, as if disturbed by some emotion from a previous life (Kuntaka, p. 224, refers to the curse and the following verse in discussing contextual figurativeness, where the details of the original story have been changed; Bhoja quotes the verse for 'reflection' [56] : *Śṛṅgāraprakāśa* II p. 570):

Seeing delightful things, hearing sweet sounds,
since a man becomes sad even though they please him:
Surely he remembers in his heart something he is yet
unaware of,
— friendships in another life, whose emotion is constant.
(V. 2)

He does not remember Śakuntalā even when he sees her, but his heart is convinced, being strongly agitated by the meeting (V.31). In Act VI he regains his memory and suffers remorse for having repudiated her. In Act VII as he approaches the hermitage on Mount Hemakūṭa his arm trembles again and he remonstrates with it for such a portent when he has no hope of attaining his wish (VII.13). At the reunion Duṣyanta begs to be forgiven, but it was not his fault and Śakuntalā blames her own presumed evil deeds of a former life for what has happened. Being told of the curse, of which she was unaware, she supposes that it must have happened when her heart was distracted because of Duṣyanta's absence. After this the play ends with the congratulations of the gods and a prediction of Bharata's future greatness.

1422. The *Kumārasambhava*, 'Origin of Kumāra', is an epic in eight cantos on a mythological theme. Its source was perhaps *Mahābhārata* III *adhyāya* 213, or some *Purāṇa*. The gods are oppressed by the demon Tāraka, against whom they are helpless because his power came from Brahmā. Brahmā himself will not act against his own creation, but promises Indra that a son of Śiva will have the power to destroy Tāraka. This son will be Kumāra, the God of War, also known as Skanda and Kārtikeya. Śiva has as yet no son and is moreover at that time engaged in a course of strenuous asceticism, oblivious of everything, including the desperate situation of the gods. Indra's problem is to interrupt Śiva's meditations and make a father of him. Kālidāsa delightfully describes the intrigue which Indra then prepares. Umā, daughter of Himālaya (the Mountain, personified as a god), known also as Pārvatī (which means daughter of a mountain), is known to be Śiva's predestined consort. The great ascetic remains oblivious of her, but Indra commissions Kāma, the God of Love, to undertake the extremely dangerous task of arousing Śiva by shooting him with one of his arrows. Śiva catches sight of Kāma in the very act of taking aim at him, and burns him down with a flash from his Third Eye. Thus Kāma lost his body and has ever since been known as 'Bodiless' (Anaṅga). After this disaster, no other course remaining, Umā herself engages in severe asceticism in order to become worthy of her future husband. At length Śiva recognises her efforts, tests her devotion to him, declares his love and asks her father for her hand. In Canto VII they are married and Śiva restores Kāma's body. Canto VIII describes the lovemaking of Śiva and Umā [1520], with their visit to Gandhamādana, concluding with their great happiness.

1423. Some have supposed this poem to be unfinished, for eight is a rather small number of cantos for an epic, whilst Kumāra is not yet born, his birth or even his infant victory over Tāraka being thought a more suitable conclusion. But it is quite reasonable to take the marriage of Śiva and Umā and its consummation, ensuring the 'origin' of Kumāra, as a proper conclusion to the action proposed. The alternative view would suppose either that the poem was interrupted by the poet's death (we treat it here as if it was his last work, but this is mere conjecture) or that criticism of the eighth canto, such as we have noted above, caused him to abandon the work. It is rather strange that similar suppositions have arisen in connection with Kālidāsa's other epic, the Line of Raghu, whose last canto describes the dissolute life of a Solar emperor and might offend the same kind of sensibility which disliked the description of the lovemaking of the highest deities. If Kālidāsa's public had such scruples, would he have made the same kind of mistake twice, at the cost of leaving both his epics unfinished ? It is possible, in view of the fact that it does appear to have been the habit of Indian poets to circulate their poems canto by canto at times, or to read current work to their friends, to imagine epics abandoned under criticism, but there is no tangible evidence for this in Kālidāsa's case. There exists a sequel of nine cantos composed by an anonymous but apparently fairly recent poet, which adds the story of Kumāra's birth and victory. It is not referred to by the old critics or commentators, though recently it has been claimed that it is authentic Kālidāsa.

1424. There are many beautiful descriptions in this poem [1267]: in Canto I the Himālaya Mountain, followed by the birth of his daughter Umā and a description of her (the mountain is described as a mountain, his daughter as a very attractive girl); in Canto III spring; in Canto VIII sunset, night and moonrise on Mount Gandhamādana. In Canto II the gods praise Brahmā with an interesting theological hymn based on Vedic speculations, after which Brahmā describes the appearance of the gods after their defeat. Canto IV is devoted to the lament of Rati (Love, the wife of Kāma) after Śiva has reduced her husband to ashes.

1425. Himālaya:

> Who protects the darkness, which is as if afraid of the day,
> from the Sun, concealing it in his caves:
> Surely those whose heads are lofty show affection
> even to low persons who come for refuge, just as to the good. (I.12)

This is an example of the figure corroboration [208], of which Kālidāsa is very fond, at the same time the verse contains a 'fancy' *utprekṣā* in its personifications (Namisādhu p. 139: mixture of figures).

1426. In spring (as 'cause of 'emotion', Dhanika p. 99):

The bee, following his own beloved,
drank honey from the same cup of a flower;
And the black antelope scratched with his horn
his mate, who closed her eyes at the touch.
(III.36)

The female elephant from love gave the elephant
a trunkful of water scented with the pollen of lotuses;
The ruddy sheldrake honoured his wife
with a lotus stalk of which he had eaten half.
(III.37)

Kuntaka (p. 50) quotes the first of these to illustrate his natural, unstudied, 'delicate' style [288]. Other critics (*Sarasvatikaṇṭhābharaṇa* p. 629, etc.) quote these in discussing the production of *rasa*; they might therefore be regarded as illustrating the 'having *rasa*' figure [215], otherwise simply as 'naturalistic description' *svabhāvokti* [197].

1427. Sunset:

See, shy one, the Sun
hanging in the West has made
With his long image in the water of the lake
a causeway as of gold.
(VIII.34)

This is another example of fancy.

1428. Then at night another:

The Moon, combing the darkness with his beams,
as if with his fingers the massy hair of night,
Seems to kiss her face
whose eyes — the lotuses — have closed into their buds.
(VIII.63)

Bhoja (*Sarasvatikaṇṭhābharaṇa* p. 438) argues that this is 'partial fancy' *utprekṣāvayava* [234], arising from metaphorical transfer of the various actions (cf. Kuntaka p. 176, same figures in connection with 'having *rasa*').

1429. These examples may show that there is much to enjoy in this poem, in the detailed imagery and fancy. There is also much humour and a generally light touch, contrasting with the more serious tone of the Line of Raghu. The aesthetic experience is of course the sensitive. Bhoja finds seven kinds of 'frustration' in the epic (*Śṛṅgāraprakāśa* ed. Yadugiriyati, p. 73). In effect the poem narrates the life of Umā from her birth to her marriage, showing how she won her husband by her asceticism and devotion, her father having failed previously to arrange it and the more direct approach with the support of Kāma having ended in disaster for him and humiliation for her. Kālidāsa's art is at its happiest in the Origin of Kumāra, in which he has found full scope for his special abilities. It seems natural to regard it as his last work.

1430. Kālidāsa is the poet of love and of women. He has produced a remarkable gallery of portraits of women in love: Mālavikā, Irāvatī, Dhāriṇī, Indumatī, Sītā, Kumudvatī, Urvaśī, Auśīnarī, the *yakṣa's* lady, Śakuntalā and Umā. They are all different, but what perhaps links them all is a certain irrepressible capriciousness, seen to be mellowed by experience into a capacity for more unselfish and constant love. Love is strengthened and character matured by separation and difficulties. In several places in his works Kālidāsa has developed the sensitive in frustration, but generally from the point of view of the man, whose love is intensified by separation.

Chapter XXV

PRAVARASENA, ŚYĀMILAKA AND SAMGHADĀSA

1431. The Māhārāṣṭrī epic *Setubandha*, 'The Building of the Causeway', appears to have been composed by the Vākāṭaka Emperor Pravarasena II (reigned *c*. +410 to 440) mentioned at the beginning of the last chapter. This seems more probable than that Pravarasena I (*c*. +280 to 340), father of Sarvasena [1265], was the author, since for example the critics who admire him give the impression that Sarvasena was an earlier writer by mentioning him or his work first (Daṇḍin, *Avantisundari*, introductory verses 12-3, Bhoja, *Śṛṅgāraprakāśa* II pp. 373 and 374). The author says (I.9):

> It is difficult for a *kāvya* story to be completed,
> having the chief aesthetic experiences,
> When it is begun by a new king,
> making good the slips; as a friendship
> <Is difficult to be completed
> with a famous connoisseur,
> When it is begun with new passion,
> making good the slips.>

There is a pun here on the Māhārāṣṭrī compound *rāāraddhā*, 'begun by a king' or 'begun with passion', and on other words. This gives us the information that Pravarasena composed his epic in the early part of his reign, amid the distractions of his royal duties, perhaps during the decade +410 to 420. The verse is also referred to by commentators, such as Rāmadāsa, as evidence that another poet, supposed to be Kālidāsa, helped the emperor to complete the composition. In style and fancy there is a considerable difference between Kālidāsa and the author of the Causeway (as it is sometimes called for short), whilst there is nothing in Kālidāsa's works to suggest that he was an exponent of Prakrit epic composition. The tradition about Kālidāsa seems to appear very late (Rāmadāsa lived in the +16) and the old critics are known to mention only Pravarasena in connection with the Causeway. Pravarasena's apology in this verse is thus probably merely a conventional one such as is found at the beginning of other epic undertakings, seeking the indulgence of the critic. It is answered in the next verse (I.10), which is quoted by Bhoja (*Śṛṅgāraprakāśa* II p. 473) as an example of the 'preliminary statement of purpose' as the 'ornament of a whole work' *prabandhālaṅkāra* beginning with sentences about one's family, etc.:

> In what way do *kāvya* narratives not delight?
> — since intelligence increases,
> Honour (good reputation) is produced, good qualities are gained
> and the deeds of good men are heard.

He seems to imply that any slips in composition may perhaps be forgiven him for the sake of the good effects such an epic should produce.

1432. It is interesting that he has in mind the moral effects, a likely concern of a ruler hoping his subjects will emulate the noble qualities of his heroes. Pravarasena goes on (I.11):

> It is difficult to produce
> a new way for one's subject matter through brilliance of composition,
> Just as (it is difficult to produce) getting rich by (merely) wishing
> or acquiring the beauty of youth (merely) by being nobly born.

We are again reminded that a king is writing. Nevertheless (I.12):

> Listen to the Slaying of Rāvaṇa, in which Sītā's unhappiness is ended,
> the goddesses are freed (from the oppression of the demons),
> Which pulls out the arrow from the heart of the whole universe
> and which is marked by 'devotion'.

As Bhoja points out, *Śṛṅgāraprakāśa* II p. 474, the word *aṇurāa* occurs at the end of each canto as a kind of mark of the intention of the poet, which he calls an 'ornament of a whole work' *prabandhālaṅkāra*, a practice perhaps started by Sarvasena [1267] and followed in several later epics though apparently borrowed from the biography [425]; but Pravarasena surely intends here also to announce 'devotion' as his theme for the epic, the devotion of Rāma and Sītā and also of Rāma's allies in the great struggle. We may understand that he is presenting the old story of Rāma's war against Rāvaṇa in a new way, not just by brilliant poetic effects (though there are plenty of these) but by bringing out the theme of devotion or loyalty, in love and in friendship. Bhoja quotes the verse (II p. 472) for its 'declaration of the matter to be narrated', another example of the 'ornament of a whole work' beginning with sentences about one's family, etc.

1433. The Building of the Causeway, also known as the Slaying of Rāvaṇa (*Dasamuhavaha*, sometimes *Rāvaṇavaha*), in 15 cantos narrates the story of Rāma's war against Rāvaṇa from just after the consecration of Sugrīva as King of the Monkeys, Vālin having been killed by Rāma, to the slaying of Rāvaṇa by Rāma and his return to Ayodhyā with Sītā. It thus covers almost the same part of the Rāma story as Bhāsa's play The Consecrations [1026]. As a brahman, and probably a champion of the Vedic tradition and everything connected with it, like his ancestors, Pravarasena follows the *Rāmāyana* of Vālmīki in detail, perhaps deliberately upholding his version of the story against Vimala's criticism (cf. Chapter XVI above [854-7]) in the *Paümacariya*, also a Māhārāṣṭrī epic. Thus the central episode, after which the Causeway takes its usual name, is the building of the bridge or (better) causeway from India to Ceylon (Laṅkā) by the monkeys, which Vimala objected to as impossible (as well as objecting that the 'monkeys' were not real monkeys). Formally, Pravarasena's epic resembles Sarvasena's and not Vimala's, using the *skandhaka* (*āryāgiti*) metre, not the *āryā*, and the fully developed *kāvya* epic techniques of Aśvaghoṣa and his successors in Sanskrit. It is likewise an *āśvāsabandha* [cf. 413, 1266] (Bhoja, *Śṛṅgāraprakāśa* II p. 370 as standard example of a Māhārāṣṭrī epic; Śāradātanaya p. 282). As regards the language of the Causeway, we should note that Pravarasena, like Sarvasena, is continuing the tradition of Māhārāṣṭrī literature in its homeland, so that he was presumably writing in something close to the actual vernacular of his country, though no doubt heavily overlaid with poetic *kāvya* vocabulary.

1434. Pravarasena begins with invocations to Viṣṇu and Śiva, then introduces his story in the way we have seen above. Sītā is already in Rāvaṇa's hands and Rāma is in a state of despair, he does not wish to live (I.15). The rains have ended and autumn is described at some length, in the manner proper for an epic description but with strong hints at the coming action, autumn being the proper season to begin military campaigns. At this appropriate time, the great monkey Hanumant returns to Rāma, having succeeded in finding and visiting Sītā in her captivity. He reports that she is weak and grieving for Rāma, but she is alive. Having learned Sītā's whereabouts, Rāma determines to march on Laṅkā and sets out with his new ally Sugrīva and the army of monkeys.

1435. Having marched from the vicinity of the Vindhya past the Sahya and Malaya mountains, the army reaches the coast opposite Laṅkā and is shaken by the sight of the Ocean lying in its path: the Ocean is described at length in Canto II. Sugrīva then makes a rousing speech to his troops, promising them honour, or shame if they fail when others have succeeded in even more difficult circumstances, ending with a vow to reach Laṅkā somehow, if it means uprooting the Vindhya Mountains to use them as a bridge, turning the water into dry land joining the Mountains Malaya and Suvela (the latter being on the Laṅkā side). This speech takes up the whole of Canto III.

> Those good men are few
> who without talking bring about the objective stated;
> Those trees too are only few
> which without a display of flowers give fruit.
>
> (III.9, corroboration [208]:
> *Sarasvatikaṇṭhābharaṇa* p. 503)

The ancient King of the Bears Jāmbavant, also an ally of Rāma, who remembers a time even before the Churning of the Ocean (IV.20), adds his advice and exhortations, encouraging Rāma also by reminding him of his past heroic deeds in previous incarnations of Viṣṇu.

1436. Then Rāvaṇa's brother Vibhīṣaṇa arrives from Laṅkā, where he had already seen Hanumant. He is a friend (because he had wanted peace between the 'demons' of Laṅkā and Rāma), so Rāma declares he will allow the demon *rākṣasa* dynasty to continue through him and consecrates him king of Laṅkā. During the night, the Ocean fears Rāma's anger at finding him an obstacle:

> As the night ended;
> its image fallen into the trembling waves,
> The disc of the Moon whirled like Ocean's heart
> bewildered over what should be done.
>
> (V.10)

The following morning Rāma, his distress turning into anger, seizes his bow and shoots a fiery arrow into the Ocean.

> The pall of thick smoke clings
> to the basin of the Ocean's blood-like coral,
> Blackening it,
> spreading like a surge of poison.
>
> (V. 50: *Sarasvatikaṇṭhābharaṇa* p. 433, 'implied simile' [791])

The arrow burns its way right down into the Underworld (Pātāla), tormenting the Ocean and all its inhabitants, particularly the dragons who live beneath it. These tremendous effects are described at length (most of Canto V), with luxuriant fancy and very long compounds. Thus harassed, wounded, burned and smoked, the Ocean (God) comes out, supported by his consort Gaṅgā (Canto VI). He complains of the ill treatment but approves the building of a causeway to seal the fate of Rāvaṇa. Rāma then gives the order for the monkeys to start work and they proceed to uproot mountains as building materials, from the Malaya and Mahendra ranges, and transport them to the coast, all of which is described at great length. In the seventh canto the monkeys are described setting to work on the causeway itself with great gusto, throwing the mountains into the Ocean and causing a terrific upheaval; but even after prolonged efforts they do not seem to be nearing the completion of the task and grow tired.

1437. At the beginning of Canto VIII the monkeys cease work and the Ocean becomes calm. Then Sugrīva speaks to Nala, a monkey chief famous for his engineering skill, for he is the son of Viśvakarman himself, the divine engineer, and orders him to make the mountains Malaya and Suvela one and the Ocean two. Nala promises to complete the causeway and re-starts the work in a properly organised manner. First a mountain red with ores of gold is set in position as an auspicious beginning, then others are carefully planted side by side so as to support one another and stick together when they become wet, despite the buffetting of the waves, with their heavier bases downwards to ensure stability. Thus the causeway is completed and the army marches across it to Mount Suvela on the far side.

1438. The whole of Canto IX consists of a description of Mount Suvela as the monkeys see it on their arrival. It is in effect a single long sentence, and would have appeared directly as such in a prose description. Suvela here is an idealised mountain, reaching up into the heavens and down into the underworld, where the watery palaces of the dragons are (IX.7, quoted by Bhoja, *Sarasvatikaṇṭhābharaṇa* p. 542, for the figure hyperbole [196]). It bears all the proper wild animals, trees and precious minerals for a great mountain, especially a Southern mountain, moreover all the six seasons exist on it simultaneously. In Canto X the monkeys climb Suvela and survey Laṅkā. Rāvaṇa receives the news of their arrival with indignation and anger: he is shaken like Suvela itself when the monkeys climbed its peak. The day is ending, however, and the poet has occasion to describe the late afternoon followed at once by sunset, twilight, night and moonrise. The demonesses on Laṅkā forget their alarm in a riot of lovemaking, which is described at length. This is of course a description considered proper to an epic, but Pravarasena brings it in here with such skill as to make it fit naturally into his story at this point: the monkeys complete their building work just before the end of the day, then climb Suvela and see Laṅkā spread out before them; the evening would in any case bring lovemaking, but the alarm of the demonesses on the eve of battle, in which their lovers may be killed, intensifies their passionate feelings and removes their jealous anger (Bhoja notes the theme, *Śṛṅgāraprakāśa* II p. 476, as an example of an ornament of a whole work in connection with pleasures [1267]). Rāvaṇa, however, longs to win Sītā's love and, rejected by her, finds himself alone and suffering the pangs of separation amid this scene of passionate unions. Sītā remains devoted to Rāma, so as a last desperate resort Rāvaṇa tries to convince her that Rāma is dead, ordering his servants to make an imitation head of Rāma and show it to her. Much of Canto XI is taken up with a preliminary description of Sītā and then with the effect on her of seeing this head (52ff.). Ānandavardhana (p. 222) expresses his admiration of this passage, where the genius of the poet concentrating on the aesthetic experience (here the compassionate) produces figures of speech also, but naturally and therefore without detracting from the experience through studied effects. He does not quote, but the description begins thus:

And Sītā has fallen,
her cheek shining pale from the pressure of her
 enfeebled hand;
Her right breast raised unevenly,
pushed out by the left breast. (XI.54)

The figure here according to Bhoja is 'retinue' *parikara*, first defined by Rudraṭa (pp. 89 ff.), consisting in the significant epithets (suggesting separation and beauty) (*Sarasvatikaṇṭhābharaṇa* p. 508). After reviving a little, she laments, reflecting:

He will be the husband of Earth (only),
—(for) Royal Fortune is inconstant to many distinguished men—
Why ! Now only my widowhood
approaches unshared.
(XI.78)

Eventually she is comforted by Trijaṭā, the demoness who guards her but treats her kindly, and becomes convinced that the head is artificial.

1439. In Canto XII dawn and moonset are described: Rāma awakes and sets out with his army, whose noise Sītā hears. Rāvaṇa too awakes and the demons march out, their lovemaking suddenly interrupted, the two armies confronting each other. As they march out, the various demon heroes are described. The last three cantos are given up to the battle. First there is a general fight between the monkeys and demons, both sides determined and reckless of life, with the monkeys on the whole getting the upper hand through their superior strength, though the demons are better armed with conventional weapons. Sugrīva and others individually kill some of the demon warriors. Then in Canto XIV Rāma advances into the battle, aiming to draw out Rāvaṇa, and wreaks havoc among the demons with his unrivalled archery. But Rāvaṇa's heroic son Indrajit (called also Meghanāda) attacks and shoots the supernatural 'dragon snare' weapon at Rāma and Lakṣmaṇa: they are both entangled in it and fall, bleeding. This is the moment of greatest tension: the gods themselves, looking on from their chariots in the sky, fear that all is lost; Rāvaṇa is told that his enemy is dead and Sītā from afar sees Rāma fallen and apparently dying. But the monkeys are undefeated and Sugrīva drives Indrajit back. Now Rāma laments his fate. Lakṣmaṇa he thinks is dying gloriously, sacrificing his life for his brother, but he himself has fought in vain. He resigns himself to death, expresses his regret at having failed to secure the (demon) kingdom for Vibhīṣaṇa, and advises Sugrīva to retreat quickly across the causeway, taking his own fate as a warning before it is too late. Sugrīva ignores this, orders the monkeys to carry Rāma and Lakṣmaṇa back to their city, and declares that he himself will kill Rāvaṇa and rescue Sītā.

1440. Rāma, however, is an incarnation of Viṣṇu and has supernatural resources at his disposal at least equal to those commanded by the demons, although the latter had recently conquered the gods. Hearing Vibhīṣaṇa observe that the weapon which has felled him is of dragon or 'serpentine' origin, Rāma recollects that he has the power of summoning to his aid Garuḍa, the great bird who is Viṣṇu's mount and the inveterate enemy of all snakes and dragons. He does so, Garuḍa at once appears and the dragon snare vanishes, Rāma and Lakṣmaṇa being freed and recovering from their wounds. The battle is renewed by the demons, but again the monkeys prove stronger, Hanumant killing one demon leader and the monkey chief Nīla another. In the Fifteenth Canto Rāvaṇa himself marches against the monkeys, who retreat before him until Nīla stops them. Rāvaṇa turns back when he sees Rāma, but his brother the huge demon Kumbhakarṇa is sent forward, only to be killed by Rāma. Rāvaṇa marches again but is preceded by Indrajit, who is then killed by Lakṣmaṇa. After weeping at his son's death, Rāvaṇa marches for the last time, seeing Vibhīṣaṇa with his enemies and hesitating between shooting at him in indignation and sparing him as a brother. But Lakṣmaṇa appears and Rāvaṇa wounds him severely with his most powerful weapon. Lakṣmaṇa is healed by a wonderful herb brought by Hanumant from Gandhamādana. At this moment before the climax of the struggle Indra sends his own chariot, armour and charioteer for Rāma to use. Rāvaṇa continues to attack the monkeys and Rāma drives out to meet him and satisfy his anger. The two shower each other with arrows and both are wounded, though Rāma feels nothing but the torment of his separation from Sītā. At last Rāma kills Rāvaṇa with a well aimed arrow which severs his ten-faced head. The Royal Fortune of Rāvaṇa lingers for a time with him even after he has fallen, knowing his valour and thinking she is deceived. Vibhīṣaṇa weeps for him and Rāma orders the proper rites to be performed. Now Sugrīva can feel he has succeeded in returning Rāma's friendship, Indra's charioteer takes his leave and Rāma goes with Sītā, her faithfulness attested by a fire ordeal, to Ayodhyā to make fruitful the devotion of Bharata to him.

1441. Pravarasena's interpretation of the Rāma story will perhaps appear sufficiently from this summary. He has extracted the heroic essence and presented a study in 'devotion', a fitting subject for a royal poet. As to the character of Rāma, though he is presented as an incarnation of Viṣṇu and able to dispose of supernatural aid, Pravarasena seems to have wished to humanise him as far as possible. Rāma appears to think of himself simply as a man and to be an ordinary human being in his passions. He is shown as having weaknesses, as despairing too easily in a crisis and not having much confidence in his powers. Only when roused to anger does he feel his powers and display his irresistible archery. He needs the devotion of his friends, especially Sugrīva who shows superior powers of leadership. In this way the story is presented in a significant manner; it is a difficult struggle, not a routine parade of divine perfection, and the outcome depends on the parts played by all the characters in it, each of which has its own significance.

1442. Pravarasena's epic is rich in descriptions. Bhoja (*Śṛṅgāraprakāśa* II p. 475) notes as ornaments of a whole work [1267] particularly those of a city (Laṅkā), the seasons, a mountain and the times of day (evening, etc.). That on autumn in the first canto is fairly naturalistic, though filled with the traditional conventions of the poets and bringing in mythological references. The sky is like the lotus from which Brahmā was born, the white clouds being its thousand petals and the Sun's rays its stamens (I. 17 — simile mixed with metaphors, *Sarasvatikaṇṭhābharaṇa* p. 427). The scent of *saptacchadas* and *kadambas* is conspicuous and so are the sweet cries of the ducks (I.23). As the rains cease and the sky clears, the Moon appears to be very near (I.25). Other flowers and birds mentioned in the Review of the Seasons as characteristic of autumn are described here. The description of the ocean in Canto II is partly realistic (green with seaweed, *seāla,* on the coastal rocks, verse 31) but more mythological. That of Mount Suvela represents an ideal mountain in a mythical setting, as we have already noted. It could hardly be identified with any particular real mountain, such as those of Ceylon, except as completely transformed in poetic imagination. Its size is exaggerated until it takes its place among the heavenly bodies as well as the subterranean worlds. Indeed it is so vast that perhaps we should assume that Pravarasena already shared the later view (cf. Dhanapāla in the *Tilakamañjarī*) that Laṅkā was not identical with Ceylon but was a mythical Southern continent beyond the Southern Ocean. He may in fact have conceived Suvela as a mountain at the South Pole, corresponding to the purely theoretical Mount Meru at the North, thus as the axis round which the stars, Sun and Moon revolved. This would provide scope for the mountain described. Among the minor imaginative details we are given lions chasing the clouds on the peaks of Suvela, but getting their manes scorched by the lightning coming from the clouds (IX.79). The description of the evening in Canto X is quite short but very effective; thus when the Moon first rises it has a rather coppery colour, like the cavity of a fresh lotus flower, it sheds its rays delicately like the stamens: as it approaches it thins out the darkness but cannot yet annihilate it (X.34).

1443. When Pravarasena's descriptions rise to a climax he generally uses long compounds (some in Canto II, many more in Canto IX). He does the same thing when excitement mounts in the action (as towards the end of Canto VII, where the monkeys make tremendous efforts to fill the Ocean with mountains, without success; again in some of the battle descriptions, but not to any extent in the final fight of Rāma). He does not seem to have been regarded as an exponent of the *vaidarbha* style, as Sarvasena was [1266, 1269], and perhaps should be regarded as more inclined to the *gauḍīya*, with its fondness for long compounds and alliteration, also brilliance and exaggeration. The Causeway exemplifies all these and also double meanings, but nowhere to that excess which would spoil the artistic expression of the story. Daṇḍin condemned the *gauḍīya* style but praised Pravarasena (*Avantisundarī*, introductory verse 13; again *Kāvyalakṣaṇa* I. 34), so we are justified in saying that the Causeway used *gauḍīya* elements only moderately. Since the Māhārāṣṭrī epic does not use the great variety of metres of the Sanskrit, it is not surprising that such other methods of suiting the expression to the sense, and varying it, as passages in long compounds, should be used. With this method may be compared the metrical variations accepted within the *skandhaka* metre: syncopated forms with additional bars of the musical structure. These *galitaka* verses are rhymed (i.e. introduce *yamakas*). Twice towards the end of Canto I Pravarasena introduces rhymes in the ordinary metre. The *galitakas* are found in Cantos II, III, VI, VII, VIII and IX, thus more particularly in the descriptive parts and not at all in the last six cantos, where narrative greatly predominates. We have noticed above that Pravarasena's epic was a favourite of the critics, including Daṇḍin, Ānandavardhana and Bhoja (the latter quotes about 30 verses from it in his *Sarasvatīkaṇṭhābharaṇa* and many more in his *Śṛṅgāraprakāśa*). It remains to add that Bāṇa (*Harṣacarita*, introductory verse 15), Dhanapāla (*Tilakamañjarī*, introductory verse 22) and others praised him among the greatest *kavis*.

1444. Probably in the +5 lived Śyāmilaka (or Śyāmala or Śyāmadeva), from whom we have a satirical monologue, 'The Kick', *Pādatāḍitaka*. The discussions by Burrow and Schokker make it seem probable that the references in this play (pp. 18-21 in Kavi and Ramanatha's edn., 93-7 in Schokker's) to Indrasvāmin (or Indravarman or Indradatta) and Bhadrāyudha are to historical characters of the time of Skanda Gupta. Bhadrāyudha, Lord of Northern Bāhlīka and other provinces, apparently defeated the rebellious Indrasvāmin of Aparānta (Koṅkaṇa) on behalf of Skanda, the 'King of Magadha', about +455 to 456. Since these characters appear in the play, the action would seem to take place during Skanda's reign and it was perhaps written then. The great metropolis in which the drama is set is called simply Sārvabhaumanagara, 'Emperor's City', but is likely to be Ujjayinī. Skanda was known as Vikramāditya and we have noted above [1377] the possibility that he was a patron of Kālidāsa. Śyāmilaka himself came from the 'North' *udīcya*, which could mean anywhere in the regions of Bāhlīka (Bactria), Gandhāra and Vāhīka (Panjab) and perhaps even as far as Pañcāla. We learn from Rājaśekhara that Śyāmadeva also wrote some work of literary criticism, but apart from these references and quotations nothing seems to be known of it (*Kāvyamīmāṃsā* pp. 11, 13 and 17). The Kick is quoted appreciatively by Abhinavagupta and Kuntaka (p. 70), critically by Kṣemendra (*Aucityavicāracarcā* verse 28; *Suvṛttatilaka* after II.31, but after II.35 he quotes with approval a verse by the same author from an unknown work). For Abhinavagupta it is the standard example of a satirical monologue (*Abhinavabhāratī* I 176; approximate quotation also at II 299 for the characteristic 'ornamentation' [186] adapted to a comic play).

1445. The Kick is a much longer play than the satirical monologues of Śyāmilaka's great predecessors, Vararuci, Īśvaradatta and Śūdraka (48pp. in its first edition against 28 of the Lotus Gift, 31 of The Dialogue of the Rogue and the Parasite and 15 of Both Go to Meet), continuing the apparent tendency towards the expansion of dramas. It likewise has a very large number of characters: more than 50 are described, an interesting cross section of Gupta society in the imperial capital, coming from all parts of the Empire and beyond. After invoking Pleasure (Kāma), the Producer in the Prologue announces the play and thanks the author, who is named, in contrast with the prologues of the earlier satirical monologues. He then asks those tricky gentlemen *āryas*, who roam about like cranes and cats, and similarly minded ministers of the king and ascetics, to leave the audience (first half of verse 4). This most remarkable request is perhaps due to the fact that living persons seem to be described in the play: the audience should stay only if they want simply to enjoy the satire, not if they intend to denounce the play afterwards to powerful persons who might harm the author or the actors. The tradition still lives in India that the actor on the stage is free to speak as he likes of living persons, for example in *kūṭiyāṭṭam* (the jester) and in *tamāśa*. On the other hand, crazy 'beggars' (*ḍiṇḍin* or *ḍiṇḍika* [995, 1166]), who are clever in the art of the jokes of authors, are invited to stay (this can also be translated: 'those who are clever in the art of the jokes of authors who are beggars', i.e. the author is a poor beggar and appeals to the connoisseurship of the audience in comic plays). The same verse ends by saying that the circle *goṣṭhī* (27) of rogues *dhūrtas* desires to drink honey without flies. 'Rogue' is evidently quite a flattering epithet for a theatregoer, suggesting sophisticated but harmless pleasures. Why?:

> Ascetics do not attain 'release' by weeping,
> humorous stories do not obstruct a future heaven;
> Therefore a wise man should laugh with an appreciative
> mind
> after abandoning mean modes of life. (5)

At this moment the Producer is interrupted by hearing the parasite striking a bell in the Parasites' Pavilion and making a proclamation. This parasite, who acts the rest of the play, is none other than the author Śyāmilaka himself, described as bald and also as the *cākrika* of the rogues, where the exact sense of *cākrika* seems uncertain, perhaps 'speaker' (of a circle or assembly). In this play 'rogue' and 'parasite' seem almost synonymous and moreover the membership of their circle seems very wide and not restricted to a few professionals. Śyāmilaka's first verse is then heard from off stage: it is an invocation to Pleasure's Banner, which is the upraised foot of a charming woman when her lover is entreating it with his head (i.e. he is bowing at her feet, but she lifts her foot, spurning him). Apparently this verse, with which the 'speaker' seeks attention for his proclamation, is not meant to describe the incident which produced the action of this play but is simply a conventional invocation, whilst its mention of an upraised foot does, as if by coincidence, indicate the 'seed' and suggest the 'objective' of the action. The Producer then makes his exit and the Parasite Śyāmilaka enters and recites a more explicit verse on the foot raised in a lovers' quarrel, at which he hears someone laugh. It is Dadruṇamādhava, with whose imagined presence Śyāmilaka now enters into conversation. From this we learn that Śyāmilaka has been appointed to convene the assembly of parasites to rule on a legal case brought before them, but apparently he did not till now know the details of the case. Dadruṇamādhava on the other hand was an eyewitness of the incident which caused the plaint and now tells Śyāmilaka the story (which of course he repeats as 'speech in space' according to the satirical monologue convention). Madanasenikā, a geisha girl from Saurāṣṭra, yesterday 'favoured' his honour Tauṇḍikoki Viṣṇunāga on the head with her lotus foot. At this Śyāmilaka quotes the popular verse: 'Joy comes to a living man even after a hundred years !' [634]. The foolish brahman Tauṇḍikoki ('Cuckoobeak'?), however, was enraged at her lack of respect in touching his sacred head with her foot and abused her. Śyāmilaka expresses surprise on hearing that the girl then tried to conciliate Cuckoobeak, a miserly, cowardly vampire of a man. Of course, he is the son of a minister and also a superintendent of edicts *śāsanādhikṛta*, so it seems she has disregarded gifts and pleasure (love), because women like speech ! Dadruṇamādhava remarks that her pursuit of speech has led her to a disaster of speech (getting abused instead of flattered) and then continues his story. He had intervened and rebuked Cuckoobeak as a 'space-needling' (equivalent to 'hairsplitting') grammarian, who ought not to crush jasmines with a pestle nor try to get sounds from a lute by using a firebrand on it (a speech which Abhinavagupta quotes at II 299 apparently in a corrupted form, to illustrate that for comic effect in comedies, etc., a dramatic 'characteristic' [184] becomes a 'quality' *guṇa* and enhances the beauty of the language of the piece, as when addressing a dry scholar with pedantic words devoid of the 'qualities' expected in *kāvya*). We may remark here that the author has evidently developed his character Cuckoobeak from Śūdraka's grammarian Dattakalaśi, 'Offered Waterpot', in the Lotus Gift [1222]. Both use correct, learned and harsh language. Śyāmilaka has placed the character, appropriately and credibly as a superintendent of edicts, and invented an actual situation in which he uses his harsh language on a woman and makes a laughing stock of himself, by taking himself and his priestly birth so seriously when apparently engaged in the pursuit of pleasure. Dadruṇamādhava continues that Cuckoobeak disregarded him and went to the house of Lord (Prince?) Jīmūta ('Cloud'), the dean or president of the parasites. He then comforted Madanasenikā, ridiculing Cuckoobeak who did not deserve the honour she had conferred on him. In the morning Dadruṇamādhava decided to go to the 'bench' *piṭhikā* or tribune of the brahmans, i.e. their court, in case there was any trouble. Cuckoobeak was there already, in great distress appealing to them to save him from this insult to his head by a helot girl. The brahmans, secretly much amused, declare that they have surveyed numerous books of legal institutes (*dharmaśāstras*, a list of eleven, 'etc.', is enumerated) but have not learned of any expiation for such a great sin. The despairing Cuckoobeak complains bitterly at this threatened loss of his priestly status and reduction to that of helot (this being the effect of a 'great sin'). After the brahmans have enjoyed this spectacle, nudging each other, making remarks on his stupidity, a great scholar and also joker among them raises his right hand for permission to speak. He then explains to Cuckoobeak that the law is that a local, or occupational, or clan, or other group of people is authoritative in the matter of its own customary law, provided that it does not come into conflict with the universal traditional law. In the present case the caste *jāti* of parasites is the proper group to decide on the expiation for this sin, which should therefore be sought through their assembly. This suggestion is greeted with cheers by the assembly of brahmans and Cuckoobeak thanks them and departs.

1446. After discussing the definition of a 'parasite' with Dadruṇamādhava, Śyāmilaka proceeds on his way through the city, calling upon the parasites to attend their assembly. As to the definition, let us quote from the discussion:

> Having spent the whole day in argument with litigants,
> as the day ends you enjoy food somewhere in a friend's
> palace;
> Then at night you play with the geisha girls and put in
> your weapon:

there isn't even water in your house, yet you swagger
about ! (15)

On his way, Śyāmilaka meets about twenty people, including several of the parasites. It appears that they have all heard already about the assembly to take place that afternoon to settle Cuckoobeak's problem, so that there isn't much to do and he can pass the time with friends on his way (pp. 88-9 of Schokker's text). It may be noted here that being a parasite is evidently not a full time occupation, but a social position which may be combined with various other stations, offices or professions. There are several princes (a Śaka, an Ābhīra, the defeated Indrasvāmin mentioned above and others), a brother-in-law of the Emperor who works at the War Office (pp. 75 and 95), a doctor from Bactria (p. 87, Hariścandra Kāṅkāyana), writers, musicians and a judge (p. 77), all parasites. The doctor is on his way to visit a geisha girl to cure her headache, which Śyāmilaka refuses to take seriously. The various encounters in the streets are presented on a somewhat larger scale than those of the earlier satirical monologues. Seeing a great crowd of people blocking Market Street (p. 80), which apparently would be the direct way from the Parasites' Pavilion in High Street to Jīmūta's palace in Geisha Greatway Square, Śyāmilaka decides to make a detour, turning right into Flower Street, so that after crossing Pūrṇabhadra Square he can reach Geisha Street through Fish Street. This will be useful also because he can expect to find most of the parasites in the geisha quarter (this is before he finds out that they all know about the assembly already). From this brief itinerary we can construct a rough sketch map of Emperor's City, probably Ujjayinī, which makes this *kāvya* more realistic and should also be helpful for future archaeological work in the neglected metropolis. In Flower Street Śyāmilaka sees the drunkard Bāṣpa at a tavern, dancing with a drinking cup raised in his left hand. Further on, he passes the ancient harlot Dharaṇiguptā and remembers the horrific *bibhatsa* experience of his friend the drummer and parasite Sthāṇumitra three days before:

Impassioned for a kiss
he felt in his own mouth at the root of his tongue

Her tooth fallen with its root,
—and coughed and spat it out. (33)

Kṣemendra (*Aucityavicāracarcā* verse 28) objects to this because the comic effect is pervaded by the horrific, which spoils one's pleasure by its disharmony. The critic is perhaps too fastidious, but that is a matter of opinion. After this, Śyāmilaka enters the geisha quarter and gives a long description of its elaborate palaces with beautiful gardens. He also describes some of the people he can see: a girl conciliating her angry lover, another being made up by hers, one singing, one making a mynah talk, another making a peacock dance, one painting, one reading a biography, and so on. There are ladies' carriages, but horses and elephants waiting outside indicate that their masters are visiting the palaces; for example Śyāmilaka recognises the horse of a general's son he knows at the gate of Puṣpadāsī's palace and goes in to talk with him. He sees a girl playing the flute on the balcony of her palace and the 'minister of private affairs' of Prince Indrasvāmin coming out from it, with whom he gossips for some time. Next he sees the victorious Bhadrāyudha, mentioned above, leaving another geisha's palace, surrounded by swarms of beggars *ḍiṇḍins*. Śyāmilaka contemptuously describes the crowd of Lāṭa people [256], who apparently make up a substantial part of the cosmopolitan population of the metropolis, or perhaps are merely those who have come over, anxious to offer their services, to the winning side after the war, for their strange dress and ornaments and peculiar dialect with no 'y' sound (for which they substitute 'j'). Watching Bhadrāyudha among them he remarks: 'Certainly there is no sovereignty free from fiends *piśācas*!' (p. 97). But it is proper for Bhadrāyudha to display the Fortune of the Dynasty of Magadha (i.e. of the Guptas), moreover:

The Aparānta beauties sing his deeds,
the ends of their tresses tangled by the soft sea breezes,
As they hold on to the creepers of the trees and bend playfully
along the palm-garlanded shores of the great ocean. (61)

Kuntaka quotes (p. 70) this verse for the quality 'sweetness' *mādhurya* used in the 'intermediate' style [293] (we here follow the reading 'bend playfully' in the edition of Kuntaka's text; the text of the play has instead 'are eager'). Śyāmilaka then meets a Buddhist layman at the Temple of Pradyumna [526] and reproaches him for his lack of Buddhist compassion in disregarding a girl who loves him. The parasite here makes fun of the ancient Buddhist practice of the four 'immeasurable' meditations which eliminate the obstacles to freedom of the mind from attachment (Sthaviravāda version in Pali, Saṃyutta V pp. 115ff.; Sarvāstivāda version preserved in Chinese, Taishō 99 section 27 No. 32), saying sarcastically: 'It is proper that you should live with equanimity *upekṣā* towards a woman who has sympathetic joy *muditā* in you, when you cultivate loving kindness *maitrī* and are the essence of compassion *karuṇā* !' (because the layman's name is 'Disregard', meaning that he cultivates detachment). The layman objects that Śyāmilaka has accepted a deceiver's interpretation: such is the nature of transmigration (i.e. that kind of compassion is not the way to *nirvāṇa*). But Śyāmilaka insists on his own understanding of the teaching of the Buddha and also that that teaching is the authority concerning this very girl. The Buddhist of course accepts the authority of the Buddha and eventually agrees that, since in any case he admits that he is not free from passion, he ought to apply compassion in this particular case and rescue the girl from the ocean of grief. (Schokker's notes and references on this passage are so extraordinary that it is difficult to pass them by without an exclamation of amazement.) Later on, Śyāmilaka comes to the house of his old love Śūrasenasundarī and sees the side gate open. He goes through into the garden and sits down to rest on a stone seat in an alley shaded by *priyaṅgu* creepers. As he does so, he notices a verse written on it, a complaint of a woman whose lover has disappointed her. Śūrasenasundarī then comes out and greets him. He of course offers her the seat, but immediately checks her to save the verse. However, she at once rubs it off and then tells him a long and amusing story about a friend of hers and the man she loves but who failed to satisfy her. Next, Śyāmilaka jokes about the purely 'verbal' love between Madayantī, chowrie (insignia of royalty) bearer and 'reciter of books' *pustakavācikā* to a prince, and her husband who also is a reciter of books, as well as her new lover, who apparently is a bureaucrat. 'Verbal' love has been criticised as 'neuter' by Dattaka's School (of harlotry) [1123]. Among several more encounters, Śyāmilaka meets near the Temple of Pleasure a relative of Cuckoobeak, Sūryanāga, who visits cheap 'flag harlots' on the outskirts of the city. Hariśūdra, governor of the city, describes a show to which he was invited, in which the Sinhalese geisha Mayūrasenā, whom he loves, performed faultily in the first strophe or scene *vastu* [367, 382, cf. 379] of her *lāsyavāra* [362, cf. 347], as a result of drinking too much. Nevertheless he had supported her, against the rest of the audience, thereby conciliating her after previously having been unfaithful by making love to the Tamil girl Kāverikā. Now he has just left her house, as Śyāmilaka saw, and he describes how they made love, in the course of which he received a kick. This only spurred him on to more passionate efforts and a successful consummation. Of course, the parasite on hearing this urges him to attend the assembly for Cuckoobeak's expiation, but Hariśūdra objects: as far as he is concerned the favour of a kick with a lotus foot is sufficient expiation. After this, Śyāmilaka realises it is getting late and hurries on. Now he describes the sunset and the beauty of Geisha Greatway Square, which he is now approaching, with its crowds of young people, open and closed carriages, horses and elephants, the newly plastered walls and other signs of prosperity, as well as the sound of a *viṇā* and singing as circles of people meet on the upper terraces of the palaces and drink whilst the Moon rises (107). Among the remaining encounters, the Śaka prince from Saurāṣṭra is attached to a slave girl and the Greek geisha Karpūraturiṣṭhā is loved by the Ābhīra prince from Mālava. Śyāmilaka has a poor opinion of the last couple, though he regards the girl as his 'friend', considering them well matched: the Greek geisha who is a monkey dancer with the Mālava lover who is a donkey singer.

1447. At last Śyāmilaka makes his way into the palace of Lord Cloud for the assembly of parasites (p. 129). The forecourt is already jambed with the vehicles of the parasites. In the arched gateway servants are ready with their silver pitchers of water raised for washing the feet. The palace is brilliantly decorated with flowers, incense and lamps. People are greeting one another in various ways, politely, familiarly, affectionately or respectfully. There is music and talk and the parasites are joking. Śyāmilaka as 'speaker' now calls the meeting to order and announces the business before them. They take their seats, trying to appear serious and full of concern at the shocking calamity of the kick, Lord Cloud even shedding tears as, through the speaker, he asks the parasites to proceed to deliberate on the question of expiation. Various suggestions are made, such as that it is Madanasenikā who is at fault, not Cuckoobeak, for her lack of judgment concerning his love, in putting her foot on this 'sacrificial animal's' head at the wrong time, or that he should make expiation by washing her feet, or that she should kick his head again, or that he should wash his head with the same water after washing her foot, or drink it, or that he should shave off his hair made dusty by her foot. Cuckoobeak thanks Rudravarman for the last suggestion, but thinks that his violated head should be cut off, let alone his hair. Lord Cloud intervenes to rule this out: he should rather keep his hair unwashed as long as possible and his expiation should be this:

> Let him see her, her eyes rolling with languid passion,
> her girdle held firm by one hand placed on her loins,
> Favour *my* head
> with her lac-painted ankleted foot. (147)

The parasites applaud this solution and Cuckoobeak says 'thank you very much' and departs. The play ends with a 'consummation of the *kāvya*', through Lord Cloud asking Śyāmilaka what desired thing he can offer him, and an appropriate final benediction by the parasite [150]. It is rare to find in a Sanskrit *kāvya* such a direct portrayal of contemporary society and such undisguised social criticism. Such is the function especially of the satirical monologue, and The Kick is perhaps the most extensive as well as the most circumstantially historical example we have, justifying Abhinavagupta's selection of it as representative of the type.

1448. To about the +5 seems to belong the *Vasudevahiṇḍi*, 'Wanderings of Vasudeva', by the Jaina writer Saṃghadāsa. References to it in Jaina literature indicate a date not later than about +500. For example Jinabhadra, *c.* +600, refers to it in his *Viśeṣaṇavatī*. The *Āvaśyakaniryukti* of Bhadrabāhu, which is believed to be earlier than Varāhamihira (died +587), refers to the Dhammilla story (*gāthās* 1614-5) which forms part of Saṃghadāsa's work, though this may have existed in some form earlier (on which there seems to be no evidence). The 'Jaina Māhārāṣṭrī' language in which the *Vasudevahiṇḍi* is written is full of archaisms suggesting a much earlier date. It is possible that these result merely from imperfect translations from an original Paiśācī text and do not represent the usage of Saṃghadāsa's period. Alsdorf argues for an early date on the grounds of these archaic linguistic forms (see 'The Vasudevahiṇḍi, a Specimen of Archaic Jaina-Māhārāṣṭrī', in the *Bulletin of the School of Oriental and African Studies*, London, Vol. VIII, p. 320). He also regards the occasional passages in the *veḍha* metre, which highlight descriptions in the prevailing prose of the novel, as an archaic feature, on the ground that their structure resembles that of the *veḍhas* in Jaina canonical texts. He thinks these are of Saṃghadāsa's own composition, not translations or borrowings, because they occur both in the matter taken from the *Bṛhatkathā* and in that from Jaina legend (*Asiatica*, Leipzig, 1954, pp. 1-11). Of course, the composition of the Jaina canonical texts we now have continued over many centuries, though the present writer believes the *veḍha* or 'hypermetre' to be very ancient and perhaps the earliest form of *gaṇacchandas* (*Pali Metre*, p. 156) [2532]. We may suppose that the composers of canonical texts attempted to maintain the ancient style, whilst we await more precise clarification of the evolution of metrical structures within the *veḍha*, which might determine the date of Saṃghadāsa. Some stray details possibly suggest for the *Vasudevahiṇḍi* a date not far removed from that of The Kick. There are a number of references to the Koṅkaṇa country (a name for part of Aparānta, namely the coast of Mahārāṣṭra, which seems to have come into vogue only in the Gupta period) and one to the Hūṇas (p. 148). Whilst Guṇāḍhya's *Bṛhatkathā* is at any rate the ultimate source for the story of 'Vasudeva', Devacandra (+12) says that Bhadrabāhu wrote a *Vasudevacarita* (in the introduction to his *Śāntināthacarita*). Nothing further seems to be known of such a work, which might be earlier than Saṃghadāsa's. There are several Bhadrabāhus in Jaina tradition, one a contemporary of Candragupta Maurya, another the supposed author of the commentaries called *niryuktis* at an uncertain date between the +1 and +6. Saṃghadāsa's work seems to be complete in 29 chapters (called *lambhas* or *lambhakas* as in the *Bṛhatkathā*) plus introductory narratives and a conclusion. The introductory matter consists of a preface *kathotpatti* on the source of the story (the Jina Mahāvīra, as in the case of the *Paümacariya* [854]), a narrative called the 'Dhammillahiṇḍi' and three sections of introduction to the main Vasudeva narrative (they are called *pīṭhikā*, *mukha* and *pratimukha*). Vasudeva and Dhammila (m.c.) are named as the *Hiṇḍis* by Uddyotana (*Kuvalayamālā* p. 281). A later writer, Dharmasena, added 71 new chapters to make up a grandiose narrative in 100 chapters. This actually fills in episodes from the *Bṛhatkathā* narrative which Saṃghadāsa had eliminated, notably the delightful one of Prabhāvatī, including the trial scene [684], whose authenticity is thus confirmed (an edition of this *Majjhimakhaṇḍa* of the *Vasudevahiṇḍi* is being prepared from MSS in the Ahmedabad L.D. Institute by Bhayani and Shuh). Part I, 1988. A

1449. Saṃghadāsa calls (p. 26) his composition a novel *kathā* illustrating all the four ends of life (virtue, wealth, pleasure and liberation) [446]. It should perhaps be regarded as belonging, amongst other things, to the series of Jaina novels of virtue *dharma*. But Saṃghadāsa presents his work as history, incorporating in it (as emboxed stories) a great part of the Jaina version of universal history. His hero is the supposedly historical character Vasudeva, the father of Kṛṣṇa [1047], presented against the background of the history of the Yādava family, here called the Harivaṃśa (the Jainas give their own version of its ancestry). By substituting the name Vasudeva for Naravāhanadatta and making various other adaptations, Saṃghadāsa inserts into Jaina universal history substantial parts of Guṇāḍhya's *Bṛhatkathā* [667, 678 ff]. The adventures of Naravāhanadatta in different countries, in which he acquires numerous wives, thus become the 'wanderings' of Vasudeva. As in the original novel, the hero is presented telling his own story in the first person. The *Vasudevahiṇḍi* seems to reproduce the prose style of the *Bṛhatkathā* fairly closely and possibly, as we have noted above, to bear direct traces of the original language. In Saṃghadāsa's adaptation some of the characters retain their original names (for example Mānasavega, Vegavatī and Gandharvadattā), but many have been changed. The relationships with wizards remain prominent (and wizards seem to have popular in Jaina literature at all times), but Naravāhanadatta's conquest of their world beyond the Himālaya has been discarded, presumably as inconsistent with the new historical framework. The wanderings of Vasudeva begin (Chapter I) when his eldest brother, Samudravijaya, forbids him to go out because he is too attractive to women. He escapes by staging a mock suicide (burning an unclaimed corpse on a pyre in a cemetery and leaving a suicide note) and disappearing. In Chapter XXVII, as a result of being married by Rohiṇī at her self-choice, he becomes embroiled with Samudravijaya, is recognised and the two are reconciled.

1450. Since there is evidently little which is original in this story of 'Vasudeva' its importance for us may seem small, except for the purpose of trying to restore the contents of the *Bṛhatkathā*. It shows the continuing elaboration of the Jaina version of universal history [869], gradually incorporating miscellaneous stories found to be of interest and worth appropriating as part of the Jaina heritage. It also shows the development of literary ideas in medieval India along the borderline between history and fiction, the deliberate blending of the two in a manner horrifying to the historian but widely accepted for artistic or instructive purposes. Saṃghadāsa is perfectly aware of what he and others were doing: at the beginning of his Tenth Chapter there is a discussion which distinguishes between stories as either *carita*, 'lived', or *kalpita*, 'imagined'. The former describe what has actually been seen or heard; in the latter the narrator adapts them to his own (instructive) purposes. Saṃghadāsa has adapted his narrative, amongst other things, to the criticism of Vedism (Brahmanism). In subsidiary stories in Chapters III and V he describes the supposed origin of the two *Vedas*, one 'aryan' and the other 'unaryan', with the abominable practice of animal sacrifice with which the brahmans were still reproached, no longer with much justice except for the persisting sacrifice of goats.

1451. Some episodes apparently not from Jaina legend cannot at present certainly be attributed to Guṇāḍhya, in the absence of evidence from the other available versions of the *Bṛhatkathā*. Such is the story of Kokkāsa (incorporated in the 'Dhammillahiṇḍi' section), who voyages to 'Greece' (presumably either Ptolemaic Egypt or Seleucid Mesopotamia) and there learns how to construct flying machines (pp. 62-3), eventually meeting disaster for himself and a king who becomes his patron. Some episodes in the adventures of Cārudatta (Sānudāsa in the *Saṅgraha*) are not exactly paralleled in the other versions.

His travels by sea as far as China and Greece end in shipwreck off the coast of Gujarat and a perilous adventure with an alchemist (*jaiahiraṇṇa, yatitahiraṇya*), who converts iron into gold by means of an elixir *rasa*. The alchemist needs assistants to obtain the elixir from a subterranean 'diamond pool', lowering them into the chasm with a bottle and rope for the purpose. But each assistant in turn is abandoned to die in the chasm, so that they shall not live to share the secret. Cārudatta escapes by clinging to the tail of a monitor, which drags him out through a crevice (Chapter III). Adventure stories of this type resemble the old Buddhist stories of the foolishness of pursuing wealth at all hazards (e.g. in the Pali *Niddesa* [702]).

1452. Saṃghadāsa explains the extraordinary adventures of Vasudeva as being the result of his action in a former life, in conformity with received Jaina doctrine. In Chapter I we read that formerly Vasudeva was Nandisena, an orphaned son of a poor brahman who was brought up by his uncle. The uncle promises to marry him to one of his daughters, but when the time comes they all reject him: he is ill-favoured in being repulsive to women as well as orphaned. Eventually he runs away in despair and attempts to commit suicide. He is stopped by an ascetic, who persuades him to take up asceticism in order to improve the moral balance of his actions so that he will be more fortunate in future. It is because of the severe asceticism he then undergoes that, after being reborn in due course as Vasudeva, he is extremely attractive to women, which leads both to the trouble with his brother and to his acquisition of so many wives.

1453. The point of the prefixed 'Dhammillahiṇḍi', 'Wanderings of Dhārmika', is simply to illustrate the doctrine that the result of action may appear in the same life (in 'this world', as the Indian expression has it), instead of in another life (in the 'other world'). Dhārmika's experiences are similar to those of Nandisena-Vasudeva, but they all take place in one life. He is the son of a caravan merchant in Kusargapura (fictitious? — apparently in Magadha): his story is not connected to the scheme of universal history but stands by itself. In his youth, though he is already married his mother encourages him to enjoy himself. He attends a dancing show organised by the king and falls in love with the beautiful dancer Vasantatilakā, the daughter of a geisha. He goes to her and stays at her house until his money is exhausted, whereupon the girl's mother agitates for him to be thrown out. After long arguments the mother eventually succeeds in getting him abandoned, though Vasantatilakā really loves Dhārmika. The wretched Dhārmika then wanders in an old park outside the city and several times attempts suicide, though without success. Finally he meets a Jaina ascetic, who exhorts him not to act rashly, telling him of his own former sufferings because of women. Dhārmika becomes an ascetic under his guidance and for six months lives an austere life, fasting and so on. The ascetic predicts that as a result of this asceticism Dhārmika will have thirty two wives and become as rich as a wizard. All this comes to pass immediately afterwards. First Dhārmika is picked up by two beautiful girls in a chariot and driven to Campā, protecting them heroically from the dangers of the road. The girls turn out to be princesses who have heard of his good qualities and wish to become his wives. At Campā he begins to live luxuriously and more and more girls (mostly 'wizard' girls with extraordinary powers) come to him. A princess of Campā chooses him for husband at her self-choice and he forms other royal alliances, thus becoming powerful and rich. At the end a kind hearted wizard girl who knows about Vasantatilakā takes Dhārmika by air back to his home, to be reunited with his family, including his first wife, and legally married to Vasantatilakā (royal consent had to be obtained for the girl to give up her geisha status). The source of this 'Dhammillahiṇḍi' is not known, except that some episodes in it derive from the *Bṛhatkathā*, and it is possible that Saṃghadāsa himself invented it.

1454. Compared with the Jaina novels of 'virtue', such as Pādalipta's *Taraṅgavatī* [840] and the later examples by Haribhadra, Siddha and others, the *Vasudevahiṇḍi* makes a rather strange impression. Like Nanda in Aśvaghoṣa's epic The Handsome Nanda, Saṃghadāsa's two heroes take up asceticism in order to secure afterwards the pleasures of love. Unlike him (admittedly the cases are rather different in detail) they are never led to suppose that there might be anything contradictory in such a course. On the contrary their investment in discomfort is shown simply as a businesslike exchange for future comfort, seemingly with considerable profit.

Chapter XXVI

AMARUKA

1455. The date of Amaruka seems more uncertain than that of any other well known Indian poet, moreover his very existence has been seriously doubted. The position of our present chapter is therefore provisional. Some would delete it altogether, though they might embellish other contexts with verses scattered from it. It is suggested,[1] with apparently strong arguments, that the 'Hundred' generally known as Amaruka's, the *Amarukaśataka*, is in reality an anthology of verses from many different poets, not the unitary work of one. The anthologist perhaps was called Amaruka or Amarūka, variant forms, that is all we may affirm about the name (Amaru is a shortened form originally metri causa, sometimes used, generally in inferior manuscripts). The main argument here is that Vidyākara (*c.* +1100) quotes about a quarter[2] of the 'Hundred' in his anthology *Subhāṣitaratnakoṣa*; he gives ten of the verses anonymously but attributes sixteen more to twelve named authors; to 'Amarūka' he attributes only two other verses not found in our available recensions of the Hundred. From this it is concluded that Vidyākara used a copy of the Hundred similar to the texts we now have, but that it was an anthology and in it the names of the

1. By Kosambi, *Subhāṣitaratnakoṣa*, Introduction p. lxxi, and Ingalls, *An Anthology of Sanskrit Court Poetry*, pp. 44-5.

2. Not a third; whether we count all the verses attributed to Amaruka in all the available recensions of the Hundred (138 in the edition used by Kosambi and Ingalls, not including verses found only in anthologies), or reduce the Hundred to about 100 verses by eliminating those found only in one recension, we get about 25%. It is odd that Vidyākara appears to quote from all the known recensions of the Hundred, as if he used an edition like that of the Nirṇaya Sāgara Press, which combined them in one volume. Thus he quotes at least one verse each from the recensions used by Vemabhūpāla (e.g. 614, 649), Rudramadeva (e.g. 622) and Ravicandra (e.g. 479, 671, 803) which is not to be found in any other recension; as for Arjunavarman, his recension contains only one verse peculiar to itself (102), which is not quoted, but Vidyākara sometimes has readings peculiar to it (e.g. *tāraṃ*, in 621).

original authors were generally noted after their verses, just as we find in manuscripts of Vidyākara's own anthology. Since his time these authors' names could have dropped out of the manuscripts of the text as it has come down to us.

1456. Against this suggestion it can be urged that the Hundred is quoted by many other anthologists and critics, none of whom seems to attribute any of its verses to any author but Amaruka. Several of these writers are earlier than Vidyākara, so that his aberrant ascriptions appear to have been unknown before his time as well as after it. The first critic known to quote from the Hundred is Vāmana (+8), but he does so anonymously (verses 19 and 34 according to Arjunavarman's recension, Vāmana III.2.4 and IV.3.12). Ānandavardhana (+9) praises the verses of 'the poet Amaruka' (*Dhvanyāloka* p. 325), as exemplifying independent verses *muktakas* of the kind which pour forth aesthetic experience *rasa* — i.e. they are models of the form. Elsewhere in his work he quotes several verses from the Hundred, though without naming their author: in most cases he quotes them in connection with questions about the aesthetic experience. Thus he quotes verses 9, 81 and '104' — the last only in Vemabhūpāla's recension — to show how the poet skilfully avoids letting figures of speech interfere with the *rasa*, or actually uses them to increase it (pp. 232 and 368, 221, 308); he quotes verse 2 to illustrate the combination of *rasas* in one verse (pp. 195 and 369). He also quotes verse 82 (p. 525) in order to compare it with what he calls a later verse on the same theme: the author of this later verse is unknown, but the juxtaposition indicates that for Ānandavardhana the verses of the Hundred were relatively old. Indurāja (+10) also names 'the poet Amaruka' as the author of verse 75 of the Hundred, which he quotes as having qualities *guṇas*, namely sweetness, strength and clarity, but no figure, using moreover the same expression about 'pouring forth aesthetic experience' *rasasyandin* as Ānandavardhana had used — he probably borrowed it from him, which would confirm that by 'Amaruka' Ānandavardhana, like Indurāja, meant the author of the Hundred (Indurāja's commentary on Udbhaṭa's *Kāvyālaṅkārasārasaṅgraha*, p. 82; incidentally, as a follower of the school of Bhāmaha and Udbhaṭa, Indurāja seems to accept only the three qualities named here as valid qualities, thus finding them all combined in Amaruka's verse). Abhinavagupta (*c.* +1000), explaining Ānandavardhana's praise of Amaruka in his commentary on the *Dhvanyāloka* (*Locana*, p. 325), quotes the same verse (75) to illustrate Amaruka (naming him) and show how he produces *rasa* in a single verse, through the conjunction of the causes and effects of emotion (i.e. according to the *Nāṭyaśāstra* method). This again confirms that Ānandavardhana had the author of the Hundred in mind when mentioning 'Amaruka'. Abhinavagupta also quotes verse 23, anonymously, in this commentary (*Locana* p. 79). In his commentary on the *Nāṭyaśāstra* he quotes it twice more, for excellence of *rasa* (I p. 303, II p. 222). Afterwards he quotes another verse (62), as by 'Amaruka', to illustrate the characteristic *lakṣaṇa* 'prohibition' *pratiṣedha* defined in his recension of the *Nāṭyaśāstra* (II pp. 311-2).

1457. Dhanika (*c.* +1000), working in a different part of India, quotes 14 verses as from the *Amarukaśataka* (2, 9, 12, 18, 19, 31, 38, 41, 51, 52, 57, 60, 76 and 99, all in Arjunavarman's recension — 52 being only in that and Rudramadeva's). He also quotes, without naming any author, 4 other verses found in Arjunavarman's recension (64, 77, 92, 101) and 4 verses found only in Vemabhūpāla's recension ('104', '106', '107', '109') (Dhanika: *Avaloka* on *Daśarūpaka*, attributed verses on pp. 39, 45-7, 49-50, 83, 85, 88, 104-5, anonymous verses on pp. 39, 44-6, 49, 81). Bhoja (+11) quotes verse 60 as in the *Amarukaśataka* (*Śṛṅgāraprakāśa*, Vol. II p. 585, Josyer's ed.) and a number of verses anonymously. Kṣemendra (+11) quotes as by 'Amaruka' verse 3 (*Aucityavicāracarcā* verse 107) and another verse (*Aucityavicāracarcā* 50) not found in the available recensions (the Nirṇaya Sāgara edition gives it as '163', taking it from Kṣemendra).

1458. The commentators available on the Hundred, of whom the earliest is Arjunavarman (+13), speak only of the poet Amaruka as the author and discuss among other things how he arranged his verses. The later anthologists, except those who have taken verses directly from Vidyākara, do not seem to know of any author of the verses in the Hundred other than Amaruka.

1459. As for the ascriptions of Vidyākara to poets other than Amaruka, none of the verses so ascribed seems to have been found in any of their extant works. Dharmakīrti and Harṣa are known to have written works on literary criticism, so that it is possible that Vidyākara took (or quoted from memory) verses quoted by them in those works and noted only the critics' names as his immediate sources, instead of the ultimate source. At least one verse is ascribed to a fanciful author coined out of a word occurring in it, *jhalajjhala*, 'sobbing'. There are parallels to this kind of identification in other anthologies, suggesting that verses were sometimes known by unusual words occurring in them and referred to by those words, which in time came to be mentioned as if they were the names of the authors.

1460. There is no conclusive argument here. A much more thorough text-critical study of all the verses associated with Amaruka's Hundred than has yet been accomplished may produce a decisive argument to settle the authorship problem. Meanwhile we are left on the whole with largely impressionistic judgments about the style and techniques of the verses themselves. If we feel that there is a certain unity of method, and of outlook, in the verses we take to belong to the original Hundred, contrasting with the work of other poets (particularly those mentioned by Vidyākara in this connection), then we shall believe in a single authorship, an individual personality which has created these miniatures. But that will always be a subjective judgment. Each reader will make a judgment one way or the other after studying the verses we are about to discuss. It must be noted that, if the Hundred is an anthology and we accept Vidyākara's ascriptions, then it was compiled not earlier than the +7 (Dharmakīrti and Bāṇa lived in the first half of that century); one poet named here by Vidyākara (Śatānanda) lived as late as the beginning of the +9, but the verse ascribed to him ('133') is found only in Ravicandra's recension and is therefore most unlikely to belong to the original Hundred, whilst it is actually a variant of verse 28 of the *Śṛṅgāratilaka* (which is translated at the end of Chapter XX above [1247]).

1461. On the identity of 'Amaruka', we must mention finally the fantastic legend about him, which seems to appear first in the *Śaṅkaradigvijaya* of Mādhava or Vidyāraṇya (+14) and to have been copied and further elaborated by the latest commentators on the Hundred. This epic describes the imaginary 'conquest' of India by the Vedāntin teacher Śaṅkara (beginning of the +7) in debates with his opponents. This 'conquest' bears no relation to any historical facts and is meant only to glorify a revered ancient teacher. Being an ascetic, Śaṅkara was ignorant of the science of pleasure and was thus threatened with defeat when debating on that subject. To remedy this deficiency, he seized an opportunity to project his soul into the body of a king named Amaruka who had just died. In the king's body he experimented with love and recorded his impressions in the Hundred attributed to Amaruka, then returned to his own body, invincible henceforth in debates on the science. The latest commentators embellish the story somewhat, making this 'Amaruka' a king of Kaśmīra (it is hardly worth remarking that no king of Kaśmīra of that name is known to history).

1462. Ultimately the available recensions of the Hundred seem to reduce to two. One was an inflated text, apparently of 114 verses, which was current in Āndhra and Mālava (Avanti) by *c*. +1000. In the +13 Arjunavarman, King of Mālava, wrote on this his commentary, called the *Rasikasaṃjīvinī*, in which he excluded 14 verses as spurious *prakṣipta*, i.e. not in Amaruka's manner, quoting some of them (we may note that they include descriptions of nature, direct description of a girl and a pun: the verses he accepts as genuine are 'indoor' poetry with hardly any reference to nature, the characters are described indirectly by one another or through their own words and verbal tricks like punning are avoided). Arjunavarman added two verses from some other source. At the end of the same century or early in the next, Rudramadeva (identified by Devadhar with Pratāparudra II Kākatīya, King of Āndhra, see his Introduction to the Poona edition, p. 14) wrote his very brief commentary on all the verses of this recension, without considering whether any are spurious. The 'recension' of Ravicandra (whose date does not seem to have been determined) is an inferior derivative from that of Rudramadeva, with 6 extra verses, many corruptions (even unmetrical readings, as if the commentator was not acquainted with Sanskrit metres) and probably deliberate changes in the text to facilitate the secondary interpretation which the commentator imposes on it, as producing the calmed *śānta* aesthetic experience (this is in conformity with the legend that the real author was Śaṅkara).

1463. The other recension also was current in Āndhra, at least by the +14. It was commented on there by Vemabhūpāla (early +15), the Rāṣṭrakūṭa ('Reḍḍi') king Peṭa

Komaṭi Vema, also known as Vīranārāyaṇa (see his biography by Vāmana (II)). It has 87 verses in common with Arjunavarman's text, two others found in Ravicandra or Rudrama, but a dozen peculiar to itself yet apparently in Amaruka's manner. The commentary is entitled *Śṛṅgāradipikā*. Vemabhūpāla says that he has rejected spurious verses (without quoting any), he thus produces a total of 101. His text became popular all over South India, as far as Kerala, and consequently is known as the 'Southern' recension.

1464. The various other commentators known followed one or other of these versions, or sometimes seem to have selected verses from both according to their taste. For example Acyutarāya (early +19?) mixed the two recensions and wrote a commentary (the *Śāradāgama*) on a text of 103 verses thus produced. He gives a double interpretation in accordance with Vedānta mysticism, having in view Vidyāraṇya's legend. It is worthy of note that the religious fervour of the later middle ages gave rise to many such artificial reinterpretations of Indian classics [1098]. It is also of interest that at least three kings honoured Amaruka with a commentary, a distinction perhaps unique in literature.

1465. We have no independent recension from anywhere in the North of India, the manuscript traditions drawn on by the Kaśmīra critics, or the anthologist Vidyākara in the North East, having apparently been extinguished. We may infer that they were somewhat different from the recensions we have, since these writers attribute to Amaruka verses otherwise unknown to us. For our present purpose we have to take the verses common to Arjunavarman and Vemabhūpāla as most likely to be genuine 'Amaruka'.

1466. Among the commentators the best guide to the understanding of Amaruka seems to be Vemabhūpāla, who attends carefully to the aesthetic effect *rasa* and the delineation of types of character, especially the types of 'heroine' represented. Arjunavarman also is an excellent commentator and very thorough, but he is more interested in the figures of speech, though these are surely of very limited importance in Amaruka. At the same time he shows his critical acumen and appreciation of the primary aim of the Hundred in his rejection of spurious verses as noted above.

1467. The verses of Amaruka are perfect examples of Indian poetic technique, and more especially of the aesthetic technique first presented in the *Nāṭyaśāstra* and afterwards elaborated and analysed in various ways by such writers as Ānandavardhana, Rājaśekhara, Abhinavagupta and Dhanika. In a way it is difficult to comment on them, because to state baldly what emotions they express, and to classify the characters who appear, spoils the effect. Though these characters are typical, and that is why they appeal to us, we see them and remember them as individuals. It is just through this delicate quality of being spoiled by comment that we can understand the theory and techniques of the production of the aesthetic experience *rasa* and of implied *vyaṅgya* meanings. If we say that in such and such a verse the lady expresses 'alarm' or 'dissimulation' or 'joy' or 'misery' or 'eagerness' (transient emotions identified by Vemabhūpāla), the effect becomes flat: it is just by not saying these things, but showing their living action, that Amaruka is so specific and sharp. If the ingredients which produce the aesthetic experience, when conjoined, are thus themselves indirectly suggested, the production of *rasa* itself is doubly indirect.

1468. It is interesting that Vemabhūpāla points out to us (on verse 7), quoting the *Nāṭyaśāstra* (XXIV.255-63 [57, 803]), that the 'sensitive' experience has two states or positions, in 'union' and in 'frustration'; that the latter is again of two kinds, 'not yet united' and 'separated'; that the latter is of three kinds, through (jealous) 'anger', 'going abroad' and just 'compassionate'; that the first of these is of two kinds, through 'jealousy' and 'preceded by a lovers' quarrel'; that, finally, the first of these is of four kinds, produced by 'depression', 'deception', 'dislike' or 'anger'. And so on. Most of these he illustrates in the course of his commentary, from the Hundred. These classifications do not add to our enjoyment of the verses, but on occasion they do suggest possible ways of understanding the situation depicted and what might have gone before it.

1469. Another classification Vemabhūpāla makes, again based mostly on the *Nāṭyaśāstra*, is of the kinds of 'heroine' according to their relations to the 'hero'. They may be 'his own' (usually) or 'another's' (rarely, including girls still living with their parents) or 'common' (geishas — only two very doubtful cases). Heroines may also be 'innocent', 'bold' or 'middling'. They may further be in any of the eight situations such as 'whose lover is dependent on her', 'whose lover has gone abroad', 'separated by a quarrel', 'who goes to meet her lover', etc., some of which we noted in the Seven Hundred Songs [802, 805 807] and in connection with Śūdraka's The Lotus Gift [1227-31]. Heroines may be 'firm' or 'uncertain' in their actions. The heroes are usually found to be either 'false' or 'agreeable' (in about equal numbers — but the 'agreeable' ones are not invariably faithful), rarely 'rude' or 'skilful'. Perhaps Amaruka had ideas of this kind in mind when he composed the poems, as a traditional framework, but fortunately he did not label his studies conventionally nor arrange them systematically. They completely transcend any theoretical basis, so that we have the pleasure of finding that the commentators disagree with one another over their attempts at classification.

1470. Let us now look at a selection of verses from the Hundred with a minimum of comment (these verses are found in all available recensions; A = the text accepted by Arjunavarman, V = the version of Vemabhūpāla, followed by the verse numbers). In the first two of these the 'heroine' is being chided by a girl friend:

> Your loved one waits outside, downcast, scratching at
> the ground;
> your friends are without food, their eyes swollen with
> continual weeping;
> The parrots in their cages have renounced all humorous
> talking;
> and you are in this state! — Hard hearted girl, give up
> your anger now... (A7, V8)

> Women are innocent and false! They steal a lover
> and won't be stopped,
> so why be distressed? Why go on weeping? Don't
> play their game!
> Your lover is so attractive, likes play, is young and
> susceptible, timid one!
> Why don't you conquer him with tenderness[1] and

1. Reading *varkara* with some manuscripts; see the article by Fris.

cruelty, with hundreds of endearments, and buy
him back ?

(A8, V9)

These show heroines of different characters and also lovers of different characters, though in both cases evidently at fault. Arjunavarman thinks the second verse is an example of the figure 'revolution' *parivṛtti* [228], by implication, since the heroine can exchange her tenderness and cruelty for the man she wants.

1471. Next let the poet describe more directly (or are these also said by girl friends supposed to have witnessed the scenes, as gossip ?) the actions of two more heroines when their offending lovers reappear, each showing anger according to her character :

Angrily catching him firmly in the meshes of her soft
and trembling creeper-arms,
his beloved, leading him to the bedroom, deliberately
in front of her friends,
Indicated his misconduct with faltering and gentle
speech: 'Yet again he was acting so !'
But the lucky lover, intent on denial, was smiling,
though she was beating him, whilst she wept.

(A9, V10)

She avoided being together on the same seat by rising
to meet him at a distance;
his impetuous embrace, too, she prevented on the pre-
text of bringing the betel;
And she did not enter into conversation with him, by
making the servants work nearby;
— the clever girl satisfied her anger at her lover by
conforming to the civilities.

(A18, V17)

Arjunavarman notes the heroine's transient 'dissimulation' *avahittha* [56] in this last verse, as well as Rudraṭa's figure 'mingling' *milita* [260], because her anger shows itself as politeness, whilst Bahurūpamiśra, naming Amaruka, quotes it for a 'firm' *dhīrā* heroine (on *Daśarūpaka* II. 17).

1472. In another case the heroine complains to her girl friend of a faithless and cruel lover who took her rebuke (which should have been an example of *vakrokti* in the popular sense of 'crooked expression') too literally, and also of herself:

> Somehow, friend, I said: 'Go !' — With pretended wrath,
> but that hard hearted one roughly left the bed and went off;
> Yet, for that one whose love has suddenly perished and who is without pity,
> again my shameless heart is yearning: what shall I do?
>
> (A15, V14)

1473. The commentators disagree on the exact implications of the following incident:

> Seeing both the girls he loved together on the same seat he approached them carefully from behind,
> and covering the eyes of one as if intending to have a game,
> The rogue turned his neck sideways and kissed the other
> — whose heart thrilled with the merriment of love and the surface of whose cheek glowed with secret laughter.
>
> (A19, V18)

According to Vemabhūpāla the girl whose eyes were covered is an 'innocent' heroine, the other either 'bold' or at least 'middling'. Arjunavarman has a different theory: the girl whose eyes were covered is an old love for whom the hero still has affection; the one who was kissed is a new love for whom his affection is greater, as he has cleverly demonstrated to her, to her great delight. The latter view is a modification of theories of Rudraṭa (his conception of the figure 'distinction' *viśeṣa* [230], p. 123) and Dhanika (types of heroine, p. 47), which this verse was adduced to illustrate. Rājaśekhara (p. 47) quotes the verse simply as an example of an incident imagined by the poet (a 'contrivance'), whilst Vāmana admired its compact style ('union' as a quality of the meaning pp. 38-9 [243]), cunningly arranged but not excessively so. He adds the remark that this kind of thing is to be seen extensively in the works of Śūdraka [1234] and others: we have already had occasion to refer to The Lotus Gift for ideas which may be compared with Amaruka's [1469], but Vāmana implies that we should push the comparison deeper and seek a model for Amaruka in some of Śūdraka's verses, perhaps tracing here a movement, in drama and poetry, which eschewed any kind of complexity and sophistication in figurative language, in the interests of effective expression of situations and emotions, thereby associating lyric poetry closely with the techniques of the theatre. Such a connection would suggest a fairly early date for Amaruka and there seems to be no obstacle to placing him in the +4 or +5.

1474. The following verses hardly require comment:

During the night, when the couple were talking intimately, the pet parrot heard their words,
then repeated them too much in the morning in the presence of the elders:
Afflicted with shame the bride put into the crook of its beak a cut ruby earring she was wearing,
pretending it was a pomegranate seed in order to check its speech.

(A16. V15)

1475.

Though on the same bed they were distressed, because their faces were averted and they wouldn't speak;
conciliation was in both their hearts, but pride held them back;
Slowly the couple's eyes turned to their outer corners and met —
their lovers' quarrel broke and, laughing, they turned impetuously to embrace.

(A23, V21)

1476.

Her lover had come, after she had spent the day
with difficulty because of hundreds of desires;
then they went to the bedroom, but the stupid
servants went on talking for a long time;
Saying: 'I'm getting bitten', the slender one, her heart
tremulous for lovemaking,
suddenly waved her silk garment and extinguished the
lamp.

(A77, V86)

1477. An inexperienced girl sets out to meet her lover and runs into a more experienced girl friend, who remarks:

On your bosom you have put a loud necklace, round
your broad loins you have tied
a noisy girdle, on your feet you have jangling jewelled
anklets:
Innocent one! — If thus you go to meet your lover,
beating the drum,
why do you look all round as if agitated with intense
terror?

(A31, V29)

As she is going at night to a secret assignation it would be more suitable to wear something quiet and dark (both commentators interpret the first clause as referring to a brilliant necklace worn 'high', which would show up in the dark). Vemabhūpāla points out the 'crooked expression' *vakrokti* of this rebuke in the last line.

1478.

Where anger was just a frown, where a quarrel was
just silence,
where conciliation was just a mutual smile, where
grace was just a glance:
Of that very love now see the destruction which has
happened!
— You grovel on the ground near my feet, but I am
mean and find no release from my anger.

(A38, V33)

According to Vemabhūpāla the heroine is using a crooked expression when she says she is mean, because she wants her lover to understand that he is mean, her apparent meanness is only a reflection of his, i.e. his faithlessness. Really she wants a reconciliation, but it depends on him. The hero here is identified as 'rude'. The heroine is said to be 'his own', 'bold', 'firm' but 'ill-treated' *khaṇḍitā*, another of the eight types according to situation. Arjunavarman ignores most of this, partly because he admits the term *vakrokti* only in the special sense of 'equivocation' (as used by **Rudraṭa** [257]). Instead he finds here one of the figures of speech first known to us from Rudraṭa, *avasara*, 'opportunity' or 'sally', a kind of circumlocution or euphemism [260]. We have already noted that Arjunavarman's primary interest in his commentary seems to be the figures of speech (he finds in the Hundred about 45 different figures, following primarily Rudraṭa), under the varieties of which he tries to bring as many as possible of the forms of expression which occur. His comment on this verse is typical of his approach, of the application, and thus justification, of Rudraṭa's special doctrine of the figures of speech as basic in all poetry. Vemabhūpāla on the other hand just casually notes the figure he sees in each verse (there always is one, but frequently it is merely 'genre' or 'naturalistic description' [197, 259]), but finds only a dozen different figures altogether. By far the commonest, besides 'genre' *jāti*, he finds, is 'spurning' (*ākṣepa*, insinuation or apparent prohibition [207]), and the present verse is one of his examples of this.

1479. The heroine of the following dialogue verse also uses crooked expression according to Vemabhūpāla (the first speaker is her husband):

> 'My dear !' 'My lord ?' 'Angry one, give up your
> rage !' 'How have I shown any rage ?'
> 'You have tormented me !' 'You have not offended
> me, all the offences are in me !'
> 'Then why do you speak falteringly, and weep ?'
> 'Before whom do I weep ?
> 'Isn't it me ?' 'What am I to you ?' 'My beloved !'
> 'I am not, because of that I weep.'
>
> (A57, V50)

The husband's words also are 'crooked', because he is trying to get round her, to conciliate her and put his offence out of her mind. But she outmanoeuvres him by denying that she has any anger for him to conciliate and maintaining on the contrary that it is she who has offended. This gives her the initiative so that after the third line she can make the discussion direct and frank. The characters, says Vemabhūpāla, are similar to those in the last verse we quoted except that the heroine is only partly 'firm' and partly 'uncertain' (which she shows by her weeping, it appears) and the hero is 'false' (not 'rude'): thus we can understand that the conflict between them takes place at a slightly different level from the previous one, with different weapons. Dhanika (p. 45) indicates an interpretation similar to Vemabhūpāla's, adding that the heroine uses irony *utprāsa*. Abhinavagupta quotes this dialogue verse to explain the *uktapratyukta* limb of the *lāsya* [363] (*Abhinavabhārati* III p. 76).

1480. Here is the verse which both Indurāja and Abhinavagupta quote from Amaruka to illustrate how his verses pour forth aesthetic experience, Indurāja adding that it has (all) the three desirable qualities but no figure:

> When, a reconciliation having been effected with much
>   difficulty, her lover made a slip in his reply,
> the woman, emaciated through their separation,
>   covered up by pretending not to have heard it,
> But, fearing it should have reached the ears of her
>   intolerant friends,
> she looked round in confusion: as the house was empty
>   she sighed again with relief.
>
> (A75, V76)

The 'causes' and 'effects' of the heroine's emotion (love) are vividly depicted here; Vemabhūpāla notes the 'transient' emotion 'alarm' *śaṅkā*. Bhoja (*Sarasvatikaṇṭhābharaṇa* p. 742) finds all five dramatic conjunctions in this single verse : the opening in the first phrase (reconciliation), the re-opening in the second (slip), then the embryo in the second line (covered up), the obstacle in the third (fearing) and the conclusion in the last line.

1481. Let us quote three more verses which need little comment:

she did not cling with her arm-creeper to the hem of
his garment, nor wait in the doorway,
She did not let herself fall on his feet, nor say the word:
'Stay !'
Only, as the false one prepared to leave in weather
darkened by rows of clouds,[1]
the slender one stopped her lover with a swollen river
made of the flood of water of her tears.
(A62, V53)

1482.

Despondently she looked as far as the eye could reach at
the way her beloved should come,
when. the roads became quiet as the day declined and
darkness crept on,
Taking one sad step towards the house, the traveller's
wife,
thinking: 'He may have come at this moment', quickly
turned her neck and looked again.
(A76, V91)

1483.

Though he knows his beloved is separated from him by
provinces, by hundreds of rivers and by masses[2] of
mountains,
and that even with a great effort she cannot be
brought within range of his eyes,
Even so the traveller, stretching his neck and only half
touching the ground with his feet, wipes the tears
from his eyes
and looks constantly in her direction, rapt in meditation.
(A99, V92)

1. The onset of the rains, most unsuitable both for travelling and for leaving one's beloved.

2. An interpretation suggested by Fris. Otherwise 'by hundreds of rivers and mountains and by forests', as understood by the commentators.

1484. These sixteen verses seem typical of the collection and should sufficiently demonstrate its characteristics. The style is simple, though very compact. For example: it is very much simpler than Kālidāsa's Cloud-Message, which contrasts with it as descriptive poetry though formally a lyric and moreover a 'hundred'. Amaruka's lyrics, however, might, not inappropriately, be classed as dramatic poetry, which as a rule is simpler than other kinds. Arjunavarman calls the style *vaidarbha*, having the ten qualities defined by Daṇḍin, with the exception of the first verse, an invocation to Durgā (p. 3). Compounding of words is very limited despite the advantage in compactness it might seem to offer. Figures of speech are inconspicuous, unless we redefine them and enlarge their scope as Arjunavarman does. The figures of sound (alliteration, etc.) are almost totally absent (the first verse, being in a different style, is again an exception). Conventional metaphors ('lotus-eyes', 'Moon-face' and the like) are generally excluded, but 'creeper-arms' is used very appropriately in verse 9 to suggest both trembling and binding, thus enhancing the aesthetic effect; the idea (perhaps then a new one) pleased Amaruka, for he used 'arm-creeper' in verse 62 to emphasize clinging.

1485. The predominant metre in Amaruka is the *śārdūlavikrīḍita* (the original text seems to have had 61 verses in this out of just over 100 verses), which in the medieval period became perhaps the most popular of all metres in Sanskrit lyric poetry [584, 647, 657, 767, 1369]. Amaruka was perhaps the first to use it prominently and popularise it. There are about 15 *hariṇīs* and 12 *śikhariṇīs* [647, 1293], other metres are only sporadic. One might entertain the idea that the original collection consisted only of *śārdūlavikrīḍitas*, but on the one hand there are too many verses in other metres for this to appear probable and on the other it seems more likely that Amaruka, to avoid monotony, deliberately interrupted the sequence of verses in his favourite metre with contrasting rhythms. It can also be suggested that the metres used reflect the content to some extent: the *hariṇī* bursts out with an initial succession of short syllables (verses A15, 31 and 75 among those we have quoted), expressive of surprise or alarm; the *śikhariṇī* seems suitable for insistence (verse 7), cajoling and urging with its single short initial syllable followed by five longs and then five shorts and a questing cadence (but it seems equally useful for contrasting the actions of two different characters — verse 41 — and with a different intonation it can be wistful — verse 43); the *mandākrāntā* (cf. Kālidāsa's Cloud-Message [1412]) seems very appropriate to express nostalgia (verse 38); the other verses translated above are all *śārdūlavikrīḍitas*, the beautiful rhythm of which is more flexible, and adaptable to a great variety of emotions, whilst it seems particularly suitable for 'crooked expression'.

1486. The verses in this Hundred present situations in private life, basically between two persons who are, or at any rate have been, lovers, but often involving additional characters closely connected with them. If we compare them with other lyrics we notice first that there is hardly any reference to nature, such as flowers or birds (only the household parrot) or the spring (there is an indirect indication of the rainy season with reference to starting on a journey). Love here is not under the influence of nature, nor are any of its phenomena compared with the phenomena of nature in this text which eschews the distraction of comparison. There is also a total absence of mythological or traditional (to legends) allusions, except in verse 67 to Love and Death (also in 71 to Love, but Arjunavarman declares this verse is spurious). As a matter of fact the gods ('Viṣṇu, Śiva, Brahmā etc.') are summarily dismissed in verse 3 (after the conventional invocations to Durgā and Śiva), in favour of the face of the Beloved as a more effective protection. Verse 36, which in Vemabhūpāla's recension more appropriately follows this as verse 4, adds that it was silly of the gods to churn the ocean, since it is those who kiss a proud but responsive girl who obtain ambrosia (cf. verse 594 of the Seven Hundred Songs). We are also remote from the village and country milieu of the Seven Hundred collected by Sātavāhana, with its peasants at work and its women busy in the kitchen or the fields, though that too deals with situations between lovers. Amaruka's heroes appear to be aristocrats: perhaps he really was a king or prince. Comparison with the Seven Hundred shows how specialised the Amaruka Hundred is in content and method: it is difficult to find a verse there which, if translated into Sanskrit, could be interpolated in Amaruka.

1487. These single-verse poems are well described as miniatures, but if miniature paintings are thought of as a parallel it may be observed that Amaruka's poems usually have a strong time dimension, which it would be difficult or impossible to suggest in paintings of the situations. The loves usually have a history and sometimes quite a lot of action is directly described. With a long metre such as the *śārdūlavikrīḍita* (19 syllables in each of the four lines) Amaruka can set a great deal of action or talk in one verse. With his unsurpassed power of suggestion he can add hints of much more which had taken place previously.

1488. Generally the verses contrast the feelings of two characters, a contrast which gives poignancy to the emotions. Occasionally there is a touch of humour, always gentle. But the all-pervading spirit of the Hundred is that of tenderness. There is none of the scepticism or cynicism about love of the philosophical poet Bhartṛhari. The emotion is not simply valued highly: there is nothing higher, as Amaruka expressly states at the beginning where he puts it above religion, or rather in place of religion. Nowhere in the verses is the possibility suggested that there might be any other happiness or anything at all worth pursuing except love. In every relationship and situation described, the characters are treated with sensitivity and deep sympathy, especially the women: it would be difficult to find another writer anywhere who has depicted women with equal accuracy, insight and understanding. Men are amateurs at love and write as amateurs. Women are professionals but as a rule do not care to write. For this reason the work of Amaruka is almost unique.

Chapter XXVII

BHĀRAVI

1489. The date of Bhāravi has not been much discussed, even the one fairly definite piece of evidence available not having attracted much attention, perhaps partly because of textual difficulties. He is mentioned in a Cālukya inscription of +634, along with Kālidāsa, as a famous poet. The Cālukyas had succeeded the Vākāṭakas in Mahārāṣṭra and Āndhra in the +6, but their capital was further South, in Karṇāṭaka. The inscription merely indicates that Bhāravi was recognised in the Cālukya Empire as a great poet, who may have lived at any time before it was written. A further reference is found in other inscriptions, of the Gāṅgeya king Durvinīta, where the king himself claims to have written a commentary on the fifteenth canto of Bhāravi's *Kirātārjunīya* (this is a canto of *citrakāvya*, for which a commentary is especially useful). The Gāṅgeyas (or Gaṅgas) ruled the Southern part of Karṇāṭaka from the +4, usually as feudatories of the Pallavas, who in that period ruled over an empire which extended from coast to coast across India, immediately South of the Vākāṭaka dominions. The date of Durvinīta has been contested by historians, but is usually placed in the second half of the +6. He also claims to have made a (Sanskrit) version of the *Bṛhatkathā*, though none of his works appear to have survived. It is sometimes supposed that Bhāravi lived at his court (at Talavanapura on the upper Kāverī), but that is simply a conjecture (except when based on an incorrect reading of the corrupt text of Daṇḍin which we must now examine).

1490. The only definite statement we have is that by Daṇḍin, where he mentions Bhāravi as having been a friend of one of his ancestors (*Avantisundarī* pp. 9f, clarified by *Avantisundarīkathāsāra* p. 4). Daṇḍin lived at the Pallava capital, Kāñcī, and from the references to historical events in the autobiographical introduction to his *Avantisundarī* we find he was born in the middle of the +7 (*c.* +650 to 660). His great grandfather, Dāmodara, was a writer who was patronised by Durvinīta, also by Simhaviṣṇu Pallava (reigned *c.* +580 to 600). The available text of Daṇḍin's novel is corrupt, so that some have read it as identifying Dāmodara with Bhāravi. That this is a misreading is shown clearly by the *Sāra*, since published in a better edition. Dāmodara was born in Mahārāṣṭra (presumably in the first half of the +6). Through the friendship of Bhāravi, he was introduced to a king named Viṣṇuvardhana. On account of a ritual impurity incurred on a hunting expedition (eating meat, because no other food was available: presumably he was attending the king), he left the court and went on pilgrimage by way of expiation. After that, Dāmodara went to Durvinīta's court (whence Simhaviṣṇu heard of him and invited him to Kāñcī). Bhāravi thus appears only in connection with Viṣṇuvardhana.

1491. There seem to be two kings named Viṣṇuvardhana in this period of history. One was a Cālukya, the younger brother of Pulakeśin II (+610 to 642, whose inscription mentioning Bhāravi we have noted above), who some time after +631 became independent in Āndhra, founding the line of 'Eastern' Cālukyas. He would appear to be too late to have been a contemporary of Bhāravi and Dāmodara. The other is Yaśodharman Viṣṇuvardhana, of the Aulikara family, known from his inscriptions, one of which is dated in +533/4. He was apparently a Gupta feudatory who asserted his independence at the time of the Hunnish invasions, with his capital at Daśapura in Avanti (or 'Mālava'). In his inscriptions he claims to have conquered most of India, from the Himālaya to the Western Ocean and from the Lauhitya (River Brahmaputra) to the Mahendra Mountains (in Southern Kaliṅga). This is probably an exaggeration and certainly his empire proved ephemeral, nothing further being heard of it, but it is generally accepted that he inflicted a major defeat on the Huns. It is also generally accepted that he conquered at least part of Mahārāṣṭra from the Vākātakas. Thus Yaśodharman Viṣṇuvardhana seems the most likely king to have been associated with Bhāravi, though the evidence is not quite conclusive, and the poet's floruit may be placed *c.* +530 to 550. Whether Bhāravi wrote with an eye to the military and political struggles of the period of the decline of the Gupta and Vākāṭaka empires is a matter of pure conjecture.

1492. Bhāravi's only known work, the *Kirātārjunīya*, 'Arjuna and the Kirāta', is perhaps the most perfect epic available to us. The epics of Aśvaghoṣa [714-5, 743-64] may be considered equally fine, and the *Buddhacarita* possibly more profound in content, whilst Bhāravi shows the form at a later stage of its development, with more concentration and with a higher polish given to every detail. The greater force of expression is Bhāravi's original genius rather than merely the result of the trend towards concentration, for the other epic poets known to us hardly attempt it, generally seeking a light touch. The only known poet who can really be compared with him is Meṇṭha [1328]. Our fragmentary knowledge of the 'Slaying of Hayagrīva' suggests an equally forceful narration but a very different individual manner: Meṇṭha's expression is linguistically simple but generally full of ambiguity and figurativeness of meaning; his force derives largely from subtlety and humour [1340, 1347]. Bhāravi's language on the other hand is extremely difficult. Like Aśvaghoṣa he rejoices in the finer points of Sanskrit grammar, whilst he applies them to attain the utmost conciseness. The resulting impression is one of an irresistible directness, the weight of which resides in the heavy load of meaning carried by each word. At the same time he selects and arranges his words in such a way as to produce a crisp texture of sound dressed with a limited but regular application of alliteration. His choice of metres beautifully corresponds to the changing content of the narrative.

1493. Arjuna and the Kirāta is based on an episode in the *Mahābhārata* (III *adhyāyas* 28 ff.), during the exile of the Pāṇḍavas, in which Arjuna goes to the Himālaya and engages in severe asceticism in order to propitiate the gods, and especially Śiva, so that they will give him divine weapons which alone will enable him to overcome the enemy. The episode begins with an argument among the Pāṇḍavas as to what they should do, in which Draupadī in particular upbraids Yudhiṣṭhira for doing nothing. Then the sage Kṛṣṇa Dvaipāyana (the supposed author of the *Mahābhārata*) appears (in what is supposed to be his own poem) and advises Yudhiṣṭhira to send Arjuna to obtain divine weapons. The gods test Arjuna and Śiva himself, disguised as a Kirāta (a mountain tribesman of the Eastern Himālaya region), picks a hunters' quarrel with him, after they both shoot a demon in the form of a boar which had attacked him. Arjuna fights heroically against the invincible might of Śiva and is eventually overpowered, but Śiva is pleased with him and grants him the weapons he desires. Afterwards the other gods appear and also give him weapons.

1494. This episode, which in the original occupies fifteen cantos, Bhāravi redevelops as an epic in eighteen cantos. He changes little in the details of the narrative, but makes everything succinct, both narrative and dialogues (of which latter there are many), makes some rearrangement of the action, brings out the fullest significance of every detail, enhances the whole with a few new details and charges the verses with the 'weight of meaning' for which he is justly famed. It is necessary to enrich the content in order to realize the ideal of an epic, rather than of a mere episode. In addition, Bhāravi develops the characterisation of his heroes in a brilliant manner. Apart from stressing the significance of the actual story, which carries the mythological and mystical overtones of Tradition as well as the philosophical content of *kāvya*, Bhāravi's 'weight' includes many particular insights into the problems of human life, presented in his characteristically forceful style.

1495. Bhāravi begins his epic by presenting us at once with the thread of the action. There is no invocation, though commentators draw attention to the fact that the first word is the auspicious one 'fortune' (*śrī*, i.e. sovereignty). As a matter of fact this 'fortune' referred to is that of the enemies of the Pāṇḍavas. The argument of the poem is, how is it to be won from them by the Pāṇḍavas? Fortune is referred to again at significant crises in the action, as when Indra tries to deter Arjuna from seeking her (personified as a goddess) because she is indiscriminate (XI.24) and the hero replies defending her: she does resort to a real man (XI.61) and he is determined to restore her to his family (XI.69); by the concluding verse of the epic (XVIII.48) Fortune (*lakṣmī*, a synonym) is virtually in his possession already, since he has the weapons which ensure victory. To underline this theme, the word *lakṣmī* occurs in the last verse of every canto of the epic. Here Bhāravi follows the convention of 'ornament of a whole work' (*Śṛṅgāraprakāśa* II p. 474) we have found already in Pravarasena's Building of the Causeway, where the word *aṇurāa*, 'devotion', is used in the same way [1431-2, 425].

1496. The first verse of Arjuna and the Kirāta informs

us that a secret agent sent by Yudhiṣṭhira has returned with news of the actions of the king of the Kurus (i.e. Yudhiṣṭhira's enemy Duryodhana, the Kaurava). The agent presents his report carefully, because the news is bad, namely that Duryodhana's government is calculated to ensure that he is prosperous and invincible. This report, which is a model of a good speech, takes up the first half of the first canto. After the agent has taken his leave, Yudhiṣṭhira tells his wife, Draupadī, and his brothers. The second half of the first canto then consists of an angry tirade by Draupadī, reproaching Yudhiṣṭhira for his stupidity and for his calm acceptance of their miserable condition. He should break the agreement (by which they are supposed to remain in exile for thirteen years after Yudhiṣṭhira has lost his kingdom through gambling) and take immediate action to restore their honour.

1497. In the first half of the second canto Bhīma supports Draupadī with a speech urging action and not allowing Duryodhana to consolidate his position further, moreover it would be shameful meekly to receive their kingdom back as a gift from the enemy at the end of the stipulated period instead of fighting for it: death is better than dishonour for a self-respecting person. Yudhiṣṭhira then replies to Bhīma with a slightly longer speech, criticising impetuous action and praising discrimination and endurance. While he is speaking, the sage Dvaipāyana arrives and the canto ends.

1498. In Canto III Yudhiṣṭhira greets the sage, who then makes a short speech, advising that the enemy is not to be depended on, consequently the kingdom will have to be won back by valour. But the enemy is stronger, therefore action must be taken to excel him in arms. The warriors on the other side, such as Bhīṣma, Droṇa and Karṇa, are almost invincible, therefore Arjuna must practise asceticism and acquire divine weapons which will make him stronger than they are. Yudhiṣṭhira commands his brother to follow the sage's instructions and Dvaipāyana inspires and instructs Arjuna, then says that a sprite *yakṣa* will lead him to a beautiful mountain where he will practise asceticism to propitiate Indra. The sage then vanishes and the sprite appears in his place. As Arjuna prepares to depart, Draupadī incites him, reminding him of the outrage she had suffered, dragged as a slave before the assembled nobles by

Duryodhana's brother Duḥśāsana (when Yudhiṣṭhira had gambled her away). Arjuna then puts on his armour, takes his weapons and sets out with the sprite.

1499. The fourth canto describes their journey through the autumn countryside. The first half is direct description, then in the second half the sprite describes the autumn to Arjuna, indicating that it is an auspicious time for his task (the season of fruition, also the customary time to begin a military campaign). As he speaks, the Himālaya Mountains come in sight.

1500. In the fifth canto the Himālaya is described as they approach it, being compared with Śiva in appearance (light one side, like Śiva's smile, dark the other, like the elephant skin He wears) and associated with Him in various other ways. Then the sprite speaks to Arjuna, saying that just seeing the Himālaya removes people's sins. Afterwards he points out Mount Indrakīla, a mountain of golden colour 'which is dear to your father' (because Arjuna is supposed to have been the son of the god Indra by his earthly mother Kuntī: the Pāṇḍavas so called were not in fact the sons of Pāṇḍu, since he was prevented from having children by a curse, consequently he permitted his wife to have sons by any of the gods she liked; thus Yudhiṣṭhira was the son of Dharma, Bhīma of the Wind God, etc.). He tells Arjuna to practise asceticism there, as instructed by the sage, then, with good wishes, leaves him.

1501. In Canto VI Arjuna climbs Indrakīla, whose beauties are described, and reaches a wooded and pure spot near the summit, in which secluded place he begins his ascetic life. The description contrasts with that of the Himālaya in the previous canto, in that it is direct and naturalistic and described at close quarters, instead of concentrating on mythological associations. After a few days the forest rangers, the sprites *yakṣas* guarding the mountain, report Arjuna's presence to Indra. They do not know who he is, but his warlike dress and weapons suggest his intention of gaining some great conquest through his asceticism. He may be a demon striving to acquire extraordinary might, a threat to men and even to the gods (there were plenty of precedents for this). Indra, however, knows who the ascetic is and is glad because he is acting rightly, but decides to test the firmness of his asceticism. He sends the nymphs *apsarases* with orders to destroy Arjuna's asceticism, attended by their 'ministers' the celestial musicians *gandharvas*, and watches the brilliant crowd set out.

1502. In the seventh canto this celestial army proceeds through the heavens (stars, planets, etc.), which are disturbed in various ways by its passage. The poet finds here scope for the figure 'exaggeration' *atiśayokti* [196], as when he says that the rows of flying mansions *vimānas* become banks to the rivers of heaven (which ordinarily have no banks; the 'rivers' are the nebulous streams of the Milky Way and the 'mansions' are stars moving from their proper places as they convey the army). With shouts of encouragement, the army then descends on the summit of Indrakīla like the river of heaven. The canto concludes with a description of the elephants of the celestial army and of the beauty of the trees as the nymphs rest against them after their journey.

1503. In the eighth canto the nymphs create mansions for themselves on the mountain and enjoy themselves in the forests. Afterwards they bathe in the celestial river (the Ganges in its course through heaven, i.e. the Milky Way).

1504. In the ninth canto the day ends and there is a description of evening, the time appropriate to begin lovemaking. Then comes darkness and moonrise, the Moon destroying the darkness. Night consecrates Love with the Moon, as if with a silver urn which pours out the flood of glittering water (32). The nymphs prepare for lovemaking and send messengers to their lovers. Then they join their lovers in drinking parties (they have mead made with lotuses). In this way they shorten the night and the canto ends with the morning.

1505. The tenth canto describes how the nymphs then go to distract Arjuna from his asceticism, soon realising from his appearance that this will be difficult. At their command, all six seasons appear simultaneously with their peculiar seductive beauties such as flowers, whilst the celestial musicians play lutes and drums (the rainy season is described first). However, instead of Arjuna falling in love with the nymphs it is they who fall in love with him. They redouble their efforts, accosting him, appealing to his compassion, one of them finally striking him on the chest with a lotus, but he ignores them.

1506. Then in Canto XI Indra, disguised as an old sage, goes up and speaks to Arjuna, first praising his asceticism and then praising liberation as the proper aim: but, he goes on, Arjuna's armour and weapons completely contradict this supposed purpose. With this, Indra launches into a criticism of Arjuna's evident intent for victory and satisfying anger, instead of practising forbearance. The quest for wealth conduces to unhappiness, for Fortune is indiscriminate. Therefore he should renounce war and instead seek calm. The aim should be to end rebirth, for pleasures are as illusory as dreams. Replying, Arjuna first praises this speech, but then says that the sage does not understand his situation. Consequently the speech, fine as it is, is irrelevant and Arjuna is not a fit person to receive it. He then explains the situation and Dvaipāyana's command to worship Indra (to whom he is unwittingly speaking). The outrage to Draupadī in particular, when her upper garment was pulled off in the assembly hall, cannot be forgiven, though at the time Yudhiṣṭhira had endured it. It is no good seeking friendship with bad people, for this only leads one into doing wrong actions oneself. It is difficult to make out the actions of the bad, just like those of fate, since for them good qualities and faults are equal. Thus the situation must be remedied (and conciliation with such enemies would be bad).

1507. Arjuna here further elaborates his ideas about the right course of conduct, which invite careful attention since they form the heart of the epic, explain the springs of his action. People lacking in self-respect, he says, who are without firmness and therefore allow themselves to be oppressed through this defect of power, are contemptible. Their condition is equal to that of grass (they will be trampled on). Fortune and honour resort to a man only as long as he does not lose his self-respect: only then is he a real man. Among those who serve as models in benedictions (those one would wish to resemble), the wisest are those who let their indignation fall on their enemies (the commentator Mallinātha gives Rāma as such a model, but his interpretation is otherwise difficult to follow). I do not wish for happiness or wealth or for the state of *brahman* (liberation), he says, but I do wish to wipe away this dishonour by killing the enemy. Perhaps I shall be ridiculed by good people, perhaps I am mistaken, or perhaps you will be ashamed of having taken trouble inappropriately (trying to advise me), but unless I can restore the fortune of my family and destroy its enemies I consider even *nirvāṇa* an obstacle (or danger). He concludes by again affirming that he must be a real man and guard his honour. Indra then reveals his real identity to his son, commands him to worship Śiva, who can transfer Fortune to him from the enemy, and vanishes.

1508. In the twelfth canto Arjuna, pleased with this, proceeds accordingly to practise very severe asceticism in order to propitiate Śiva. As a result, the 'successful ascetics' (great sages) in the region cannot endure Arjuna's splendour (the power radiated by his asceticism) and take refuge with Śiva. A description of Śiva follows, then the sages complain of the disturbance caused by this unknown ascetic and the threat his extreme practices and warlike appearance imply for the gods: with such strength he may easily conquer the whole universe and they cannot endure him. Śiva replies, explaining who Arjuna is. He is an incarnation on the Earth of Nara, part of the primaeval Man (*puruṣa*=Viṣṇu according to Mallinātha). (The other part, Nārāyaṇa or Acyuta, has also gone to the Earth as Kṛṣṇa the Yādava.) Nara and Acyuta have been asked by Brahmā to go among men to protect creation by killing demons. His asceticism is for my worship, because he wishes to expel enemies who oppress the entire Earth, having surpassed (even) Indra's strength (i.e. Indra could not give him weapons powerful enough and referred him to me). Even now the demon Mūka, knowing this, has taken the form of a boar and is on his way to kill Nara, therefore I must go there quickly. I will take the form of a Kirāta king and kill this boar, Nara too will shoot it: then he will engage in a hunting quarrel with me and you will see his strength. Śiva then disguises himself, and disguises his attendants *gaṇas* [649] as a *kirāta* army which advances through the forests. Śiva intercepts the boar just as it reaches Arjuna.

1509. In Canto XIII Arjuna sees the boar approaching and draws his bow. Śiva does the same and both shoot and hit the boar, Śiva's arrow piercing right through its body and disappearing into the Earth. Arjuna goes to retrieve his arrow but finds a forest ranger (one of the supposed *kirātas*) there, who speaks to him politely but then rebukes him for trying to take the arrow which belongs to his King. He should apologise and then seek the King's friendship.

1510. At the beginning of Canto XIV Arjuna is angry

but firm and replies even more politely to the *kirāta*, claiming the arrow and telling him to look elsewhere for the King's. He does not desire friendship with this envious and wicked king, who is not a warrior but a low person unworthy of either his friendship or his enmity; but if he tries to take this arrow the result will be as if he had tried to take a gem from the head of a poisonous serpent. In the second half of the canto the *kirāta* reports this to Śiva, who orders his army to attack Arjuna. Arjuna repels them, wounding the *gaṇas* with his arrows.

1511. In the fifteenth canto the army retreats until it is stopped by Śiva's son (Skanda, the War God), who makes a long speech rebuking them. Śiva also bars their retreat and then himself starts to fight Arjuna with arrows.

1512. Arjuna in Canto XVI is puzzled at the Kirāta king's ability to stand against him, after the whole army had fled. His arrows having failed, he decides to try other weapons and launches first the *prasvāpana* (sleep-inducing) missile and then the *āgneya* (fiery) missile. Śiva withstands both.

1513. These missiles having failed, Arjuna in Canto XVII returns to his arrows. Śiva intercepts them and replies with a shower of his own arrows. Then Arjuna draws his sword, but Śiva smashes it with an arrow. Arjuna continues fighting with stones and uprooted trees.

1514. In the final canto Arjuna and the Kirāta fight with their fists, then wrestle. At last Śiva springs in the air and Arjuna grasps him by the feet (thus unconsciously assuming the proper attitude before his God). Śiva is more pleased with Arjuna's 'virtue' *sattvatā* than with his asceticism and reveals himself. Arjuna praises him with a hymn and then asks for the strength to obtain victory. Śiva gives him his own flaming *raudra* weapon and the Veda of Archery (this science is regarded as a subsidiary *veda* [480]), which appears personified. Indra and the other gods appear and also give Arjuna various weapons. Then Śiva tells him to go and conquer the enemy and Arjuna returns to Yudhiṣṭhira, bearing the Fortune of victory.

1515. The manner in which the action rises from the opening verse to the rapid conclusion will perhaps be clear from this summary. The tense narrative easily carries the incidental descriptions characteristic of epic poetry. The entire action also reflects the various relationships between the characters, in which there is generally an element of ambiguity: we understand that it is in the gods' interest to help Arjuna, but first they want to test him to make sure that he is capable of becoming their champion; he himself encounters them as opponents because they conceal their identity from him. The resulting contest is played out with Indra and then in a different way with Śiva. Since Arjuna himself is the divine Nara we are probably not wrong in feeling some element of real rivalry in these trials of strength: we are expressly told that Arjuna has to surpass the strength of Indra, his father, though this father's feelings after his son has refuted his arguments and told him, with a touch of humour, that his splendid speech is irrelevant, are not described; in the case of Śiva there is the eternal rivalry with Viṣṇu, of whom Arjuna is part. But these are the mysteries which underlie the *Mahābhārata* as it was told in Bhāravi's time and about which theologians still argue. Since Arjuna really acquired power sufficient to conquer the universe, as reported by the sprites and then by the sages, Indra and Śiva would feel obliged to test, not so much his physical prowess as the strength of his character: they must not be satisfied until they have proved there is no trace of corruption in him, that nothing will deflect him from the course of duty and honour. The relationships of Arjuna with his brothers and with Draupadī, again, are complex. Though brothers, they have different fathers, which largely explains their different characters. Yudhiṣṭhira is just, Bhīma impetuous, Arjuna brave. Draupadī is their common wife and so appears to Arjuna both as his elder brother's wife and as his own wife, thus combining the superior authority of the former with the affection of the latter. This seems to give Arjuna a certain advantage over Yudhiṣṭhira, with whom her relationship is simpler and who has to endure all her fury.

1516. The ends attained by the hero are firstly 'wealth' *artha*, or power, in the sense of the virtual restoration of his family's fortune. But there is clearly a strong element of 'virtue' *dharma* in this, as far as Arjuna is concerned, for he is not seeking his personal fortune but rather doing his duty. 'Pleasure' *kāma* is inconspicuous but not totally absent: it is evident that Arjuna will win Draupadī's special regard by his action; moreover he is said to win the love of the nymphs, though this is supposed to be a matter of indifference to him.

'Release' *mokṣa* appears only as an obstacle offered by Indra.

1517. The epic can be analysed, as Bhāmaha requires, according to the five conjunctions of plot construction. It may be suggested that the 'opening' is set where Dvaipāyana gives his advice (in Canto III), recommending the course of action to be followed towards the objective of winning Fortune. The 're-opening' may be placed where Arjuna begins his asceticism (Canto VI). The 'embryo' might be discovered in Canto XI in the encounter with Indra. The 'obstacle' is presumably in the fight with Śiva, where Arjuna finds his arrows useless (Canto XVI). The conclusion is right at the end of Canto XVIII, where Śiva reveals himself and grants Arjuna's desire. The apparently late (+17?) commentator Citrabhānu gives (p. 5) a similar analysis as follows. The opening conjunction is established in the first three cantos and marked by the commencement stage. The re-opening conjunction is in Cantos IV to the middle of VI, with the undertaking. The embryo conjunction is in the Cantos from the middle of VI to the end of XI, pregnant with the 'hope' (i.e. possibility) of attainment. The obstacle conjunction is in the six cantos XII to XVII, mixed with the 'certainty of attainment'. The conclusion conjunction is in the last canto, in relation to the 'arrival' of the fruit. This analysis does not contradict ours (made before seeing Citrabhānu's) and it is interesting to find that the precise 'conjunctions' in the action as understood by us occur at the ends or climaxes of the stages as demarcated by Citrabhānu [127-34, 405].

1518. In this story of the winning of Fortune by Arjuna, Bhāravi has in effect concentrated the essence of the entire Great Epic. The battle with the Kauravas is already virtually won, so that the story is complete without further details. Dvaipāyana has explained that the struggle can be decided only by valour, Arjuna has demonstrated that he has enough of this to win and Śiva has confirmed that this is so and placed the supremely powerful weapon in Arjuna's hands. The previous part of the story is also sufficiently indicated to make the main action clear: Yudhiṣṭhira has 'thrown away' his kingdom (says Draupadī, I.29) in his passion (for gambling), but this defeat was due to deceit on the part of his enemies (I.30); the humiliation of this defeat, the degradation of the Pāṇḍavas (on which Draupadī then dwells), was intensified by unbearable insult, namely the outrage to Draupadī when she was rough-handled as a slave girl by the Kauravas who had won her from Yudhiṣṭhira (as she reminds Arjuna in Canto III and as he tells Indra in Canto XI, where the events are briefly recapitulated in verses 45ff.); nevertheless they submitted to the agreement proposed by the elders to resolve a situation intolerable for the imperial family, whereby the Pāṇḍavas and Draupadī were released from slavery but sent into exile for a stipulated period (the agreement is mentioned by Draupadī, I.45; the defeat and exile alluded to by Arjuna, XI.58). Given this background of earlier events, Bhāravi presents the moral problem of the Pāṇḍavas and the decision on how to solve it, which Arjuna then puts into practice but also defends with arguments. One could continue indefinitely drawing out the implications of Arjuna and the Kirāta, but perhaps these indications will satisfy our present purpose.

1519. The aesthetic experience produced by this epic is of course the heroic, with a good deal of the marvellous but only a minimum of the others. That minimum is, however, provided: for example the comic, which might be unexpected in so serious a work, is sufficiently satisfied in the encounter between Arjuna and Indra, in the form of delicate irony. Citrabhānu (p. 5) says that the dominant heroic is enhanced by the sensitive, marvellous and calmed [1516, 1524]. The characters from the outset express the strong emotions which the struggle with the Kauravas has caused, especially in the period when they were defeated and humiliated. The appropriate transient emotions can be found: for example Dhanika (p. 86), in order to illustrate 'reflection' *mati*, chooses a verse from Arjuna and the Kirāta (II.30), in Yudhiṣṭhira's reply to Bhīma's impetuous speech:

> One should not act rashly,
> — lack of discrimination is the basis of the greatest
> misfortunes:
> For Successes,[1] greedy for good qualities,
> themselves choose one who acts after reflection.

After resolving on the proper course of action, following Dvaipāyana's advice, Yudhiṣṭhira gives his command and Arjuna

1. Personified; Mallinātha interprets as 'Fortunes', with allusion to self-choice marriage. The figure is 'corroboration'.

carries out the plan with unshakable singlemindedness, developing the basic emotion of 'energy' *utsāha* until success is achieved.

1520. An epic poem is expected to contain a variety of episodes of action and description, as noted particularly by Rudraṭa (see Chapter VI above [408]). All these, as we can understand from Rudraṭa's principle of 'harmony', or 'appropriateness' *aucitya*, discussed in connection with the relation of various elements in *kāvya* to the aesthetic experience [256], must be strictly subordinate to the main story and be developed only as they occur naturally in it. Bhoja, in discussing ornaments of a whole work in epics, etc., has pointed out a number of episodes in Arjuna and the Kirāta by way of illustration (*Śṛṅgāraprakāśa* II 475 f.) [1267]. Thus political debate or counsel *mantra* is obviously very prominent in this poem, particularly in the first three cantos and again in the eleventh. In this connection we may note Bhāravi's interest in eloquence, in the qualities of a good speech, which he makes his characters discuss several times and which we take up below when we consider the 'qualities' *guṇas* in his epic. Bhoja notes the obtaining of desired objects, namely in this case Arjuna obtaining divine weapons, which of course is the concluding episode of the main action here. The battle is of the variety 'equal-unequal', because the opponents, Śiva and Arjuna, are partly equal in strength and partly unequal. The descriptions of mountains (Cantos V and VI), night and moonrise (Canto IX) are noted, then the nymphs' enjoyment of the forest, picking flowers, drinking (Bhoja says this takes place in the pavilions they have created for themselves there) and lovemaking, along with the descriptions of the seasons and of the nymphs' water sports in the celestial river (Cantos VIII and IX). The lovemaking in this case is a 'general festival of love' (contrasting for example with that of Śiva and Umā in Kālidāsa's *Kumārasambhava*, which is a 'particular festival', i.e. of one couple only). Bhoja also says that the epic includes a description of a hermitage: this presumably refers to the place chosen by Arjuna for his asceticism (Canto VI), not the forest hermitage where Yudhiṣṭhira is spending his exile, which is hardly described.

1521. Bhoja also discusses how poets sometimes rearrange the natural order of things, his illustrations including some from Bhāravi (p.478). This is one of his 'ornaments of a whole work' *prabandhālaṅkāras*. Thus it is a rearrangement of time when all six seasons appear at once (he quotes X.18). There is a rearrangement (substitution) of persons when Dvaipāyana vanishes, introducing the sprite in his place to take Arjuna to the mountain (III.29). It is a rearrangement of action when the elephants (of the *kirāta* army) cannot endure it, when ordered to advance into battle against Arjuna, though they are mounted by brave men (XVI.2), i.e. they retreat unexpectedly. Bhoja also quotes this last verse, with two others from the same Canto, to exemplify a context *prakaraṇa* which is imagined *kalpita* by the *kavi* and to which there is nothing corresponding *nirābhāsa* in the source (*Śṛṅgāraprakāśa* I, 117-8).

1522. On several occasions in Arjuna and the Kirāta the characters praise one another's speeches, or the poet directly describes the qualities of a speech. The qualities mentioned can be compared with the 'qualities' *guṇas* recognised by writers on style and may help to make clear Bhāravi's own style, the qualities he himself valued and wished to present in the dialogues, the speeches, which form a large part of his epic. Thus at the beginning the secret agent makes his report. Since he desires the welfare *hita* of his master the speech is truthful even when unpleasant (i.e. he is not a flatterer). Then his speech is characterised as 'effective' (*sauṣṭhava*, meaning excellent or powerful in its expression, conveying the meaning effectively) and 'exalted' *audārya*, also as having 'decisive meaning' (*viniścitārtha*, i.e. the reverse of doubtful) (I.3). The agent himself explains as he starts (I.4) that he is going to report the truth and his master should excuse him whether it is good or bad, because a speech which is both beneficient and agreeable is a rarity. In the second canto Bhīma considers Draupadī's speech to have been very serious *garīyas*, having a happy result but disturbing to one whose strength is impaired, like a very potent medicine (II.1 and 4). He supports her with one which is 'relevant' (*upapattimant*, applicable to the situation) and based on what is exalted (*ūrjita*, superior) (II.1). Afterwards Yudhiṣṭhira praises Bhīma's speech as free from confusion, clear, delightful and salutary (II.26); as distinct *sphuṭa* in its words, having 'weight of meaning' *arthagaurava*, having its meanings distinct *pṛthak* and having power *sāmarthya*; as relevant and authoritative (II.27-8). In the eleventh canto Arjuna praises the qualities (the word *guṇa* is used here XI.41) in Indra's speech. These are clarity *prasāda*, strength *ojas*, having seriousness *garīyas*, conciseness *lāghava*, 'expectancy' (*sākāṅkṣā*: this is a grammatical term meaning the mutual expectancy of words in a sentence, i.e. that the words are grammatically well-knit), absence of ellipsis *anupaskāra*, comprehensiveness *viṣvaggati*, being without confusion (*nirākula*, i.e. consistent), having its essence *sāra* determined by logic *nyāyanirṇita* and being thus independent and authoritative, irrefutability *aprakampatā*, inescapability *alaṅghyatva* making it exalted *ūrjita*, exalted in its wealth of meaning *audārya arthasampatti* and therefore calmed *śānta* (XI.38-40). Finally in Canto XIV Arjuna, addressing the *kirāta* (*gaṇa*), again mentions the qualities of a good speech, that it is distinctly pronounced (*viviktavarṇa*, having distinct phonemes), euphonious *sukhaśruti*, is clear *prasanna*, deep *gambhīra* and agreeable (XIV.3); it is relevant and of deep meaning (XIV.4). He adds that some people praise weighty wealth of meaning and others excellence of expression: a speech which pleases everybody is extremely rare (it is very difficult to combine these two qualities).

1523. These qualities are presented here in a poetic manner, but we can compare them with those set out more systematically in the theory [189, 237, 240, 243, 292-7]. It would appear that Bhāravi stresses clarity, strength, exaltation and lucidity among the traditional ten qualities. Of these, exaltation seems by far the most important. It is stressed and clarified through a series of apparent synonyms (*audārya*, closest to the old *udāratā*; *ūrjita*; *arthagaurava*; *gambhīra*; *garīyas*; perhaps *viṣvaggati*), though these also express different shades of meaning which could almost be taken as different qualities. Bhāravi here is insisting on serious, weighty or deep meaning as the most important quality in a speech and by implication in a *kāvya*. Lucidity may be taken as covered by the logical qualities mentioned by Bhāravi: logical, irrefutable, relevant, without ellipsis, without confusion, having decisive meaning, etc. Here again Bhāravi makes more distinctions than the traditional analysis. Bordering on this quality is the corresponding clarity with reference to the expression, the words, concerning which we find such terms as 'distinct in its words'. We should note that Bhāravi is firmly committed to the idea of a grand distinction into expression and meaning. As far as we know, this conception in *kāvya* was first formulated by Bhāmaha, whom Bhāravi very probably follows. Bhāmaha was critical of the old idea of the qualities, perhaps largely because of the confusion among them, the lack of clear distinctions, still more critical of the idea of styles founded on them. Bhāravi may be seen as meeting this problem by applying Bhāmaha's distinction of expression and meaning to it and probably as revising the qualities accordingly. Later on Vāmana tried another solution, accepting the traditional terminology but with a dichotomy of each quality into two, of expression and of meaning.

1524. Bhāravi relegates 'sweetness' *mādhurya* to an inferior position, not naming it but occasionally using words meaning 'agreeable' or 'delightful' or 'euphonious'. His view evidently is that it is very acceptable if it can be achieved but difficult to combine with weighty meanings, lucidity, clarity and strength, all of which are more important and must be given priority over it. His main quality on the side of expression, namely the very general 'excellence' *viśuddhi* or 'effectiveness' *sauṣṭhava* or 'power' *sāmarthya*, which terms seem to be more or less synonymous, is not easy to relate to the traditional qualities. Conciseness and 'expectancy' might be related to 'union' *śleṣa*. Finally, the quality of 'calmed' arises out of wealth of meaning. This would lead us into a discussion on whether Bhāravi accepted 'calmed' as a *rasa*, aesthetic experience produced by a work of art. It also suggests the view of the Great Epic, his source, as 'calmed'. Perhaps Bhāravi intended to suggest a connection between the qualities he valued and the aesthetic experience, with a possible *śānta rasa* arising from his 'exaltation', perhaps again he thought of 'calmed' as an essential element in the 'heroic': the single-mindedness of the hero is similar to that of a detached ascetic seeking *nirvāṇa*, their 'energy' similarly overlaps. But of course this quality is found only in the speech of Indra advocating withdrawal from the world, so we must be cautious in trying to infer too much of Bhāravi's general theory from his particular examples. As so often in his epic, he here opens up vistas of implications for us to explore.

1525. Although no known critic seems to have referred to the question, we might perhaps surmise from Bhāravi's ideas on good qualities that he favoured the *gauḍiya* style. Daṇḍin seems to have held him in high regard, though very critical of that style, which might authorise the conclusion that this is a moderate kind of *gauḍiya*, seeking as far as possible to incorporate the qualities of the *vaidarbha* as well. Thus there is plenty of 'strength' in the epic, but not to the extent of having an excessive number of long compounds. Bhāravi likes alliteration, but again is quite restrained in using it (Daṇḍin says this is the *gauḍiya* version of 'union'). His figures of speech are most effective and serve the purpose of the subject matter. Lucidity and exaltation are favoured by Bhāravi (though on occasion the reader may complain that lucidity is sacrificed to sonority, as in I.1) and accepted in the *gauḍiya* according to Daṇḍin; concentration (ambiguity) and grace, the latter interpreted as exaggerated expression, which Daṇḍin also notes for *gauḍiya*, may be found in the epic though Bhāravi does not appear to mention them directly. From Vāmana's point of view Bhāravi's style might seem to be on the borderline between *gauḍiyā* and *vaidarbhi*, but leaning towards the former. There is strength and grace, in Vāmana's senses, but most of the other qualities are present too. From Kuntaka's point of view it seems clear that Bhāravi belongs to the *vicitra* (beautiful) style which replaces the *gauḍiya*. In view of Bhāravi's cultivation of exaltation and deep meaning, however, it may seem preferable to regard him as an exponent of the 'Western' or *lāṭiyā* style recognised by Bāṇa and Rudraṭa [239, 256].

1526. Kuntaka quotes (p. 73) a verse (VIII.6) from Arjuna and the Kirāta to illustrate his general quality (which is the same for any 'style') 'appropriateness' or 'harmony':

> The *aśoka* branch with its young shoots trembling
> as the bees drink up from its clusters,
> Appears to be imitating brides who shake their hands
> when their lips are sharply bitten.

Much of the harmony of this verse is in its sounds, but it is present also in the figurativeness: there is 'condensed expression' *samāsokti* here according to Mallinātha, which as Bhāmaha defines it implies an advantageous comparison; but one could think of other figures too, on account of the parallelism of actions. The verse harmonises perfectly with the aesthetic experience to which it contributes.

1527. Bhoja multiplied the 'qualities' far beyond even Vāmana's. He illustrates (*Sarasvatīkaṇṭhābharaṇa* p. 722, *Śṛṅgāraprakāśa* Vol. II. p. 453) four of them in a verse of Bhāravi's (V.33):

Here Śiva playfully took the hand of Pārvatī (in
 marriage),
which was decked with auspicious and powerful herbs
 (remedies for snake bites, etc.);
While her unsteady eyes trembled
at his hand with its slipping snake-amulet.

Here Bhoja finds two distinct kinds of exaltation of expression (*udāttatva* and *udāratā*), in the use of eulogistic words and in the spaciousness or boldness *vikaṭatva* of the composition, and clarity and grace in the meaning, 'grace' being the brilliance of the aesthetic effect. The whole verse is said to exemplify the mixture of 'qualities' with aesthetic experiences in which the latter predominate. The *rasas* he then identifies, however, are not any of the regular ones but four of Bhoja's peculiar *rasas* at the level where they are 'many' and even limitless. They are named after the emotions 'fright' *sādhvasa*, 'play' *vilāsa*, 'devotion' *anurāga* and 'union' *saṅgama*, but clearly relate to the sensitive among the regular aesthetic experiences, with an admixture of the apprehensive. From such qualities as grace (defined following Vāmana) we might assign this verse to the *gauḍiyā* style. Bhoja in his two works on literary criticism quotes a number of verses from Bhāravi's epic to illustrate the various emotions, for example from the description of the nymphs bathing in the celestial Ganges:

Their thighs touched by the quivering fish,
the nymphs, their eyes wild with terror
And their tendril-hands shaking, became
attractive even to their girl friends. (VIII.45)

This illustrates the transient emotion 'terror' *trāsa* [56] and the particular case when there is no real cause for fear (*Sarasvatīkaṇṭhābharaṇa* p. 590, also *Śṛṅgāraprakāśa* Vol. II p. 573). The commentator Mallinātha notes the 'naturalistic description' *svabhāvokti* [197] in this verse.

1528. It might seem that such qualities as euphony or distinct pronunciation could hardly be discussed in relation to a literary text as opposed to a live speech. Nevertheless the choice of expressions by the poet directly affects the reading, whether aloud or silent, and all Indian literature and criticism is very much alive to sound effects of all kinds. The critics freely discuss intonation *kāku* as implied by what is written, especially in relation to the expression of emotion. An interesting example of this is found in Rājaśekhara's *Kāvyamīmāṃsā* (p. 32), where he quotes a verse from Arjuna and the Kirāta (IX.39) which consists of four separate speeches, between a lady (a nymph) and her messenger (friend, confidante), each of which has a different intonation:

> "Tell him everything for which he should be reproached!"
> — "It isn't good, my dear, to speak harshly to one's man."
> "Then conciliate him and bring him."—"But how can one who has offended you be conciliated?"

In this we can understand that the first speech is harsh in intonation, the second has the tone of a warning or admonition, the third sounds eager, the fourth is discouraging. Rājaśekhara's view here (p. 31) is that the different intonations multiply the number of 'styles' beyond the three basic ones (which he takes from Vāmana). Dhanika (p. 104) refers to the same verse in a different kind of discussion, as illustrating a particular situation between lovers: the lover is supposed to be using 'disregard' *upekṣā* in order to overcome the lady's anger.

1529. From the point of view of 'figurativeness', as understood by Kuntaka, in Arjuna and the Kirāta we have already considered the poem as a whole, with some reference to its source in the Great Epic. Kuntaka himself, as we noted in Chapter IV above [284], refers to (pp. 239f.) Bhāravi's epic as an example of how one episode of a source is made into a complete work. It surely came close to the critic's ideal of a *kāvya* considered as a whole, as presented in his book on figurative expression. Kuntaka here quotes from three verses in cantos I and III in order to show how the great poet, leaving aside the rest of the Tradition (*itihāsa*, i.e. the *Mahābhārata*) and anything without aesthetic value, presents the action of an extraordinary hero in one episode, in such a way as to form a complete and beautiful epic, which includes in effect the whole story ending in the fall of Duryodhana and the success of Yudhiṣṭhira. First (I.3, first half) we have: 'In private, having obtained leave from the King (Yudhiṣṭhira) who wished to arrange the destruction of his enemies, (the secret agent made his report...).' This opens the story, preparing for the discussion which will result in Arjuna going on his exploit and mentioning the end which Yudhiṣṭhira hopes for. Then at the conclusion of her speech (I. 46, i.e. the last verse of I, second half) Draupadī says : 'Let Fortune again come to you, as to the rising Sun at the beginning of the day, after destroying the darkness consisting of your enemies.' This shows her extreme anger, which serves as a driving force in the epic. Lastly, from the conclusion of Dvaipāyana's speech to Yudhiṣṭhira (III.22, second half): 'These (enemies, Bhīṣma, etc.) will be uprooted by Arjuna after acquiring rare heroism (heroic power, *vīrya*).' This alludes to Arjuna's struggle to obtain divine weapons, which will culminate in the fight with the Kirāta King, where his wonderful valour is displayed.

1530. As an example of contextual figurativeness, Kuntaka refers (p. 233) to the wrestling 'context', the final stage in the fight between Arjuna and the Kirāta. Kuntaka has said that, through the kind of contextual figurativeness he is defining here, the main *rasa* of a *kāvya* can be 'tested' (like gold with a touchstone) and found to be present in each 'context' (an act of a play, a section of a canto of an epic covering one theme, etc.) [281]. In Bhāravi's epic the heroic is the main aesthetic experience and it is clearly produced by the wrestling scene.

1531. Kuntaka also quotes (p. 42) from Arjuna's speech to the *kirāta*, as an example of contextual figurativeness in that the poet has changed the story at this point: the *kirāta* has used gentle persuasion in order to try to get Arjuna to accept a falsehood (XIV.7), whereas in the source there is no such argument but merely the mutual challenge in which the *kirāta* claims the first hit and rebukes Arjuna's pride.

1532. Figurativeness at the sentence level consists in the use of the figures of speech. Kuntaka (p. 216 Krishnamoorthy's edition) quotes Bhāravi for a simile where there seem to be two comparisons with two *ivas:*

> Then the science went out from the mouth of the great
> sage
> — as from the orb of the Sun delightful at the beginning
> of the day
> A ray bright as a spark of fire —
> approached — like a quivering lotus — Arjuna's face.
> (III.25)

But as these are in the same sentence they will fuse into one image: the science flashed from Dvaipāyana to Arjuna as a ray from the Sun to a lotus.

1533. To illustrate 'accompaniment' *sahokti* [224], Kuntaka quotes a verse which (IX.39) is given above [1528] for its intonations, pointed out by Rājaśekhara, along with the verse which follows it:

> "What is the use of (my) going? For it is not proper
> to come to him."
> "What is anger when he is (your) lover, O lucky angry
> one?"
> — Lovers who had come near and heard such talk
> among the women
> conjectured their satisfaction, with much enjoyment.
> (IX.40)

The two verses form a pair, since this is the same dialogue between a lady and her friend. Both the heroine and her friend want only reconciliation with the lover; though they appear to be opposed to each other in the argument they are saying the same thing (Krishnamoorthy pp. 228-9). From Kuntaka's point of view it is a very good example of an 'accompaniment' in which there is no trace of any simile.

1534. Kuntaka quotes (p. 216) two examples from Arjuna and the Kirāta for 'having doubt' [233], showing the element of fancy which he insists on in this figure:

Has darkness coloured the various trees and peaks?
Has it bent down the sky, has it hidden it?
Has it filled the uneven places of the earth?
Has it abolished the directions? (IX.15)

Ruyyaka (p. 57) quotes the same verse in his discussion on 'having doubt'. The second verse is from the description of the water sports of the nymphs in the celestial river:

As they plunge in, half closing their unsteady eyes but
glancing out of the corners:
when their lovers are very close, is it fatigue which
makes the women's bodies tremble,
Which lifts their breasts with a sigh,
or is their love proclaimed? (VIII.53)

1535. Lexical figurativeness [274] of various kinds is also illustrated by Kuntaka from Arjuna and the Kirāta. Thus (pp. 92f.) the *kirāta* in speaking to Arjuna (XIII. 58) adopts a haughty tone by choosing the synonyms *tapasvin*, 'ascetic' (instead of the more usual *muni*, 'sage'), to refer to Arjuna, and Vajrin, 'Thunderbolted' (among countless synonyms), to refer to Indra. The point is that *tapasvin* has a shade of meaning suggesting a 'poor thing' or 'poor wretch', whilst Vajrin suggests the mighty weapons available to the *kirātas* on Indra's mountain: we do not value your poor arrows and we have the arsenal of the gods on this mountain, thus we are not accusing you falsely to steal an arrow from you (but simply telling the truth, he claims).

1536. Another variety of lexical figurativeness is euphemism *saṃvṛti*, which Kuntaka (p. 108) illustrates by quoting the verse (XIII.49) where the *kirāta* claims that his King has saved Arjuna from death by killing the boar, but instead of saying 'death' he says that what the animal would have done to you is 'unspeakable'.

1537. Other critics have drawn on Bhāravi to illustrate the figures of speech, whilst the commentator Mallinātha has named a great variety of them in many of the verses (see the index to these by Cappeller, pp. 190-2), though he has also passed over many without notice. Mallinātha indicates 'fancy' *utprekṣā*

[213] as occurring most frequently, and simile next, with corroboration third.

1538. But the philosophical figure of corroboration *arthāntaranyāsa* [208] is surely the most characteristic figure in Bhāravi (and Mallinātha has omitted to note a number of them, so that complete statistics might rank it higher) and used with more powerful effect by him than by any other poet, commenting on his narrative. The verse (II.30) quoted above [1519] to exemplify a transient emotion (reflection), as noted by the dramatic critic Dhanika, is a case of corroboration (combined with fancy: Successes themselves choose...). Thus we see how this particular figure harmonises with the expression of an emotion significant in this philosophical poem. Ruyyaka (p. 140) quotes this same verse to illustrate corroboration. Vāmana (p. 64) quotes another verse (VIII.37) as his example of corroboration. It comes from the context of the water sports:

> One (nymph) did not throw away the garland which her lover
> had placed on her bosom with swelling breasts, after knotting it,
> In the presence of her rival, even when it became sodden with water:
> for good qualities are found in the affection, not in the external thing.

1539. Corroborations help establish the spirit of the whole epic in the first canto. Thus in the second verse, describing the character of the secret agent, Bhāravi remarks that those who desire the welfare (of others, as of their masters) do not wish to speak falsely in order to be pleasant. Then in the fourth verse: 'A speech which is both beneficient and agreeable is a rarity'. In the fifth verse the secret agent explains to Yudhiṣṭhira:

> What sort of friend is he who does not advise his lord well?
> What sort of master is he who does not listen to a good adviser?
> For where kings and ministers are in harmony
> all successes always take their pleasure.

Reporting the enemy's prosperity, however, the agent offers the flattering reflection (verse 8) that the hostility, even, of noble persons is better than any kind of association with the ignoble (i.e. it has proved to Duryodhana's advantage to quarrel with you, because it has led him to imitate your good qualities). We find another string of corroborations in Draupadī's speech in the second half of this canto, but suited to her angry and cynical mood: kings use deceit to break treaties when they want to conquer their enemies (45). Bhīma's speech in the second canto similarly contains such reflections, but suited to his heroic character, impetuous but straightforward: a great man does not wish to receive wealth from another person (as a gift) but only through his own energy. Yudhiṣṭhira's reply again includes a series of corroborations, well suited to his more reflective character, among which we have already discussed one (II.30). Dvaipāyana's speech also contains some corroborations (such as III.17). The figure appears again in all the following cantos until the last part of the poem, the battle, where it becomes rare: in fact it is rare where there are no speeches, being properly a figure of rhetoric used for persuasion. Most of its occurrences are in the speeches; for example Indra's brief exhortation to the nymphs contains three together (VI.43, 44, 45). A minority express the poet's reflections on the actions described (in cantos VIII, IX and X, among which VIII.37 is translated above). On the other hand, in the excitement of the battle we may suppose that Bhāravi felt such reflections inappropriate and did not indulge in them. In Arjuna's hymn of praise to Śiva there is no room for argument and philosophy, only for descriptions of the extraordinary qualities of the divine person and eternal nature, ending with a simple request.

1540. A good example of 'fancy' *utprekṣā*, which Mallinātha finds so frequently, has been noted above in summarising the ninth canto (IX.32) [1504]. 'Exaggeration' *atiśayokti* is comparatively rare, but appears appropriately when the celestial army marches, as we saw in canto VII.

1541. Namisādhu commenting on Rudraṭa's *Kāvyālaṅkāra* (p. 85) refers to a verse of Bhāravi's as an example of 'incongruity' *viṣama* [260] as an 'objective' figure:

On the one hand the deeds of kings, by nature hard to
understand;
on the other hand (ordinary) mankind, irresolute with
ignorance:
This is your power — that by me has been known
the enemies' political plan, whose principles were
hidden.

(I.6)

The secret agent is modestly introducing his report to Yudhiṣṭhira.

1542. Namisādhu quotes (p. 106) another verse which he says illustrates an unusual variety of 'fancy' *utprekṣā* as a comparative figure:

One who performs with slaughter as his purpose,
the rituals which ought to produce the supreme good
(liberation):
He, deluded, is one who muddies very clear waters
which ought to cut off the evil of tiredness.

(XI.19)

This is from Indra's speech to Arjuna rebuking him for practising ascetic rites for a wrong purpose. The 'fancy' here is to compare refreshing waters with liberating rituals. Mallinātha, however, says the figure here is a variety of 'illustration' *nidarśana*. For Mallinātha the standard type of 'fancy' is represented by the following verse (IX.26), quoted by the anthologist Śārṅgadhara, by Kuntaka (p. 9) and by Namisādhu (p. 69):

After rising, the Cool-Rayed (Moon) set out across the
sky
very slowly, as if very much afraid —
Attacked by the glances of jealous women,
sullied with hot tears.

1543. In the fifteenth canto Bhāravi demonstrates his command of *citrakāvya*, 'pretty' or decorative composition consisting in the use of the figures of sound instead of the figures of sense [411]. The rout of the army of *kirātas* (i.e. Śiva's *gaṇas*) is depicted with increasing confusions of rhyme and alliteration. Even Skanda, the general, is wounded:

> He (Arjuna), with his sword and bow and arrows,
> his fortune (spoils of war) won from chariot and foot soldiers,
> Flashing and firm, frolicked in fun,
> leaping and injuring Śiva's offspring.
>
> (XV.5)

—The alliteration in this verse is such that only one consonant is heard in each quarter (except for the final of the whole verse, as permitted by the rules for this figure):

> *sa sāsiḥ sāsusūḥ sāso*
> *yeyāyeyāyayāyayaḥ,*
> *lalau līlāṃ lalo 'lolaḥ*
> *śaśīśaśiśuśīḥ śaśan.*

1544. Then Skanda makes his speech rebuking the *gaṇas* for their cowardice and carrying the alliterative figures still further:

> He is not a man, who has been beaten by an inferior, O you (*gaṇas*) of various faces:
> surely a man who has beaten an inferior is no man?
> He whose king is unbeaten, though himself beaten is really unbeaten;
> he who beats (only) those already thoroughly beaten is not without sin (is a coward).
>
> (XV.14)

In translation this appears to be a fairly straightforward lecture to soldiers. (In the second quarter above Ratneśvara, commenting on the *Sarasvatikaṇṭhābharaṇa*, p. 267, reads: "A man is no man whose king has been beaten *nunnenaḥ*", i.e. who escapes with his own life, abandoning his king to be beaten.) In the Sanskrit, however, there is only one consonant (except at the end again), which appropriately is *n* suggesting 'no' or 'not' *na*, checking the cowards:

na nonanunno nunnono nānā nānānanā nanu,
nunno 'nunno nanunneno nānenā nunnanunnanut.

1545. Further on in his speech, one verse (XV.23) is the same as the previous verse (XV.22) read backwards syllable for syllable (the script being syllabic as well as phonemic this is simpler in the original than in a romanised transliteration — apostrophes for elided *a-* do not count, being silent and perhaps not used by Bhāravi):

niśitāsirato 'bhīko nyejate 'maraṇā rucā
sārato na, virodhī na svābhāso bharavān uta.
(22)

tanuvārabhaso bhāsvān adhīro 'vinatorasā,
cāruṇā ramate janye ko 'bhīto rasitāśini.
(23)

O immortals, delighting in his sharp sword, fearless,
brilliantly, vigorously, he is not shaken:
Is not the opponent
very splendid and full of (warlike) bearing?
(22)[1]

Who, that is not brave, takes delight handsomely with
his chest unbowed,
resplendent with his body-armour shining,
Unafraid in the battle
devouring all with its roaring?
(23)

1546. A variation on this reversibility of a verse (cf. the so-called 'cancrizans' or retrograde canon in contrapuntal music), giving different meanings, is that a verse or any part

1. The translation of this verse does not follow Mallinātha's interpretation (with its unwanted *visarga*): it is closer to that of the anonymous commentary on Hemacandra's *Kāvyānuśāsana* (I pp. 310-1), but departs from that too in taking the first *na* with *nyejate* and the second *na* only with *virodhī*, as an interrogative. Thus the verse becomes interrogative just like its reverse, which is surely more appropriate.

of it should sound the same when read backwards as when read forwards, giving the same meaning whichever way it happens to be read. In the *vaktra* metre of eight syllables to each quarter verse, there is the further possibility of reading at right angles to the lines, vertically, and getting the same result, since the four lines (quarters) of the verse, followed by the four lines of its retrograde version, can be written as eight lines with the syllables aligned vertically as well as horizontally. One can then read the verse and its reversed form vertically, either downwards or upwards and starting at either side. In the case where the reversible unit is the quarter verse, we then obtain the figure called *sarvatobhadra*, 'good from every side'. It may be noted that this auspicious form suggests a mystical significance, resembling Brahmā who faces in all directions or the *bodhisattva* Samantabhadra whose benevolence radiates all round. Since Bhāravi's fifteenth canto is in the *vaktra* metre, Skanda is able to pronounce the following as part of the peroration of his speech:

	de	*vā*	*kā*	*ni*	*ni*	*kā*	*vā*	*de*	
	vā	*hi*	*kā*	*sva*	*sva*	*kā*	*hi*	*vā*	
	kā	*kā*	*re*	*bha*	*bha*	*re*	*kā*	*kā*	
	ni	*sva*	*bha*	*vya*	*vya*	*bha*	*sva*	*ni*	(XV.25)
reversed :	*ni*	*sva*	*bha*	*vya*	*vya*	*bha*	*sva*	*ni*	
	kā	*kā*	*re*	*bha*	*bha*	*re*	*kā*	*kā*	
	vā	*hi*	*kā*	*sva*	*sva*	*kā*	*hi*	*vā*	
	de	*vā*	*kā*	*ni*	*ni*	*kā*	*vā*	*de*	

This may be translated as follows (the peroration describes the battle and will end with a final rebuke to the cowards):[1]

1. *devākānin*=*deva* +*ā-kai*, possessing the resounding noise of the gods, or *deva* +*ā-kan* (Caus.), inflaming the gods; *ka* +*ava-ā-dā*=bringing down the heads, or *ka* +*vāde*=confused cies; *vāhikā*=rush or reserves (Mallinātha); *sva* + *svaka* + *ā-hi*=carrying away our own property, or *su* + *asvaka*=beautiful and not one's own (the enemy's); *vā*=and; *ka*=rut +*ā-kṛ*=flow, scatter; *ibhabhara*=temples of the elephants or multitudes of elephants ; *kākā* (Voc.) =base ones (Mallinātha) or greedy for battle (Ratneśvara); *nisva*=selfless

In which (battle) there is the resounding noise of the
gods, in which heads are brought low,
and in which the rush carries away the property of our
side;
In which the rut flows from the temples of the ele-
phants — O base ones!
— in which they reproach those who sacrifice the self-
less and the worthy (saving themselves)!

It may also be translated as follows (and we may reverse the order of quarters as befits the reversed version):

In which (battle) are distinguished the concealed
(nature) of the worthless and the worthy,
in which there is a multitude of rutting elephants —
O greedy for battle! —
And in which the reserves are bearing off what is
beautiful and the enemy's,
in which there is inflaming of the gods, with confused
cries!

Moreover the vocative can mean 'O noble ones' (says Ratneśvara p. 280) if we assume the elision '*kākā*, which might be appropriate in the reversed version, where we seem to find an exhortation to fight instead of a rebuke for running away. Ratneśvara also suggests 'reproaching to increase *vya* the selfless and worthy'. Thus the words appear to be ambiguous throughout, which suits the idea of a mystic incantation, such as the gods love, as well as the need for the reversed version to have a separate meaning. Still other possibilities of interpretation can be found, such as, for 'are bearing off', 'have as their purpose', or that 'are distinguished the concealed' means 'shines the armour'. Some may think that such a linguistic game with rare words is futile or unpoetic, yet this verse has the characteristic Bhāravi property of gradually revealing more significance when carefully studied and reflected on. There is true art in it as well as extraordinary technique. It is very appropriate in its place near the

or worthless; *bhavya*=worthy; *vya*=(perhaps) sacrificing (*vyay*?) or concealing (*vye*); *bhasvan*=reproaching (Ratneśvara) or distinguishing (Mallinātha). The locatives qualify 'in the battle' mentioned previously.

end of Skanda's speech. Bhoja (*Śṛṅgāraprakāśa* II. p. 473) regards having a canto of such difficult composition as one of the 'ornaments of a whole work' *prabandhālaṅkāras* and quotes XV.12 among his illustrations of it.

1547. Bhāravi uses two dozen different metres in Arjuna and the Kirāta. Kṣemendra (*Suvṛttatilaka* III.31) gives the opinion that there is special beauty in the *vaṃśastha* metre as used by Bhāravi [646, 895, 1238, 1343]. He also says (III.18) that that metre is particularly suitable for political narrative and then quotes the first verse of the epic to exemplify this. Four cantos of the epic are mainly in *vaṃśastha* (I, IV, VIII, XIV), which is the fixed metre with 12 syllables to the quarter derived from the ancient *jagatī* of the *Veda* and the old Pali literature, as *upajāti* was from the *triṣṭubh.* There are three cantos of *upajāti* [585, 644, 646] (cf. Aśvaghoṣa, who used it much more extensively [752]) and only two of *vaktra* (in which Meṇṭha had excelled, as Kṣemendra notes [1332]). Bhāravi is in fact carrying further the process of replacing the more traditional narrative metres by the newer ones, using the latter more extensively. Where Aśvaghoṣa used only five canto metres in an epic, Bhāravi uses eleven (Kālidāsa was conservative here, using only six, including *rathoddhatā* [573] and *drutavilambita*), among which are *puṣpitāgrā* (X) [1342], *svāgatā* (IX) [583] and *pramitākṣarā* (VI) [659] (all of which are found in the old Pali literature in their original forms and are likely to have been used before as canto metres; cf. Chapter XII above) and *praharṣiṇī* (VII) [660] (apparently of somewhat later development though an example was noted at the end of Chapter XIII from Patañjali and it is occasionally used at the end of a canto by Aśvaghoṣa: it is clearly a derivative of *aupacchandasika* [555, 566, 570]). It is not very likely that Bhāravi was the first to use any of these as a canto metre; what seems new is the use of so many of them in one epic, enriching the texture. Another feature which we have not found before in epics is the use of a great variety of metres through the main part of a canto, instead of only in a few varied verses at the end. The two cantos (V and XVIII) which open in *drutavilambita* break away after twelve or sixteen verses into many different metres. The first of these excursions is the sprite's description of the Himālaya, the second the climax of the whole epic, when Śiva is revealed, hymned and grants his weapon. The first particularly displays some rare metres, thus Namisādhu (p. 7) quotes V.18 as an example of a metre not found in the standard works on metrics. This verse also has a complicated rhyming scheme and a simile in the manner of Aśvaghoṣa's 'complete' metaphors:

> Here they describe the inner part as always difficult
> to traverse,
> through being hard to approach by any entry;
> Know that dense thicket pervading all directions,
> as Brahmā only (knows) the Highest Man (Supreme
> Spirit).

The Supreme Spirit (presumably Viṣṇu, otherwise the Vedāntic World Soul) pervades the whole universe and is therefore difficult to know thoroughly, the 'entries' *āgamas* in the simile are the religious traditions supposed to teach the way to the inner reality. Mallinātha has found the name *kṣamā* for this metre.

1548. Renou in his monograph on Arjuna and the Kirāta ('Sur la structure du kāvya', *Journal asiatique*, 1959, 1ff.) has presented a fascinating study of the style of Bhāravi in terms of grammar, vocabulary and the techniques of narration (and description) and dialogue (and speeches). Whilst we can refer to his work for the linguistic technicalities, we ought to stress the attention he has drawn to the balance, proportion and harmony found in the poem and in all its structural elements. Thus there is a balance between compounding and grammatical nexus, between other grammatical variations, between the narrative and dialogue styles (characterised by precise distinctions of grammatical expression), between heavy (difficult) and light (simple) verses, between the pairs of terms in similes, in the echoes of alliteration, in the harmonies of meaning, between dilution and enrichment, and so on. There is further a tendency to begin and end a verse or line (quarter) with the more significant words (in fact these prominent positions indicate emphasis on the words placed there). Again, the expressions tend to be balanced in point of 'volume', to achieve which synonyms or circumlocutions or analytical phrases (as it were definitions instead of names) are substituted for words lacking the necessary proportions. There is, finally, a profound harmony, pervading the poem, between the expression and the meaning.

1549. These findings correspond to aspects of the 'harmony' or 'appropriateness' at all levels which is described by the old Indian critics [256, 297], as we have seen to some extent above [1520, etc.]. The point has been summed up by Ratnaśrījñāna (p. 197), quoting Bhāravi himself on it. The sprite's description (Canto V) of the Himālaya is in fact very relevant to the narrative, introducing Arjuna to the place for his asceticism and tremendous struggle. But Bhāravi himself, in a verse (V.16) introducing the sprite's speech, seems to offer a justification for such 'loquacity'. Ratnaśrījñāna quotes this as authoritative for the theory of descriptive contexts in *kāvya*. Probably Bhāravi actually had in mind controversies about excessive descriptive passages in epics and therefore incorporated here a note of explanation of what seemed to him the proper measure for them:

> Then the follower of the God of Wealth (the sprite: definition !),
> his mind filled with admiration when looking upon the mountains,
> Uttered affectionate words to him (Arjuna), with reverence,
> for loquacity is fine when there is a proper occasion.

The sprite is moved to speak by his feelings, moreover Arjuna is unfamiliar with the Himālaya and his guide should give him directions and also say something of the nature of the divine mountains. Ratnaśrījñāna makes the last line of this verse the rule for descriptive matter, when commenting on Daṇḍin's account of 'realism' *bhāvikatva*, the naturalistic descriptions which give reality and life to a whole *kāvya*. It is the appropriateness of all the parts of a composition which gives it convincing reality.

1550. The same critic quotes (p. 258) Bhāravi again over the question of 'redundancy' of words, discussed by Daṇḍin as a fault, *ekārtha*. After Daṇḍin's example of this, Ratnaśrījñāna quotes as a counter example a verse of Bhāravi (III.1) with similar imagery but the opposite quality of concentrating an additional implied meaning into a single expression:

'...Dvaipāyana, very dark but with his matted hair irradiate (reddish or golden), was like a cloud possessing lightning...'

This implies also the deep thundering of his voice, says the critic. The faulty verse on the other hand is padded out with a separate expression for 'thundering'.

1551. We may bear this example in mind in connection with the question of 'volume' discussed by Renou. Bhāravi gives volume to his expressions in order to suit the proportions of his verses, but he does it with art, charging the volume with a balancing weight of meaning and not following the rather long-winded, if sonorous, diction of much early epic poetry. Ratnaśrījñāna also quotes (p. 31) from Bhāravi on the quality of clarity *prasāda*, where (XIV.3, which has been referred to above along with other verses on the qualities [1522]) the poet makes Arjuna praise '...a speech whose words are clear and deep.' This bears again on the question of harmony: the proper volume gives clarity, setting the expression forth distinctly, whilst the weight of meaning gives the balancing depth. Arjuna and the Kirāta would probably be the best example one could give to illustrate all fifteen of Bhoja's 'qualities of a whole work' *prabandhaguṇas* (*Śṛṅgāraprakāśa* II pp. 471-2), though the critic does not offer any examples. 'Volume' extending through the whole epic would come largely under the first two of the fifteen, but 'harmony' underlies all of them. The fifteen are : (1) the book not being (too) contracted *asaṃkṣiptagranthatva*, (2) the composition not being uneven *aviṣamabandhatva*, (3) there being metres attractive to hear *śravyavṛttatva*, (4) the cantos, etc., not being too extended *anativistīrṇasargāditva*, (5) the joinings being very close *suśliṣṭasandhitva*, (6) dependence on the fruits of the four ends *caturvargaphalāyattatva*, (7) there being skilful and exalted heroes *caturodāttanāyakatva*, (8) there being uninterrupted aesthetic experiences and emotions *rasabhāvanirantaratva*, (9) there being derivation of injunctions and prohibitions *vidhiniṣedhavyutpādakatva*, (10) there being 'contrivances' [1473] with good arrangement *susūtrasaṃvidhānakatva* (this includes use of the five conjunctions and all other elements of construction), (11) the composition corresponding to the aesthetic experience *rasānurūpasandarbhatva*, (12) the languages corresponding to the characters *pātrānurūpabhāṣatva*, (13) the metres corresponding to the matter *arthānurūpacchandastva*, (14) delighting all the people *samastalokarañjakatva*, (15) there being sentences having figures *sadalaṅkāravākyatva*. [409]

1552. The discussions above should suffice to show that Bhāravi has been universally praised and enjoyed by the critics. The anthologists are sparing in their selections from his epic, though making it a rule to include some, probably because in Arjuna and the Kirāta more than in most *kāvyas* the context is generally desirable to bring out the full implications of a verse. In spite of this difficulty the critics and anthologists between them quote well over 10% of the verses in the poem (on an incomplete survey). By far the most popular verse, from this point of view, is VIII.37, translated above [1538], — which of course happens to be detachable from its context (the nymphs bathing) without loss of meaning.

1553. Apart from the inscriptions noted at the beginning of this chapter, the earliest critic to mention Bhāravi seems to be Daṇḍin. Apart from his claim of ancestral association with Bhāravi, made in the *Avantisundarī*, Daṇḍin may be conjectured to have praised him as 'emperor' and 'first' of poets, 'facing all ways', in a mutilated (the name is missing) introductory verse (18) to that novel (this conjecture is based on the chronological sequence of the writers praised in these introductory verses). Dhanapāla (+10) in his novel *Tilakamañjarī* (introductory verse 28) brackets Bhāravi's name with that of the +7 epic poet Māgha, as the two most formidable poets, a comparison often made later. Maṅkha, as we noted in Chapter XXIII, associates him with Meṇṭha, evidently from the different point of view of a splendid epic narrative, harmonious and profound, rather than from that of difficulty and delectation for scholars. From these two opinions we may conclude that Bhāravi alone succeeded in satisfying both types of reader — another kind of 'balance' in his poem.

1554. The Buddhist anthologist Vidyākara is able to select three verses (1625, 1662, 1674) whose reflections harmonise with Buddhist philosophy. Indra recommends (insincerely !) renunciation: the fortune of youth is fleeting like the shadows of autumn clouds (XI.12). Moonrise brings suffering to those birds who must separate at night — everything is unendurable to those who are unhappy (IX.30). 'If one fights him one loses one's honour; if one makes friends with him one's good qualities are spoiled: a discerning person after examining both alternatives afflicts a vulgar person with contempt' (XIV.24: 'vulgar person', *pṛthagjana*, happens to be a technical term in Buddhism for a person so ignorant that it is useless to attempt to lead him to enlightenment, though opinions varied over the long term possibilities; in Arjuna's case the objection is to the deceitfulness of the Kirāta).

1555. But the last word on Bhāravi has been said by the poetess Gaṅgā (+14) in her epic The Conquest of Madhurā (*Madhurāvijaya* I.9):

> The fragrance of the poet Bhāravi's speech
> is revealed by crushing:
> Like a *vakula* (Mimusops elengi) garland it gives
> delight to those who know this.

Chapter XXVIII

SUBANDHU (II) AND KĀVYA IN THE +6

1556. Subandhu (II) lived some time in the +6, but his date is known so far only relatively to other writers, not positively in connection with his precise time and place. He himself makes reference to the works of earlier writers, including Kālidāsa (p. 153 of the text transcribed by Gray, to which it is convenient to make reference because the numbers appear also in his translation, which discusses various readings, but the new edition by J.M. Shukla gives a much older and more authentic text, being based on a +12 manuscript). He also mentions Vikramāditya (tenth introductory verse), deploring the bad times since that monarch has left the Earth. Then (p. 235) he mentions the philosopher Uddyotakara, whose date is the +6 but not fixed precisely (between Diṅnāga and Dharmakīrti [1459f. 1922]). The *Vāsavadattā* in turn is named by Bāṇa (early +7: *Harṣacarita*, introductory verse 12) in such a way as to make it almost certain that it is Subandhu's novel which is meant (Bāṇa here uses double meanings, Subandhu's speciality, saying that the work caused the pride of other writers to vanish, presumably because of its extraordinary command of language; it is improbable that the reference is to either of the ancient *Vāsavadattās* which we have noted in Chapter XIII above [652, 653-6]).

1557. The geography of Subandhu's novel, if it can be regarded as a clue to the country in which it was written, may be construed as referring to the region of Avanti or Mahārāṣṭra, though not very decisively. The city where its hero lived is not named, but from it he went to the Vindhya mountains. The heroine lived in Pāṭaliputra and elopes from there with the hero to the Vindhya, whence the scene moves southwards to the West coast and finally back to the hero's city. If anything positive can be adduced from this it is that the Gupta domains, their axis extending from Pāṭaliputra to Ujjayinī, were Subandhu's country. He might thus in his introductory verses be deploring the state of the Gupta Empire in the +6, contrasting it with the prosperous and magnanimous age of Vikramāditya [1299-1303] (Candra II [1272] or Skanda [1444]?).

1558. Gupta history in the +6 is confused. The detailed succession of rulers is not clear: some ruled in the East (Magadha, etc.), others in the West (Avanti, etc.), apparently different branches owing allegiance to one other. At the same time their feudatories, such as Yaśodharman Viṣṇuvardhana [1491] or later the Maukharis, were powerful and even dominant. Where 'Vikramāditya' had fought his own battles and thus commanded respect as well as winning fortune, the later Guptas allowed or desired their vassals to fight the Huns for them. The vassals were successful and by the end of the + 6 Hunnish rule had been completely eliminated from India, but Fortune had transferred her allegiance from the Guptas to the Maukharis of Kānyakubja on the upper Ganges. Already in the middle of the +6 Īśānavarman Maukhari, having achieved a great victory over the Huns, was ruling as emperor *parameśvara* of Northern India, or Āryāvarta, following in the wake of Yaśodharman whom he had perhaps put down. Kānyakubja became the cultural metropolis of India under a series of dynasties and retained its pre-eminence until the end of the +12. The Guptas tried from time to time to reassert their imperial claim, but their attempts always ended in failure. In such a period it would seem more likely that Subandhu's complaints, and his regrets for Vikramāditya, were intended as a reproach to the family of Candra II and Skanda than that they were designed as encouragement to rebellious vassals. As a conjecture, one might think of the time and realm of Mahāsena Gupta, in the latter part of the +6, as the place of Subandhu.

1559. Subandhu's *Vāsavadattā*, his only known work, is one of the rare surviving Sanskrit novels, but a representative of a genre evidently popular and plentiful in its day [436, 448]. It owes its preservation to the fact that its author has superimposed on his extremely slender story an extraordinary exercise in double meanings in the *gauḍiya* style. Scholars have delighted in this feat of enclosing two meanings in every sentence and in practically every word: each sentence reveals first part of the story, or of the long descriptive passages inserted in it, secondly a comment by way of simile or contrast or other figure. The work soon became an established classic, recognised by Bāṇa,

Vākpatirāja (verse 800), Rājaśekhara [1299], Maṅkha [1328] and other leading writers and critics. In contrast with this linguistic and scholastic interest, the value of the *Vāsavadattā* as a novel is small. From this point of view it may well represent popular romantic fiction of its period, fantastic, lacking in characterisation, amusing and ephemeral. Apart from its language and learning it would surely be in no way distinguished among the mass of such stories. Since the mass of medieval Indian novels has disappeared, the *Vāsavadattā* may be more welcome to some modern readers as typical of that kind of fiction than as a classic of luxuriant language.

1560. The heroine of this novel has nothing to do with the historical Vāsavadattā famous in many *kāvyas*. She is entirely fictitious. The story is that a Prince Kandarpaketu, of an unnamed country but which seems to be Avanti, because it lies near the Vindhyas in the opposite direction from Magadha (Mahārāṣṭra or specifically Vidarbha is equally possible), dreams of a beautiful girl whom he has never seen and loves her. Distraught, he wanders off into the Vindhya Mountains, accompanied by his friend Makaranda. At night there they overhear a noisy argument between two birds: a mynah suspects her lover, a parrot, of having been with another mynah, on account of his long absence. There appears to be some truth in the accusation, but the parrot explains his absence and diverts her anger by telling her the story of Vāsavadattā, which he has witnessed and which caused him to delay his return from Pāṭaliputra. Vāsavadattā had been averse to marriage and when her father, King Śṛṅgāraśekhara ruling in that city, had arranged a self-choice for her she had rejected all the suitors. Then she had dreamed of a handsome prince and loved him, discovering in her dream that his name was Kandarpaketu and that he was the son of King Cintāmaṇi. Vāsavadattā being tormented by love, her mynah bird, named Tamālikā, after consulting with her friends set out to discover Kandarpaketu's condition. The parrot has attended this Tamālikā on her journey and she is now resting under the tree where they are talking.

1561. Hearing this, Makaranda introduces Kandarpaketu to Tamālikā, thus discovered, and the bird presents to the hero a letter from Vāsavadattā. It consists simply of the following verse, which Kandarpaketu reads:

Even when seeing with her own eyes,
a girl in love is uncertain in her heart ;
But when she has enjoyed only a dream,
she does not strengthen her trust.

In this case the double meaning which we must expect in Subandhu is perhaps just the 'crooked speech' here implying an invitation or command to go at once to her. At the same time the formulation of the two statements reads remarkably like a quotation from a book on logic and epistemology: sensation is a fairly reliable means of knowledge whilst a dream is not usually regarded as evidence at all, being totally unreliable.

1562. Kandarpaketu proceeds to Pāṭaliputra with Makaranda and Tamālikā and finds Vāsavadattā in her palace. She is desperate because, after the fiasco of the self-choice, her father has determined to marry her at once to the son of the emperor of the wizards. The Prince takes Vāsavadattā on a horse named Manojava, 'Speed of Mind', escapes from the city, leaving Makaranda there to report what happens, and returns through the Vindhya forest. They rest and sleep in the forest, but when Kandarpaketu awakes at noon, after a long sleep due to his weariness from the journey, Vāsavadattā has vanished.

1563. He wanders about searching for her and emerges from the forest on its South side, continuing along the shore of the ocean where it is joined by the River Narmadā. He welcomes the sight of the ocean and decides to end his life by drowning himself in it. As he enters the water, however, he is addressed by a speech from space (this could be understood as the Goddess Sarasvatī), which tells him he will soon be reunited with his beloved and thus deters him from suicide. He wanders for some months along the shore and in the forest, living on wild fruits, etc., until the rainy season comes. Then just as autumn begins he sees a stone statue which appears to be a representation of his beloved. He touches it and at once Vāsavadattā, for it really was her, reverts to her own nature. He embraces her and asks what had happened.

1564. She explains that she had gone to look for some fruit or other food for him, thinking he would be hungry, but after going a short distance had found an army encamped. While she was wondering whether it was her father's army searching for her, or perhaps Kandarpaketu's, she was observed and the general ran to capture her. But it happened that another army, of mountain tribesmen *kirātas*, was nearby and the general of that too ran with his men as if hunting her. She was afraid to return to Kandarpaketu because he would be killed, being alone, if found, but meanwhile the two armies met and fought one another. In a terrible battle they destroyed one another. But the woods where Vāsavadattā had hoped to find fruit turned out to be the hermitage of a sage. He came out, enraged at its destruction in the fighting, and cursed her to turn to stone, as the cause of the mischief. Feeling compassion for the poor girl, however, he modified his curse to last only until she was touched by her husband.

1565. The couple then proceeded to Kandarpaketu's city, with Makaranda who had meanwhile arrived, and spent their time there in great happiness.

1566. *Vāsavadattā* thus incorporates a number of motifs of romantic fiction: meeting in a dream, talking birds, a bird carrying a letter, attempted suicide, a curse, a girl turned into a statue and released by the touch of her lover, a voice from space, a battle in which both armies are annihilated. The scenery is appropriate for the story, but at the same time Subandhu brings in a large proportion of the recognised subjects for description in *kāvya*. He seizes opportunities to describe, besides the hero and heroine, a king and his rule, a city and a palace, also night and dawn, the Moon and moonrise, sunset, the seasons spring, rains and autumn, a battle, a cemetery (through which the eloping couple escape from Pāṭaliputra), mountain and forest (the Vindhya in both these aspects), a river (the Revā or Narmadā, which embraces the Vindhya), the ocean and coastal mountain scenery. These long descriptions, which occupy most of the text, provide unlimited scope for Subandhu's imagination fertile in word play.

1567. In the description of the wild coast there is a compound which occurs also in Bāṇa's *Harṣacarita* (p. 272). At present it is not clear whether Bāṇa lifted it from Subandhu or whether it somehow got copied from one *kāvya* into the other by a scribe or a would-be embellisher. Vāmana takes it as his example of 'luxuriant' *utkalikāprāya* prose (I.3.25 [245], he probably took it from Bāṇa since like that text he has it in the locative case whereas Subandhu's has it in the instrumental); a single compound of up to twenty three members (there are variant readings, Shukla's text reduces the number to nineteen—p.45), which we may translate literally as it stands in the *Vāsavadattā* in order to exemplify the *gauḍiya* style:

> thunderboltpointsharpclawcollectionfuriousblowtornopenwantonelephantfrontallobeplacestartingbloodspurtanointedbeautifulmanemassterriblelionmultitude (shoreline of the great ocean) (266)

This means that Kandarpaketu went along the shoreline of the great ocean, where there were multitudes of lions, terrible looking because their manes were anointed with the blood which had spurted from the elephants they had killed with their very sharp claws.... Unless the commentators were weary at this point, it appears that in this and a few other passages no double meaning was intended by Subandhu (or this may indicate that these are interpolations). Thus also in the description of the sandbank from which Kandarpaketu intended to drown himself in the ocean we have such compounds as this: (sandbank) cooled by the embrace of the cold mass of spray splashed by the sport of a tribe of very fickle porpoises (277, translated from Shukla p. 47). However, with a certain amount of ingenuity one can find a second meaning in the first of these compounds: the word translated 'multitude' also means '*kadamba* flower', 'lion' may mean 'having stamens', 'terrible' may mean 'splendid', and so on, finally *kadambas* are supposed to flower when the thunderbolts are heard at the onset of the rains.... More ingenuity is needed with the second compound, unless we accept simply the implications of 'cooling' the hero's grief and of the possible murderous intent of the porpoises.

1568. It is this polysemia of most Sanskrit words which makes a double meaning *kāvya* more feasible in that language than in most others, moreover the writer can exploit alternative possibilities of division of a series of letters into words, since the vocabulary of Sanskrit has proliferated to such an extent that almost any syllable or pair of syllables may possess at least one meaning. By the +6 Sanskrit was an old language enriched with more than two thousand years of recorded literary creativity and almost as long a period of lexicographical activity. The meaning of a word in any language may change several times in such a period, through various processes of transfer, and in the case of Sanskrit these multiplied meanings were stored in dictionaries and kept in circulation by writers greedy for vocabulary. Further, the total analysis of Sanskrit into roots and suffixes by the grammarians showed how, since almost any suffix or suffixes might be added to any root or stem, or any stem might be compounded with any other, a practically limitless number of possible words might be derived.

1569. Subandhu's usual procedures may be illustrated by the following, where sometimes the double meaning can be presented in English, sometimes not:

> (King Śṛṅgāraśekhara's policy was so excellent that...) there was binding in chains (only) in the case of composition of phonemes, there was fancy and spurning [207] (only) with reference to figures of speech in literature, there was cutting and falling of the targets (only) of arrows, there was destruction everywhere (only) of zeroes, there was contraction of buds (only) in pools of lotuses...(126)

Here 'fancy' [213] also means 'carelessness', 'targets' means *lakhs* of money (which were not 'cut' and did not 'fall away'), 'buds' means 'treasuries'. The figure of speech which Subandhu is using here was later defined (Rudraṭa is the first critic known to notice it [260]) as 'exclusion' *parisaṃkhyā*, in that the implied 'only' in each case negates the second meaning: people were not ill-treated with binding, spurning, meanness, death.

1570. Subandhu's wit is displayed in a different way in the following:

> The stars shone...as if they were zero signs written in the sky which was like a hide black with the ink of darkness, with the Moon as a piece of chalk, by the Creator (Brahmā) reckoning the extent of the universe, because of the total emptiness (of the universe) of transmigration... (182)

Or in this:

> The rainy season played with the yellow and green baby frogs as if a game of 'politics' (i.e. chess, presumably, but this 'as if' clause is not found in Shukla's text and may be simply a commentator's gloss incorporated later), making them jump over the black paddy field enclosures (squares) with the lightning, like lacquer chessmen. (284)

In the description of the beginning of autumn we find a compound of nineteen words which does not very obviously have two meanings:

> When there was joy produced by the sweet sounds of the trains of *putrikā* birds going after the beans on the banks of the ponds dug up by the snouts of young boars greedy for the bulbs of *kaśeru* (grass) (287, Shukla. p. 49)

1571. A large number of figures of speech can be illustrated from *Vāsavadattā*, the total depending on the distinctions and sub-divisions among them recognised by different critics. The two passages just quoted (182 and 284) may be described as 'fancy' *utprekṣā*, of which there is an abundance in Subandhu, often mixed with other figures. There is a moderate degree of alliteration throughout Subandhu's writing. As a rule in his novel all other figures are mixed with the pervasive 'double meaning' *śleṣa* which Subandhu himself (introductory verse 13) claims to have incorporated into every syllable of his work. It may be worth noting in passing that *śleṣa* itself has two meanings: 1) a 'pun' as figure (for which Bhāmaha uses the synonym *śliṣṭa* [226], though Daṇḍin uses both forms and later writers generally prefer *śleṣa*); 2) 'union' as the quality of compactness (variously defined in the *Nāṭyaśāstra* and by Daṇḍin and others [189, 240, 243]). Evidently the figure and the quality are not mutually exclusive and Subandhu has excelled in both. Punning lends itself to combination with such other figures as exaggeration.

1572. It would seem that Subandhu set out by introducing ambiguity into the title of his novel and into his own name as author: there was a famous ancient author named Subandhu (see Chapter XIII above [653]) who composed a *kāvya* entitled *Vāsavadattā*, actually a drama on the historical Vāsavadattā and Udayana. Subandhu perhaps chose this name for his fictitious heroine for the sake of introducing confusion with the work of his namesake: henceforth 'Subandhu's *Vāsavadattā*' would have two meanings. The dream motif which is the basic idea in the novel was perhaps suggested by Bhāsa's Dream Vāsavadattā, as Gray suggested, but of course in Bhāsa's play the 'dream' is not really a dream but only imagined to have been one by Udayana. The story of Uṣā is a more likely model [1581].

1573. Subandhu includes a very large number of references to old legends of Tradition. Some of these appear to be to *kāvya* versions of the legends, though *kāvyas* and their authors are rarely actually named. Vālmīki is named (246) and Guṇāḍhya (147) with his *Bṛhatkathā* (also 110) and its hero and heroine, Naravāhanadatta and Madanamañcukā (153, Shukla p. 25). From characteristic details we may infer that in certain places Subandhu is thinking of the *Raghuvaṃśa* and *Abhijñānaśākuntala* of Kālidāsa, rather than of the traditional sources of those *kāvyas* (30, 153). Elsewhere he may have had Pravarasena's *Setubandha* (269) or the miniatures of Amaruka (51: the embarrassing parrot) in mind.

1574. Other references also are likely to be to lost *kāvyas* based on Tradition, though we cannot at present verify them. Thus in the context (153) which clearly refers to Kālidāsa's two works and to Guṇāḍhya's we have references to the story of Nala and Damayantī (152, cf. 275) [433], to that of Nalakūbara and Rambhā (154, cf. 105) [1580] and to that of Dharmarāja (Yama) and Dhūmorṇā. References to the story of Kuvalayāśva and Madālasā (237, 274) might have had in mind the Illusion Madālasā [1309] or some other *kāvya*, but are not specific (the story is from the *Mārkaṇḍeya Purāṇa*, but Gray was wrong in thinking that Subandhu's reference to Madālasā as 'daughter' of Aśvatara is inconsistent with the *Purāṇa*, for there she becomes his daughter when resurrected [1313]). Mention of Kṛṣṇa and Satyabhāmā (122) and of the Pārijāta tree in Indra's heaven (30) suggest Sarvasena's *Harivijaya* [1265]. In the former context we find Arjuna with Subhadrā (Kṛṣṇa's sister, whom he married), a theme on which a number of *kāvyas* are known to have been written. The reference, however, is no more specific than that (63) to Aniruddha (Kṛṣṇa's grandson) and Uṣā (daughter of the demon Bāṇa, Kṛṣṇa's enemy). Still other *kāvya* subjects mentioned are Nahuṣa (273) and the nymph Menakā (44) [357], though the two are not here brought together, Yayāti and his two wives (273) [1145], Saṃvaraṇa and the daughter (Tapatī) of Mitra (the Sun) (275), Kārtavīrya and Rāma of the Axe (276) [1144], Tārā and the Moon (273), Vinatā and her son Tārkṣya (Garuḍa, King of the Birds who rescued her from slavery) (34) and any number of others [1581]. The maids of Vāsavadattā (156-7) bear names which suggest the heroines of a series of novels, some known to us and the others possibly to be inferred from this context: Anaṅgalekhā (a novel having this title is quoted several times by late critics, see e.g. Krishnamachariar 444), Madanamañjarī (Sanskrit form of Madanamañcukā, heroine of the *Bṛhatkathā*), Vasantasenā (known to us only as the name of the heroines of three dramas discussed earlier, by Bodhāyana [1088], Bhāsa [1011] and Śūdraka [1185]), Taraṅgavatī (by Pādalipta, see Chapter XVI above [835]), Madanamālinī (unknown), Citralekhā (Bhoja mentions an *upakathā* of this name, *Śṛṅgāraprakāśa* II p. 469), Vilāsavatī (there was an old novel of this name, probably in Prakrit, by Halika, see Uddyotana, *Kuvalayamālā*, p. 3) [cf. 1375], Rāgalekhā (unknown), Kāntimatī (Daṇḍin in his *Avantisundarī* makes her a reincarnation of Śūdraka's wife Vinayavatī and a princess who marries Kāmapāla and becomes the mother of Arthapāla: it is possible that as elsewhere in his novel Daṇḍin here appropriates and summarises the matter of an earlier novel, constructing a sort of synthetic fictitious history) and Yūthikā (unknown).

1575. Perhaps from these hints we may get an idea of *kāvya* literature as Subandhu saw it, spanning the thousand years from Vālmīki and his namesake down to his own time. Beyond it lay the infinite world of Tradition, which Subandhu had studied with great care as a kind of lexicon of motifs. He was a scholar and a writer for scholars and there seems moreover to be no subject which he had not studied. His novel is a sort of archaeologists' site dating from the +6, from which historians and students of civilisation have drawn inexhaustible information about such things as the state of the sciences, of games such as chess, of the history of philosophy and of course of social life.

1576. Though it occupies only a small place in his work, a most significant part of it is the brief introduction in 13 verses [440]. These have been much appreciated and quoted by anthologists and others. Here Subandhu reveals a little of himself rather than of the rich treasury of his mind. As we have already noticed, he deplores the unhappy state of the world in which he lives. There seems to be here not just a general complaint that wicked men tend to become powerful and oppress the good, but a bitter protest arising from personal experience of ill treatment and an irrepressible feeling of indignation at these things. These verses awakened a warm response in many readers who knew too well their truth, for it was not only in the declining Gupta Empire that good men suffered and were treated with contempt by flourishing knaves and charlatans and snobs.

> Villains have extremely subtle understanding
> (but only) of very dark deeds:
> For the eyes of owls see their objects
> (only) in darkness. (7)

—The owl is an evil bird which preys on others at night. Subandhu seeks hope that in the end wickedness will prove ephemeral and goodness will endure or even be enhanced by it:

> The more a villain, dark with cunning (*bhūti*),
> outrages a good man,
> As a hand dark with ashes (*bhūti*) passes over a mirror,
> the more he makes him of spotless lustre. (8)

1577. To these and other bitter verses Subandhu prefixes his positive philosophy:

> The fortune of a good man who expands the qualities of
> others is increased:
> The light of the Moon which makes the white water-
> lilies blossom carries a doubled splendour. (5)

1578. From all periods of *kāvya* we find references to works not now available to us. Not all of these are lost for ever, since manuscripts of such works are continually being retrieved from old libraries, including small private collections, and put into circulation once more. Evidently it is harder to date a *kāvya* we cannot examine, merely from a few references and quotations, than one whose text we can study freely. Most of the critical works which bring missing literature to our notice being relatively late (+10 onwards), it is hard to infer from them whether a particular *kāvya* mentioned was composed as early as the +6 or earlier, unless there is other evidence.

1579. Subandhu can perhaps help us a little here by his allusions, but as they are of the briefest kind our suggestions must be very tentative. If he really refers to novels entitled *Vasantasenā*, *Madanamālinī*, *Rāgalekhā* or *Yūthikā*, as suggested above, we seem now to know nothing further of them. We hear of an *upakathā* entitled *Citralekhā*, apparently a supplement or sequel to a well known older work, as Bhoja seems to indicate. There is a character Citralekhā in the story of Uṣā and Aniruddha belonging to the more or less fictitious extension of the Kṛṣṇa saga. She was Uṣā's confidante who enabled her to find Aniruddha and who brought him to her. Thus a *Citralekhā* might be an invented story of that girl herself. We know at least the name of the author, Halika, of a *Vilāsavatī*, which Uddyotana ranges with the classic novels of old, mentioning it between *Taraṅgavatī* and the *Bṛhatkathā*. For the possible story of a *Kāntimatī* we may go to Daṇḍin, whose own *Avantisundarī* has something of the character of a gigantic *upakathā* to all previous history and fiction. His Kāntimatī was the daughter of a King of Kāśi, who secretly loved Kāmapāla, a dissolute and vagrant son of a minister of the neighbouring kingdom of Magadha. Kāmapāla barely escaped with his life after being detected near the palace in Vārāṇasī, but afterwards returned unobserved. He entered the King's apartments and threatened to take his life, forcing him to consent to the marriage and make Kāmapāla his minister. From an *Anaṅgalekhā* we can read quotations describing a king and elephants, which contain word play not unlike Subandhu's own, but in a simpler style (Jayaratha, early +13, commentary on Ruyyaka's *Alaṅkārasarvasva*, pp. 19 and 123).

1580. Where Subandhu refers to stories from Tradition, it is possible that some of the references are to dramas or epics based on the original stories, as suggested above in certain cases. From the later critics we hear of old plays on some of the stories he mentions. Thus Sāgaranandin (290) refers to a *Nalavijaya*, a *nāṭaka* on the story of Nala and Damayantī (in eight acts, Bahurūpamiśra on III. 38), to illustrate the point that dramatic convention excluded the showing of the hero losing his kingdom. This happens in the Nala story, when the king gambles away his realm and then spends a long period in misery and exile before regaining it, so in the play the disaster is reported by two minor characters in an introductory scene *praveśaka* to one of the acts [126]. The same critic (949ff.) quotes from a *Rambhānalakūbara* on the story of Nalakūbara and Rambhā. Nalakūbara was the son of Kubera, God of Wealth, who eventually won Rambhā, the most beautiful of the nymphs of heaven. The quotation is of an incident between them, in which Rambhā imagines through an unintentional pun that Nalakūbara has mentioned the name of another girl and becomes angry ('blunder in names' [141]).

1581. From Bhoja (see Raghavan, *Bhoja's Śṛṅgāraprakāśa*, p. 797) we learn of the existence of an epic on the story of Kuvalayāśva and Madālasā, the *Kuvalayāśvacarita*. For Bhoja this story exemplifies the strongest form of love, 'madder' *mañjiṣṭhā* passion, in a 'passionate' *rājasa* hero, who is noble and honourable, which nothing can remove. He notes that this epic contained as ornament of the whole work [1267] a good description of the heroine (*Śṛṅgāraprakāśa* II. p. 475). Bhoja also names (see Raghavan, pp. 796f.) an epic, *Subhadrāharaṇa*, 'The Abduction of Subhadrā', on the story of Arjuna and Subhadrā, the title of which indicates the main theme: Subhadrā, who loves Arjuna, is carried off by him despite the opposition of her brother Balarāma (Kṛṣṇa's elder brother). The work was ornamented with a description of the heroine (*Śṛṅgāraprakāśa* II p. 475). From the same source (p. 796) we hear of an epic on Aniruddha and Uṣā, *Uṣāharaṇa*, in which the stages in the action are developed by 'fate' *daiva* rather than as a result of the efforts of the hero. In the usual version of this legend, however, it is the efforts of the heroine after seeing Aniruddha in a dream (this may be the real source of Subandhu's idea of having his lovers meet first in their dreams), supported by her resourceful confidante, which produce the main action. There was also a *nāṭaka* having the same title *Uṣāharaṇa*, which Sāgaranandin quotes (2869).

On Nahuṣa and Menakā there was a *toṭaka* [343] in nine acts entitled *Menakānahuṣa* (Sāgaranandin 2774, Śāradātanaya p. 238). Since the action led to the union of a human hero with a goddess (nymph, as in the Valour Urvaśī), this drama was considered to be a *toṭaka* and not a *nāṭaka*; according to Sāgaranandin it satisfied Aśmakuṭṭa's requirement for a *toṭaka* that the jester should appear in every act, whereas the Valour Urvaśī did not (it has a jester, but he does not appear in every act). Bhoja knew a play on Yayāti and Śarmiṣṭhā (Raghavan pp. 894f. and 902), possibly the *Śarmiṣṭhāpariṇaya*, 'Marriage of Śarmiṣṭhā', from which Sāgaranandin (1216) quotes the rhetorical device (*pravartaka* or *pravṛttaka*) leading from the prologue in to the play [139]. The producer asks an actress to sing about the spring, but she refuses because it would bring suffering to separated lovers and wants to sing of another season. This indicates the condition of a character about to enter (for the legend of Yayāti cf. Chapter XIX above [1145]).

1582. Whilst we are on the subject of missing *kāvyas* of unknown date but perhaps to be related to the period we have now reached, it is desirable to mention some other plays belonging to that category, beginning with some on the main stories of the *Mahābhārata* and *Rāmāyaṇa*.

1583. On the *Mahābhārata* there was a play entitled *Pāṇḍavānanda*, 'Joy of the Pāṇḍavas', the Prologue of which referred to the situation in the Epic where the Pāṇḍavas were living incognito in the city of King Virāṭa of Matsya, as in Bhāsa's Five Nights (Dhanika p. 65, Abhinavagupta II p. 454, Śāradātanaya p. 230, Rāmacandra and Guṇacandra p. 132). The verse quoted is a dialogue between the producer and an actor constituting the rhetorical device *udghātyaka* for leading in to the play [139]:

> What is the ornament of the strong ? Forbearance. What is humiliation ?.That which is produced by one's kinsmen.
> What is unhappiness ? Protection by others. Who is praiseworthy in the world ? He to whom others resort.
> What is death ? Vice. Who abandon grief ? Those who conquer their enemies.

Who discovered this ? The Pāṇḍavas remaining concealed in Virāṭa's city.

Perhaps this play, introduced by such a striking verse, presented the same matter as Bhāsa's Five Nights, but it may have continued to the Pāṇḍava's final triumph. A conjectural author for it would be Viśākhadatta [1604].

1584. Two plays on the Rāma story may be mentioned here as perhaps representing trends in the +5 and +6. The *Rāghavābhyudaya*, 'Exaltation of the Rāghava (i.e. Rāma)', is extensively referred to by Sāgaranandin, who relates it particularly to Mātṛgupta's theories, just as in the case of the Illusion Madālasā (here again it is remotely possible that we have a play by Mātṛgupta himself) [166, 1308, but cf. 1325]. Sāgaranandin (102ff.) quotes Mātṛgupta on the five stages as illustrated in the story of the slaying of Rāvaṇa, then adds that these are very clear in the Exaltation of the Rāghava. In Mātṛgupta's description here the 'commencement' contains the destruction of the demons Khara, etc. (Khara was the half-brother of Rāvaṇa and his governor in South India; after the incident with Rāvaṇa's sister Śūrpaṇakhā, Khara marched against Rāma with an army of demons, Rāma with his skill in archery slaughtered them and killed Khara), in other words the first embroilment of Rāma with Rāvaṇa's demons. The 'undertaking' is where Śūrpaṇakhā organises the abduction of Sītā by Rāvaṇa in revenge. In the 'possibility of attainment' Rāma secures the friendship of Sugrīva. The 'certainty of attainment of the fruit' comes with the destruction of Kumbhakarṇa and other demons in the battles on Laṅkā. The final 'attaining of the fruit' is the slaying of Rāvaṇa, which brings Rāma success in virtue, wealth and pleasure (the three ends).

1585. It would appear that this play followed the original *Rāmāyaṇa* fairly closely. It also followed the original in keeping Kaikeyī in mind as the ultimate cause of all Rāma's troubles: Sāgaranandin says (174f.) that she is mentioned in every act. At the same time there are innovations which Sāgaranandin notes. As an 'other conjunction' in the action (contrary to the *Nāṭyaśāstra* [141, cf. 126]) he quotes (1042ff.) the voice of the Wind God heard by Lakṣmaṇa from space (or off stage), telling him the curse (we do not know what curse) will last until the slaying of Rāvaṇa. Then Rāvaṇa, foreseeing defeat, makes a false peace offer to outwit Rāma (Sāgaranandin 1300ff., 1430ff.). This constitutes the 'pause' and specifically 'beguiling' *vilobhana* [133]. He offers to give up Sītā, but it is really a demoness impersonating her whom he offers. It seems (conjecture by Raghavan) that Rāvaṇa on that occasion himself impersonated Indra as mediator. Rāma is in a dilemma: he cannot accept peace now because he has promised to make Vibhīṣaṇa king of Laṅkā in Rāvaṇa's place. Finally Lakṣmaṇa sees through the deception, which Sāgaranandin (1283 ff.) notes as 'revolution' *parivartaka*, a 'limb' of the 'expressive' *sāttvatī* mode of acting, Rāvaṇa's fury being provoked as he throws off his disguise and again threatens force [181]. The 'expressive' mode is also noted by Sāgaranandin (1250ff.) in the scene where Jaṭāyus attacks Rāvaṇa as he abducts Sītā, as being used for the furious aesthetic experience. One gets the impression from these and other quotations that this whole play was composed in the expressive mode (cf. the end of Chapter III above).

1586. The *Jānakīrāghava*, or play on the Rāghava with Jānakī (Sītā) especially prominent, contrasts with the Exaltation of the Rāghava in departing considerably from the *Rāmāyaṇa* original. This was another of Sāgaranandin's favourites and he finds in it many illustrations of the methods of construction of a plot. There seems to be no clue as to its authorship, but it might be supposed to have been composed as a model drama. As the title suggests, the action centres round the character of Sītā. Amongst other details, Sāgaranandin notes (2515) that this play depicts in the character of Sītā nine of the ten stages of love recognised in the *Nāṭyaśāstra* (the last, dying, cannot be represented in a drama) [142]. By altering the story, the author of the *Jānakīrāghava* produces a unity of action from the events of Sītā's marriage with Rāma down through the exile to the final triumph and her rescue. The alteration consists in bringing Rāvaṇa into the story at the beginning as a rival suitor seeking Sītā's hand at her self-choice. An opening benedictory verse (Sāgaranandin 148ff.) already foreshadows (hence it is called a *chāyā*) the 'seed' of the action by praising Viṣṇu for having (in his Boar incarnation) rescued the Earth when she had been carried off to the bottom of the ocean by a demon. The first 'limb' of the opening conjunction is the 'hint' [146]:

This story of Rāma, the comet of doom to the family of
Rāvaṇa,
is an ocean of ambrosia which spreads delight;
The poet's words may fill the jewelled receptacles of the
connoisseurs' ears
or they may not — be done with worrying !

The last word here may also mean 'planet' — a planet is usually a bringer of evil but here it is not feared because the powerful comet is present. So the story is bound to be a success, whatever the merits of this particular dramatist. Probably these are optimistic words spoken by the producer in the prologue, after the announcement of the play.

1587. One of the varieties of introductory scene or scene 'hinting at the matter' is technically known as *cūlikā* (literally 'crest'): it means a voice from behind the curtain (which in the Indian theatre is held across the stage) [126]. In Act I of the *Jānakīrāghava*, says Sāgaranandin (432ff.), a speech of Rāvaṇa is heard as a *cūlikā* by Sītā (on stage, or entering): he vows that he, who has defeated the King of the Gods, will carry Sītā off no matter who wins the contest at the self-choice. Evidently the suitors are assembled, Rāvaṇa and Rāma among them, and Rāvaṇa here challenges them all. Overhearing this, Sītā calls upon Rāma, whom she already loves, to save her (Sāgaranandin 90ff.). Her companion Priyaṃvadā reassures her that if the demon did this Rāma would kill Rāvaṇa and bring her back after crossing the wilderness and the ocean, thus anticipating all the action and indicating in the opening the objective which will be attained at the conclusion. [3742]

1588. On the topic of 'continuity' [124], Sāgaranandin (177ff.) quotes one of the final verses of the play, where Rāma says that he has observed his father's command to go into exile for the period wished by Kekayī (Kaikeyī), moreover the enemy are slain and Sītā rescued, therefore what else could he wish for from Indra? Evidently this is from the 'consummation of the *kāvya*' *kāvyasaṃhāra* limb at the end of the conclusion [150]. The critic's point presumably is that these intertwined themes, Rāvaṇa's enmity and the exile which enabled him to abduct Sītā, provide the continuity through the whole action.

1589. It is not clear exactly how Rāvaṇa was foiled at the self-choice, but in Act II, where Sāgaranandin finds various limbs of the re-opening [147] (651ff., 684ff., 692ff., 700ff.), Rāma and Sītā are happily united. Here there is 'play' *vilāsa* between them (Rāma's delight in her), then 'tracing' *parisarpa* when Sītā was upset by not seeing Rāma for a time and showed her annoyance, but her eyes showed her love. In this act there is the incident of the arrival of Rāma of the Axe, an enemy of Rāma. On hearing of it Sītā is alarmed, which constitutes the 'check' (*nirodha*, or in the Sāgaranandin text 'opposition', *virodha*, which word is actually used by Sītā here). Perhaps the illustration of the next limb is from the same play, though this is not made clear, since it is Daśaratha's rebuke to Rāma of the Axe for wanting to fight the young Rāma: this is 'apology' *paryupāsana* for the purpose of conciliating an angry person. In any case a 'flowery speech' *puṣpa* follows, when Sītā is told that Rāma has defeated Rāma of the Axe.

1590. But in the same act Sāgaranandin (642ff.) points out the 'sprouting' *udghāṭana* of the 'seed', required in this conjunction by the theory [131]. Rāma in a wooded garden with Sītā shows her a flowering Aśoka tree which he thinks perhaps will captivate her with its blossomy branches; but his words have a double meaning: perhaps he who holds power in Laṅkā (*laṅkā* also means 'branch'), i.e. Rāvaṇa, will capture her! This double meaning device is further identified by Sāgaranandin (1035ff.) as an example of the fourth variety of 'injection of subsidiary matter' *patākāsthānaka* [143]. Rāma's chance words unexpectedly disturb the couple's happiness with an omen of the impending danger. Near the end of the act and of the re-opening we find a 'proposal' *upanyāsa*: Śatānanda, chaplain of Janaka (Sītā's father), says he is delighted at Daśaratha's speech. Perhaps this is at the leave taking of the two fathers (as Raghavan suggests), but the exact significance of the felicitations about ruling the kingdom and the weakness of enemies is not made clear.

1591. After this the action moves very quickly, for in Act III we find Rāma already in the forest, Sītā already abducted and the friendship with Sugrīva being begun. Presumably most of the intervening events (exile, etc.) were reported in an introductory scene. Sugrīva discusses Rāvaṇa's actions with Hanumant, who makes a 'declaration of truth' *mārga* concerning the exploits of Rāma, a most desirable person for an ally (Sāgaranandin 730ff.) [148]. In this act we have the embryo and the 'germination' of the seed, namely Rāvaṇa's action in abducting Sītā, as mentioned by Sugrīva (Sāgaranandin 713ff.) [132]. Further on Sāgaranandin (746ff.) finds the 'limb' called 'inference' *anumāna*, where Rāma infers that Sugrīva is the son of the Sun and invulnerable (see Raghavan p. 68).

1592. From this point on the division into acts is not clear. For the obstacle an act entitled 'Illusion Lakṣmaṇa' is referred to, where Rāvaṇa is prominent [133, 149]. First there is 'reproach' *apavāda*, of Rāvaṇa for his faults now leading to disaster (Sāgaranandin 801ff.). In the same act there is an instance of a 'characteristic' peculiar to Sāgaranandin's theory (1701ff.), which he calls 'contraction' (*saṃkṣepa*, if the reading is not corrupt; one of the *Nāṭyaśāstra* lists has 'agitation', *kṣobha*, here), where a character describes the troubles of another whilst thereby indicating his own similar troubles. Rāvaṇa describes Sītā's sorrows and complains of his own unrequited love for her, comparing the two states but criticising her lack of compassion for him. The nature of the 'illusion' in this act is not explained; it was probably some trickery by Rāvaṇa in his attempts to seduce Sītā, such as a report of Rāma's death.

1593. The obstacle conjunction continued into Act VI, where Sāgaranandin notes (832ff.) Rāma's 'fatigue' *kheda* in the series of battles against the demons, whilst he thinks of Sītā waiting anxiously for news. Later in that act there is 'anticipation' *prarocanā*, when Lakṣmaṇa reassures Rāma because Kumbhakarṇa, Indrajit and other demons have been killed and only Rāvaṇa, who moreover is old, remains (Sāgaranandin 850ff.). Sāgaranandin further explains (84ff.) that this verse indicates the stage of 'certainty of attainment of the fruit' [127].

1594. Act VII was probably the last in this play, consisting of the conclusion with the 'attaining of the fruit' [134, 150]. Sāgaranandin (864ff.) points out the limb 'knotting' *grathana* as in the final act of the *Jānakīrāghava* and in the usual order of limbs (though this could be departed from) this comes near the beginning of the conclusion, whilst the 'anticipation' comes at the end of the obstacle or pause conjunction. The 'knotting' here is a reference by Lakṣmaṇa, speaking to Rāma, to several objectives attained: the slaying of the demons, including Rāvaṇa, enemy of Indra (we have seen already that Indra appears at the conclusion of this play), the obstacles to the asceticism of the sages (who had been disturbed in their hermitages by the demons) have been removed, fortune has been bestowed by you on Vibhīṣaṇa. Later on Vibhīṣaṇa reports to Rāma that Sītā has survived the fire ordeal. Sāgaranandin (886ff.) gives this incident as an example of a 'limb' not found in the standard list, called 'enquiry' *anuyoga*: Rāma, full of joy, asks Vibhīṣaṇa to reassure him that she has really not been burned. The last limb of the conclusion has been referred to above: Sītā is rescued.

1595. This play thus illustrates dramatic construction not simply in broad outline but in many minor details. We have no indication of the details of the sub-plot, which in this story is the matter concerning Sugrīva in his rivalry with his brother, success in which consolidates the forces of Rāma and Sugrīva for the war against Rāvaṇa [122]. We may infer that this was worked out in Act IV, between the embryo and obstacle conjunctions in the main action. The 'Illusion Lakṣmaṇa' Act would thus be Act V. Apart from its evident technical perfection, the *Jānakīrāghava* appears a masterpiece for the interest of its incidents, presentation of the story with all its implications and originality of organisation and of numerous details, all contributing most effectively to the main plot. Its language is very simple, which would contribute to its success in the theatre but not with the pandits.

1596. There are probably other lost plays, among the many mentioned by the later critics, which belong in this period, but it is a matter almost entirely of speculation which they are, until further evidence comes to light. The earlier critical works available have nothing like the copious illustrations from the repertory which we find in writings from about the +10 onwards. If we had the means of spreading this whole repertory over its proper dates we would presumably find plays of most types falling in the period from the +3 to the +6 (cf. the end of Chapter XIX for the earlier period). There would seem to have been very few 'cooperations' and 'fights', which had become obsolete even earlier, whilst 'fictions', 'comedies', 'satirical monologues', 'heroic plays' and no doubt 'street plays' (which hardly interested the critics) were in regular production alongside the *nāṭakas*. A small but definite place seems to have been retained for 'rapes' (as short plays on abduction themes represented also among the *nāṭakas*) and 'pathetic plays'. As for the minor types of theatrical performance which became increasingly popular during this period, but which generally were ephemeral, most of what can be said about their history has been noted in Chapter V above. Besides 'musical plays' *toṭakas* and 'light plays' (*nāṭikā*, 'little play'), some of which we have noticed in the classical repertory, there were the ancient *lāsya* dances, the more recent 'ballets' *rāsakas*, many other types of dance and various minor dramas referred to in early sources.

1597. Something should be said about comedies *prahasanas* in this period, since they are so poorly represented in the extant literature. Comedies tend to be topical and therefore ephemeral, thus they are fairly plentiful only from recent centuries. The critics and scholars have practically no time for them, as of small 'literary' value, but for the sake of completeness in their handbooks on drama give brief notices of them. Thus we know at least the titles of a few famous old comedies.

1598. Whereas the Master-Mistress (see Chapter XIX above [1085]) is a 'mixed' comedy according to Sāgaranandin (2902), because it has a geisha in it, other comedies were 'pure' in having only ascetics, sages and priests of humorous character, an example being the *Śaśivilāsa*, 'Śaśin's Play' (Śaśin or 'Moon' is probably the name of the chief character, likely to be a bogus ascetic). Bahurūpamiśra names a Śaśikalā as 'pure' (on Dhanañjaya III.54f.) and says that *Śaśikalā* is the heroine (on II.66), presumably therefore she is a 'respectable', or rather 'family', heroine [1213]: thus he adds a point from the theory of fictions to that of comedies. Some authorities recognise as a third kind the 'transformed' (*vikṛta* or *vaikṛta*) comedy, in which eunuchs, ascetics, etc., appear in the guise of lovers, suitably attired and speaking (Dhanañjaya p. 74, Śāradātanaya p. 247, Śiṅgabhūpāla p. 297). Śāradātanaya (p. 247) notes as example of this a *Kalikeli*, 'Play of Kali' (presumably the Kali Yuga, the present age of wickedness). The same writer notes as 'mixed' a *Sairandhrikā*, presumably the name of the heroine: it is a name suitable for a maidservant. Also mixed was the *Bṛhatsubhadraka*, 'Great Subhadraka'. According to Śiṅgabhūpāla (Āndhra edition, see Veṭūri's edition of Bodhāyana's *Bhagavadajjukīya*, p. iii), giving this play as an example, a 'mixed' comedy has a 'rogue' *dhūrta* (perhaps Subhadraka himself?) and is also 'mixed' with all the limbs of the street play [325-6], in other words various kinds of equivocation and the like.

1599. A very famous ancient comedy was the *Vikaṭanitambā*, 'Broad Buttocks' — the name of the heroine. It is referred to or quoted in some of the leading critical works (Namisādhu on Rudraṭa p. 73, Rājaśekhara quoted by Bhoja (Raghavan p. 833 and Jalhaṇa (p. 47), Dhanika p. 90) and anthologies (Vidyākara, verses 572, 659, also Śārṅgadhara and Vallabhadeva). Gradually it seems to have been supposed that the heroine's name was also the name of the authoress of the comedy, thus Raghavan enrols her among the honoured poetesses of India. Her reputation was perhaps artificially enhanced by attributing to her verses which seem to belong to Amaruka (e.g. those quotes by Vidyākara [1455, 1459]).

1600. Among the quotations we find the following :

He says 'beans' about time, 'months' about vegetables,
and what is near is eating Śakas;
In 'camel' (*uṣṭra*) he loses *r* or *ṣ*
—to him Broad Buttocks was given !

This is her friend making fun of her husband's inability to pronounce Sanskrit (Namisādhu p. 73).

1601. From Bhoja we learn that Broad Buttocks was a remarried widow, for whom another character expresses his devotion as follows:

Those who are delighted by Broad Buttock's
composition of speeches,
Do they not blame the sweet but innocent
talk of their own beloveds ?

It was this verse which seems to have suggested that Broad Buttocks was a real writer instead of a learned lady with an ignorant husband in a comedy: it is quoted by Jalhaṇa as from Rājaśekhara as if the latter was praising her, but it is more likely that Rājaśekhara himself was quoting the play. Since Bhoja quotes the same verse as illustrating a particular situation in love (in his Chapter XXII, p. 33 of Yadugiriyati's ed.), it could hardly be the critic's admiration of another writer.

1602. M.R. Kavi states that he is quoting from the comedy *Vikaṭanitambā* (*Abhinavabhārati* II p. 362), in which the character Vikaṭanitambā says :

> O bee (or 'libertine'), among other jasmine creepers
> which can endure being crushed,
> you should now divert your unsteady mind !
> Why, at the wrong time, do you ill treat the young bud
> in the new garland,
> Whose face is innocent and which has no pollen ?

According to him the lady here intends herself as one of the 'jasmine creepers' ready to be loved. The verse illustrates the *Nāṭyaśāstra's* 'characteristic' 'wish' *manoratha*, in which the wish is expressed by speaking about something else [186]. We do not know Kavi's source for this. Dhanika quotes the same verse (with variants, p. 90) to illustrate 'rashness' as a transient emotion [56]. Vallabhadeva (735) attaches the name 'Vikaṭanitambā' to it.

CHAPTER XXIX

VIŚĀKHADATTA

1603. As has been noted at the beginning of Chapter XXVIII above, in the +6 the Gupta Empire declined. Various feudatories, such as the Maitraka governors or dukes of Saurāṣṭra and the Maukharis of Pañcāla, became independent during the Hunnish Wars. Īśānavarman Maukhari made good a claim to the empire of Āryāvarta, ruling from his capital at Kānyakubja. His grandson Avantivarman in the last quarter of the +6 encountered what seems to have been the final Hunnish invasion, the enemy advancing from their kingdom long established in Gandhāra. With the support of his neighbour and ally, or probably feudatory, Prabhākaravardhana Pauṣyabhūta of Sthāṇvīśvara on the banks of the River Sarasvatī in the Kuru country, he routed the Huns *c.* +582 and seems to have ended their rule in India. Apparently as a result of this victory the Kuṣāṇas or Ṣāhis, whose ruling family had survived in Kāpiśa presumably as vassals of the Huns, became independent again and re-established their rule over Gandhāra, very likely as feudatories of the Maukharis. It may be noted that the primary cultural effect of this was a powerful revival of Buddhism in Gandhāra and neighbouring countries, including Central Asia. The freeing of the Earth from barbarian (*mleccha*, presumably meaning Hūṇa) rule by Avantivarman is referred to by Viśākhadatta, probably a dramatist at his court, in the final benediction of the *Mudrārākṣasa*.

1604. Viśākhadatta (or Viśākhadeva) seems to have belonged to an aristocratic family, since in the prologue to the same play he names his grandfather as the 'vassal' (*sāmanta*, i.e. a feudal baron) Vaṭeśvaradatta and his father as the prince (*mahārāja*, literally 'king', but this title, like most others, seems to have been gradually debased during the medieval period: there is however a variant 'vassal of the king') Bhāskaradatta (variant reading Pṛthu). Soḍḍhala (+11, *Udayasundarī* p. 150) calls 'Viśākhadeva' himself a 'vassal' *sāmanta*: he imagines a session of a literary 'circle' in the roof pavilion of Sarasvatī's palace, with Bāṇa (his favourite author [484 and 489]) presiding and attended by the great *kavis*, Kālidāsa and others, by the kings Vikramāditya [1299ff.], Harṣa (Bāṇa's patron), Muñja and Bhoja and by the vassals Vākpatirāja [413], Māurāja [283 and 290], Viśākhadeva and others. Nothing further seems to be recorded of Viśākhadatta. He is known to have written at least four plays, on Cāṇakya (and Candragupta Maurya), Candra (II) Gupta, Rāma and Udayana, of which only the first is now available intact though there are quotations from and references to the others [cf. also 1583].

1605. There is very little information available about Viśākhadatta's Rāma play, the *Rāghavānanda*, 'Joy of the Rāghava'. It is clear that it deals with the main story, ending with the slaying of Rāvaṇa. Only three verses from it seem to be identified, for example one is given by Bahurūpamiśra (on *Daśarūpaka* I. 18 and 22) for the 'intervention' *prakarī* [122] of Jaṭāyus [1357]. Two others are given by Bhoja (*Śṛṅgāraprakāśa* Vol. II p. 533f. and 536) when illustrating two 'characteristics' of *kāvya*.

1606. The second of these is attributed to Viśākhadatta by Śrīdharadāsa (*Saduktikarṇāmṛta* verse 230), thus we can assign the play to its author. Abhinavagupta, Sāgaranandin, Kuntaka and Mammaṭa (IV.43) all quote this same famous verse:

> That is Rāma, who has attained the utmost renown in
> this world with his qualities of valour;
> but if the King does not know him from the reversal
> of our fortune:
> The wind in the guise of a panegyrist sings his honours
> with seven notes
> coming out from the holes he shot in a line of broad
> *sāla* trees with a single arrow.

According to Bhoja (and Māṇikyacandra on Mammaṭa p. 91) this verse is spoken to Rāvaṇa by Kumbhakarṇa, pointing out Rāma (presumably when the war begins to go against them). It illustrates the characteristic 'implication' (so also Sāgaranandin) [187]. The holes in the *sāla* trees (variant reading 'palm trees') were made by Rāma in the contest at Sītā's self-choice. Abhinavagupta (II pp. 310f.) says instead that it illustrates the characteristic 'narration' *ākhyāna*. The *Candrikā* on Mammaṭa wrongly says the verse is spoken by Vibhīṣaṇa. Kuntaka finds lexical figurativeness in the simple use of the word 'Rāma' here, suggesting transcendent heroism (I.43 and II.30) [274].

1607. The other verse illustrates the characteristic 'ambiguity' *akṣarasaṃghāta* [186] according to Abhinavagupta (II pp. 300f.), but 'description' [187] merely according to Bhoja:

> Having placed his head in the lap of the lord of the army of monkeys (Sugrīva) and put his foot in that of the killer of Akṣa (Hanumant),
> playfully, with the rest of his body on the skin of the golden deer (Mārīca's disguise);
> His younger brother (Lakṣmaṇa) having carefully fixed a sharp arrow ready to destroy the family of demons;
> he (Rāma) remains listening to your younger brother's speech, watching from the corner of his eye.

Rāma gives the appearance of being at ease after giving the monkey empire to Sugrīva, but is really on the alert to destroy the enemy. Śobhākaramitra (p. 184) considers the verse to illustrate naturalistic description [197] in his special sense of subtle description provided by the insight of a great author.

1608. Viśākhadatta's Udayana play, the *Abhisārikāvañcitaka*, 'Deceived by the Lady who Goes to Meet', deals with a part of the legend which we have not met in any earlier drama. The lady of the title is Padmāvatī, some years after her marriage to Udayana (i.e. after the events of the Dream Vāsavadattā, for example). It appears that a certain amount of rivalry has developed between Padmāvatī and Vāsavadattā and that Udayana has become somewhat estranged from Padmāvatī. Then it is reported that Udayana's son (by Vāsavadattā?—this is not clear from our scanty sources) has been murdered. Padmāvatī is suspected of destroying her rival's baby. In this desperate situation she goes into hiding in the forest and lives as a Śabara woman (cf. Nandayantī in the *Puṣpadūṣitaka*, end of Chapter XXIII above [1368], though under entirely different circumstances). In this disguise as a woman of the Vindhya tribes [1345], Padmāvatī succeeds in meeting Udayana again (probably when he is engaged in his favourite sport of elephant hunting). He falls in love with this very beautiful but unknown woman...and eventually learns the truth: her innocence is established and all ends happily. This broad outline of the plot we gather from Abhinavagupta (III p. 197) and Bhoja (*Śṛṅgāraprakāśa* Vol. II p. 501). Such a story does not seem to be known from any other extant source on the Udayana legend, but there is no way of knowing whether Viśākhadatta invented it or most of it. According to Abhinavagupta Udayana's passion for Padmāvatī is lost and then restored. Bhoja quotes from the early part of the play to illustrate 'anger' (Udayana's mistaken anger with Padmāvatī) as an 'other conjunction' [141]. Here the King reviles her imagined treachery with bitter words.

1609. From the *Devīcandragupta*, 'Candra Gupta and the Queen', some quite extensive passages are quoted by Abhinavagupta, Bhoja and Rāmacandra and Guṇacandra, whilst there are further brief references in other sources. Raghavan has collected most of the quotations in his *Bhoja's Śṛṅgāraprakāśa* (858ff.). The play is based on a decisive historical episode from the career of Candra II Gupta, 'Vikramāditya' or 'Sāhasāṅka' (cf. Chapter XXII above). That it really is historical, and not a fiction invented by the dramatist, is attested for instance by Rājaśekhara (*Kāvyamīmāṃsā* 46f., see Raghavan p. 869). Bāṇa also confirms the historicity of the story (*Harṣacarita* p. 303). The idea that the play is a 'fiction' *prakaraṇa*, and not a *nāṭaka* ('history'), appears to be a misconception based on reading too much into the fact that Abhinavagupta (II p. 433) and Rāmacandra and Guṇacandra (p. 104) quote from this play when discussing, under the topic of the *prakaraṇa*, the fact that a geisha's actions may be described without the decorum observed in the case of family women. There happens to be a geisha in this play, but that does not make it a *prakaraṇa* unless we change the usual definitions completely. It may be noted further that after this passage Rāmacandra and Guṇacandra go on to define seven varieties of *prakaraṇa*, according as the hero or the objective or the story are invented, with the possible combinations of these, but such a classification seems foreign to the *Nāṭyaśāstra* tradition (for example the first variety will be an imaginary hero in an uninvented story attaining an uninvented objective, in the second only the objective is invented, the hero and the story being in effect well-known) [337-8]. Such definitions would require us to reclassify the whole repertory. If we follow the *Nāṭyaśāstra*, which contrasts a play with a well-known story, as a *nāṭaka*, with one with an invented story, as a *prakaraṇa*, then Candra Gupta and the Queen must be a *nāṭaka*. Unfortunately our knowledge of Gupta history does not suffice for a detailed comparison of Viśākhadatta's play with his sources.

1610. Candra Gupta and the Queen appears to have opened in the Gupta camp. Prince Candra's brother, Rāma, is king and has been defeated by the Śaka ruler (who is not named); Rāma's camp is now closely besieged, but his enemy has offered peace if he will surrender his queen, Dhruvadevī. The ministers have pressed Rāma to accept these terms and he has reluctantly agreed. Candra in Act I is desperately trying to think of some alternative to this dishonour, such as raising a vampire (*vetāla*, a kind of demon), presumably to work some magic against the enemy. As he discusses the problem with Ātreya, the jester, a maid enters carrying a robe. It is one of the Queen's, which she is sending to Mādhavasenā, a geisha friend of the Prince's and also her own friend. Probably this is a parting gift before she sets out for the Śaka camp. The maid asks the Prince where the geisha is, explaining her errand, then goes on her way to find her. This incident, which Bhoja quotes as an example of the first variety of 'injection of subsidiary matter' *patākāsthānaka* [143], gives Candra the idea of disguising himself as the Queen, entering the enemy camp and killing the Śaka. He at once goes behind the curtain (off stage) and disguises himself as a woman. (*Śṛṅgāraprakāśa* Vol. II p. 503, with Raghavan's restorations.) Later, as Candra is about to set out for the Śaka camp, Ātreya expresses surprise at his recklessness going alone among the enemy ministers. Candra's heroic reply is an example of 'strength' as an 'other conjunction' (*Śṛṅgāraprakāśa* Vol. II p. 501) [141]:

> The deer are afraid of even a single lion, tossing his
> mane,
> as he leaves the entrance to his mountain cave,
> baring his teeth ready,
> When they see elephants amazed, though of good
> families and strong in many years and valour:

many run away just from the smell of a lion — what
are numbers to a hero?

1611. From Act II we have a scene between the brothers just before Candra leaves. Dhruvadevī sees her husband in the distance, apparently with another woman, and is angry with him (this is the limb 'check' in the re-opening according to the *Nāṭyadarpaṇa*, 62f.) [147]. The King expresses affectionate words: he would rather lose the Queen than his brother. A longer quotation from this scene is given (*Nāṭyadarpaṇa* 124ff.) to show the technique of the *trigata* limb of the street play [326]. We hear the King speaking to Candra, with the Queen at a distance, thinking Candra is another woman, misunderstanding his words and commenting on each phrase. Apparently this provocation of the Queen forebodes evil for Rāma, but our fragments do not allow us to know the exact sequel.

1612. In the introductory scene to Act III it is reported that Candra has succeeded in killing the Śaka (example of 'boldness' *sāhasa* as an 'other conjunction' according to Bhoja, *Śṛṅgāraprakāśa* Vol. II p. 500; probably from this deed Candra got the epithet *sāhasāṅka*, 'having the mark of boldness'). Candra returns and probably either in this act or the next belongs a quotation which shows him observing Dhruvadevī's feelings (in the *Nāṭyadarpaṇa* this is identified as 'progress', a limb of the embryo, p. 76) [148]. Now he is certain about her: she no longer loves the King but is full of shame, anger, despair, fear and discontent.

1613. From Act IV we have an intimate scene between Candra and Mādhavasenā: he asks her to bind him, with her arms, necklace and girdle, though his heart is already bound by her qualities (this is 'wish', also a limb of the embryo, *Nāṭyadarpaṇa* 74f). Perhaps she has warned him that he is literally in danger of being bound, through some plot against him or the suspicions of his brother.

1614. In the Fifth Act, which is the last one from which we seem to have any quotations, Candra is definitely in danger and protects himself by feigning madness (artifice or illusion *māyā* as an 'other conjunction' — *Śṛṅgāraprakāśa* Vol. II p. 501). From this act Rāmacandra and Guṇacandra (*Nāṭyadarpaṇa* 172f.) quote the 'theme' (*dhruvā*, see the beginning of Chapter V above

[306]) songs for Candra's entrance and exit, as he is seen in his feigned madness on his way to the court (of Rāma Gupta). He is intent on concealing the development of his feeling of love (for whom?) and also slightly afraid of his enemy (which?). The two songs are in Prakrit, in the *āryā* metre. The first describes the moonrise with implied allusion to Candra (Candra means 'Moon'):

> The Moon, having destroyed completely the flood of
> hostile darkness by his own expansion (rise),
> By the power of his own action enters the sky to pass
> over the eclipse.

Candra had two enemies in this story: he has destroyed the Śaka, but now he must face another. Can it be his brother, who formerly expressed such affection for him that he lost the love of the Queen? The exit theme is:

> Through love he hides his various intentions, very
> secret;
> He stumbles out with agitated thoughts: the mind of
> his enemy ready for blood.

1615. At present we are left to guess the rest of the story. We know from history (contemporary inscriptions) that Candra soon became king and that Dhruvadevī became his queen. The reign of Rāma was extremely short. According to a verse in an inscription of the Rāṣṭrakūṭa Emperor Amoghavarṣa I, dating from +873, a Gupta king killed his brother and took his kingdom and his queen (see Raghavan p. 870). A later Rāṣṭrakūṭa emperor, Govinda IV, is more explicit in naming Sāhasāṅka as responsible for these bad actions, in his inscriptions (dating from *c.* +925), himself being praised as an equally great king but without such sins (Raghavan pp. 878f.). The tradition thus was that Candra II killed Rāma and then began his glorious reign. Perhaps this explains the reticence of the old Indian historians on Candra Vikramāditya Sāhasāṅka, and even in part on the Guptas generally, despite the popular traditions of his greatness. As for Viśākhadatta, it would seem to have been very difficult to have concluded his play with such an action by his hero. He surely arranged the plot in such a way as to free Candra from any guilt. Indeed the real events may have been perpetrated by others, disgusted with the weak King Rāma, so that it was only by the circumstantial simplification, that Candra became emperor after his brother's murder, that the tradition arose. We can now only speculate over the many ways in which Viśākhadatta could have constructed the conclusion of his play. For example a minister might have killed Rāma and seized power during Act IV, being therefore the enemy Candra faced in Act V. In Act V the drama is clearly at the obstacle or pause conjunction and one or two more acts are needed for the action to be completed. As a matter of fact it is not clear what the main action and objective are. What is the 'seed' in Act I ? Is it the idea of saving the Queen ? The title of the play could mean merely that in it Candra Gupta appears (disguised) as the Queen and therefore does not help, though it also does not hinder, the conjecture that the union of Candra with Dhruvadevī was the objective. His love for Mādhavasenā makes him innocent of the treachery towards Rāma of having planned this union.

1616. The remaining play by Viśākhadatta, the *Mudrārākṣasa*, 'Signet Rākṣasa', has been preserved intact and enables us to see his genius fully displayed. Already from the fragments of his other three dramas it should be clear that he stands in the best dramatic tradition of the Indian theatre, following such playwrights as Bhāsa and Śūdraka, as well as neglected masters such as Brahmayaśas or the authors of Rāvaṇa and the Witch or the Rāghava and Jānakī. He does not follow the lyric or 'romantic' trend in which emotion is described in poetry rather than revealed in action. He is forceful and realistic in character presentation and seems absolutely to resist the temptation into sentimentality which a story like Rāma's offers to a poet. In fact his language is not especially impressive as poetry. It is sometimes difficult, rather than fluent, when he uses long metres and compounds to produce an effect of force. His concern is with dramatic effectiveness. All these impressions we shall find confirmed in the Signet Rākṣasa.

1617. The story of the Signet Rākṣasa concerns Candragupta, the first Maurya emperor, and the subtle minister Kauṭalya or Cāṇakya who made him emperor. The events in the play take place in —316, one year after they have taken the empire of Magadha from the last Nanda ruler. This Nanda is dead, but his minister Rākṣasa, having escaped abroad, is still loyal to his memory and is plotting to overthrow Candragupta. Candragupta is gaining popularity by conciliatory government and Cāṇakya as prime minister seeks to consolidate his position by winning over all sections of opinion to support the new ruler. The aim Cāṇakya sets himself is therefore not to destroy Rākṣasa, his enemy, but to win him over and make him a minister of Candragupta. This should finally eradicate any remaining loyalty to the old régime, for Rākṣasa is admired by everyone, by Cāṇakya most of all, on account of his honourable and incorruptible character. The winning over of Rākṣasa is thus the objective of the drama.

1618. Rākṣasa for his part is in league with a confederacy of six kings of North West India and Persia, who hope to invade Magadha and make one of themselves, Malayaketu, emperor. He has entered the service of Malayaketu and promised to make him emperor: the claim of Malayaketu is based on the alliance his father had had with Candragupta when they jointly captured Pāṭaliputra from the Nandas, but after this his father was murdered, actually by an assassin sent by Rākṣasa to kill Candragupta, for which murder Malayaketu believes Cāṇakya to be responsible. The exact position of Malayaketu's kingdom is not made clear, but it seems to be equivalent to Gandhāra. He himself is described as a barbarian *mleccha* and most or all of his allies seem also to be barbarians, together with their troops. No doubt much of Viśākhadatta's political geography here reflects the situation in his own time, with various barbarian rulers still in the Indus valley (Hūṇas, Śakas, etc.; even the Kuṣāṇas may still have been regarded as 'barbarians' though completely assimilated to Indian civilisation, as indeed were the Śakas). Whether he had accurate and detailed sources for the −4, when the Persians and Greeks ruled in the North West until Candragupta ejected them at the end of that century, is unknown. In any case, finding these frequent references to 'barbarians' in the Signet Rākṣasa, whose author clearly sees and depicts them in an unfavourable light (e.g. Act VI verse 8 on Malayaketu, his mind empty of discrimination), we have a very strong impression that Viśākhadatta is thinking of the topicality of such a theme in his own times. When we remember that the same author wrote a play on the struggle of the Guptas against the Śakas, the conclusion becomes irresistible that at the time of the triumphant end of the Hunnish wars Viśākhadatta had a message for India on the subject of barbarian invasions. He does not oppose 'Indians' or Āryans to barbarians, however. He is interested in the defence, not of a people or a nation but of a civilisation. It is wise and just government which has to be established and maintained. It is the Earth which is to be protected from oppression by the barbarians, as we read in the final benediction of the play.

1619. The means to achieve this protection, to defeat a barbarian invasion or the intrigues of a Rākṣasa, is the science of policy or politics included in the broader science of wealth *artha*. Kauṭalya (Cāṇakya) himself is the reputed author of the *Arthaśāstra* which became the standard treatise on the science of wealth. In the Signet Rākṣasa, Viśākhadatta provides an elaborate demonstration, with Kauṭalya himself as the hero, of the relevant parts of the science. Kauṭalya sends out numerous secret agents who mislead his enemies, break up the invading confederacy as its army approaches Pāṭaliputra, by making Malayaketu suspect his allies, and make Malayaketu turn against Rākṣasa. The signet ring which gives the play its title belongs to Rākṣasa: it falls into the hands of Cāṇakya's spies and is used to seal a forged letter from Rākṣasa to Candragupta reporting the supposed plot of the allies. The spies arrange for it to be intercepted by Malayaketu, who orders his allies to be put to death and dismisses Rākṣasa from his service. He means to march on Pāṭaliputra immediately, but these actions produce a revolt in the army, which disintegrates, leaving him a prisoner in the hands of some of Cāṇakya's agents who had been in his entourage. The earlier scenes of the play provide examples of various disguised agents in action, who, moreover, often do not know one another though their moves interlock and act as a series of mutual checks. In this game Rākṣasa is continually outplayed: he too has plenty of secret agents, but Cāṇakya is too alert for them and their plots miscarry, sometimes enabling Cāṇakya to draw advantages from them himself. Rākṣasa is inclined to be too generous and too trusting and for his part does not suspect in time that several of his agents are really Cāṇakya's men, planted on him through suitable pretexts. He is also shown tired through excessive work in this complex and rapid struggle, thus becoming overwrought and absent minded. The relationships of kings and their ministers are also thoroughly explored here, with possible divisions of responsibility between them. Then there is the question of public opinion, as mentioned above, which must be roused to support the king through appropriate measures.

1620. Running through this ruthless game of plotting and deception is a more hidden theme of loyalty, which provides guiding principles for the participants. In a feudalistic society this means loyalty to various individuals: to the king, to a friend, to a master, to a dependent. The scope of moral scruples tends to be limited accordingly and of course the characters are in the midst of a war: assassination of enemies can be carried out as ruthlessly as killing them in battle. It is the motive of loyalty, bringing in a spirit of honour and chivalry, which supplies a link with high ideals and satisfies the aspirations of these political heroes towards the end of virtue *dharma*. Cāṇakya admires (Act I verse 13) the devotion *bhakti* of Rākṣasa which continues even after the death of his king: it is thus disinterested *niḥsaṅga* and he is a rare person who must at all costs be won over. We may note that in the following verse Cāṇakya adds understanding and valour as two other necessary qualities in those who are to serve a king.

1621. After the fall of Malayaketu, Rākṣasa is still at large and the real objective unattained. Cāṇakya finds the appropriate means to draw him into Pāṭaliputra and bring about a capitulation which even enhances his opponent's honour. When Rākṣasa fled through an underground passage as the city fell to Candragupta a year earlier, he left his family under the protection of a close friend, a wealthy merchant-banker *śreṣṭhin* of the city, named Candanadāsa, who is loyal to the old régime. Cāṇakya has traced them and already in Act I had summoned Candanadāsa and demanded their surrender; but Candanadāsa cannot be frightened into doing this and denies that he has them in his house, adding that he would not give them up even if he did have them. For this Cāṇakya secretly admires him and compares him with Śivi, the type of the compassionate hero who makes the hardest sacrifices for others (this adds another aspect to the ideal of loyalty). He imprisons Candanadāsa, thinking that such a good friend of Rākṣasa's will be useful later if their loyalty is mutual. Now in the final stage of the drama Cāṇakya has the death sentence on Candanadāsa publicly announced, on the ground of treason, with the time of his execution. Rākṣasa gives himself up to redeem his friend and Cāṇakya further forces him to accept the office of minister under Candragupta, handing him his own sword of office. Honour is satisfied because Rākṣasa has saved his devoted friend, whilst Cāṇakya has achieved his objective.

1622. The first Act introduces Cāṇakya in the midst of his intrigues and he acquaints the audience briefly with his plans by reflecting on them in a monologue. Then a spy reports on sympathisers with Rākṣasa in the city, bringing the discovery that Candanadāsa is sheltering Rākṣasa's family and also bringing the signet ring, which Rākṣasa had left with his wife and the spy has stolen from the merchant-banker's house. In Act II the scene changes to Rākṣasa receiving his own spies with the latest information on the situation in Pāṭaliputra. The att to assassinate Candragupta have failed and several of his agents have been killed. But one of them, reported caught, was rescued by an acquaintance, apparently another supporter of Rākṣasa, and these two now appear. The supposed rescuer, however, is one of Cāṇakya's men thus insinuating himself into Rākṣasa's service; moreover he brings with him the signet ring, explaining that he found it fallen on the ground at the entrance to Candanadāsa's house: since it is engraved with Rākṣasa's name he is naturally returning it to its owner. Cāṇakya has already got the forged letter written and sealed, but the deception will be more perfect if Rākṣasa is currently using the seal in correspondence.

1623. Part of Rākṣasa's plan is to alienate Candragupta from Cāṇakya and he has agents briefed to incite the prince to rebel against the domination of his minister in all public affairs. The subtle Cāṇakya sees here an opportunity to make the effects of this plot rebound on its author. In Act III he stages a sham quarrel with Candragupta and resigns his commission, the prince declaring that he will rule himself. By doing this Cāṇakya opens the way for a rumour that Candragupta is thinking of inviting Rākṣasa to replace him and that Rākṣasa would accept this, it being asserted that Rākṣasa's quarrel is with Cāṇakya and not with Candragupta.

1624. In Act IV Cāṇakya's agents have some success in making Malayaketu believe that Rākṣasa has indeed incited Candragupta against his minister, with a view to obtaining the appointment for himself after betraying Malayaketu. This prepares the way for the interception of the forged letter in Act V. At the same time Malayaketu hastens his invasion of Magadha and Rākṣasa too thinks the dissension between Candragupta and Cāṇakya offers a favourable opportunity to attack them.

1625. Act VI, after an introductory scene reporting that Cāṇakya has marched out and rounded up the leaderless barbarian army, serves to acquaint Rākṣasa, through an agent, with the announcement of Candanadāsa's impending execution. In Act VII, the last act, Rākṣasa arrives at the place of execution just in time to save his friend. As for the captive Malayaketu, when everything is happily settled at the conclusion Rākṣasa asks for his life to be spared and he receives his hereditary kingdom back from Candragupta, evidently as a vassal.

1626. There are a number of references to the Signet Rākṣasa in the critical works and several quotations from it. They are, however, fewer and less extensive than those belonging to the Candra Gupta and the Queen. Kuntaka, as we have seen in Chapter IV above, refers to the Signet Rākṣasa as an example of a *kāvya* by a great *kavi*, which as a whole is figurative and instructive in an original manner (p. 245) [286]. He also notes the significance of the title as indicating the essential feature of the plot (p. 243) [285] and, as an example of contextual figurativeness, the scene in Act VI through which Rākṣasa is informed of the supposed execution of Candanadāsa (p. 234) [281]. Dhanika (p. 34) makes the rather surprising statement that the source for the story of this play was the *Bṛhatkathā*. A gloss which appears in some manuscripts of Dhanika's work quotes two verses from Kṣemendra's (+11, therefore slightly later than Dhanika) Sanskrit summary of Guṇāḍhya's novel (I.2.216-7), which do indeed mention Cāṇakya making Candragupta king though there is nothing relating to the episode actually dramatised by Viśākhadatta. Possibly some versions of the *Bṛhatkathā*, or even the original, contained a more detailed narrative as part of the introductory matter introducing the hero and the author (since Cāṇakya falls chronologically between them). Otherwise the source might better have been stated as the *Purāṇas* (Ḍhuṇḍhirāja names and quotes the *Viṣṇupurāṇa*, p. 53). [4405 f.]

1627. Dhanika further indicates (p. 60) that the play uses the 'expressive' *sāttvatī* mode of stage business (*cf.* the Exaltation of the Rāghava mentioned above [1585]) and specifically one of the four 'limbs' of that mode called 'crushing' *saṃghātya*, which means splitting combinations in various ways [181]. Two such ways are illustrated in the play: by the power of secret plans, whereby Rākṣasa is divided from his allies; and by the power of wealth, through which Cāṇakya puts in Rākṣasa's way an advantageous purchase of some jewellery, but the jewels had belonged to Malayaketu's murdered father and had fallen into the hands of Candragupta, thus when Malayaketu sees Rākṣasa wearing one of them it confirms his suspicion that Candragupta has bribed Rākṣasa to betray him. Among the points made by Abhinavagupta in connection with this play is that there is none of the 'tender' *kaiśikī* mode of stage business in it (II p. 410).

1628. Other critics note a number of the devices of dramatic construction in the Signet Rākṣasa. Sāgaranandin (423) finds a *cūlikā* ('crest', voice from behind the curtain) by way of introductory scene towards the end of Act III, where a bard in the pay of Rākṣasa sings a verse at Candragupta's court designed to incite the prince to throw off the domination of his minister, as Cāṇakya duly notes on hearing it [126]. At the end of the same act he finds (958) 'understanding' *dhi* as an 'other conjunction', when Candragupta in an aside shows that, though greatly embarrassed by the sham quarrel, he is keeping his head and following Cāṇakya's plan [141]. Bhoja notes as 'other conjunctions' 'split', *bheda*, where Malayaketu sees the forged letter and is split from Rākṣasa (*Śṛṅgāraprakāśa* Vol. II p. 499), 'coercion' *daṇḍa* in the scene preparing Candanadāsa's execution in order to seize Rākṣasa (also p. 499) and 'ascertaining the cause' *hetvavadhāraṇa* when Cāṇakya after hearing the bard's insinuating verse sees Rākṣasa's plan behind it (p. 502). The third variety of injection of subsidiary matter is seen by Bhoja (p. 504) where Cāṇakya doubts whether Rākṣasa will be caught by his plan of the false rescue, etc., but is reassured by the double meaning in his agent's speech, when the latter just at that moment enters and says he has 'taken' (the message) [143]. Rāmacandra and Guṇacandra on the other hand see the fourth variety in this incident (p. 41).

1629. Rāmacandra and Guṇacandra have a few notes on the construction of the main plot. In discussing different kinds of 'seed' [123], they say that in the Signet Rākṣasa it takes the form of setting about the prevention of a disaster, quoting Cāṇakya's first words when he enters, overhearing the producer's double meaning words about an eclipse of the Moon (Candra): 'Who wishes to overthrow Candragupta... ?' (pp. 38-9). (According to Śāradātanaya, p. 229, this lead-in by taking up the producer's words is an example of the device *kathodghāta* [139].) They quote from Act III (verses 4 and 5) for the limb 'declaration of truth' *mārga* in the embryo conjunction (pp. 79f.) [148], including:

She is agitated by one who is sharp, but from terror of
humiliation does not stay with one who is gentle;
she hates fools, but does not love the exceedingly wise;
She is greatly afraid of heroes, but derides those who
are timid:
Fortune is like a geisha girl having free play—violently
difficult to be courteous to. (5)

Here Candragupta is complaining of the difficulties of being king. After this Rāmacandra and Guṇacandra refer only to the conclusion, in which they point out the limbs 'derision' *dyuti*, in the scene where Cāṇakya asks Rākṣasa whether he wants Candanadāsa to live and thus forces him to accept the sword of ministerial office (after VII.15), and 'reminding' *pūrvavākya*, where a reference back to Cāṇakya's threat, about who does not wish him to bind up his hair (end the quarrel —I.8), in the opening conjunction, is suggested by his declaration of a general amnesty (before or in place of VII.17) (pp. 95 and 99) [150].

1630. Among the anthologists who quote from Viśākhadatta, Vidyākara, the Buddhist, manages to find two innocuous verses in the Signet Rākṣasa, one (278) a description of autumn by Candragupta as he approaches the Sugāṅga Palace in

Pāṭaliputra (III.7) and the other (133) an invocation to Viṣṇu by one of the court bards (III.21).

1631. Jalhaṇa quotes ten verses, for example from the complaint of the old chamberlain of the Sugāṅga Palace (p. 433):

> To be afraid of the King, then of the minister; then of the King's favourite
> and of other parasites who have obtained favour in his palace;
> With dissembling in order to appear attentive; because of poverty, the service of one taking trouble
> for the sake of alms brings about contempt: the wise have appropriately looked upon it as a dog's life.
> (III.14)

But then after seeing Cāṇakya's modest house, when Candragupta sends him to fetch the minister, he reflects (p. 439):

> They praise the King with tireless mouths for non-existent qualities,
> through poverty even truthful men become orators;
> All that indeed is the power of desire—otherwise the Lord
> would be an object of contempt, like grass, to those desiring nothing. (III.16)

1632. Jalhaṇa also quotes the following reflections of Bhāgurāyaṇa, an officer in Malayaketu's service and confidence but really an agent of Cāṇakya, on Cāṇakya's politics (p. 409):

> Now its germination is visible, now it is mysterious because it cannot be understood,
> now its parts are full, now very slender through the control of the objective,
> Now its seed vanishes, but now it brings much fruit:
> ah!—The politics of one who knows policy has surprising aspects, like destiny. (V. 3).

Here the terms 'seed', 'objective', 'germination', etc., suggest dramatic plot construction and in fact Viśākhadatta has other allusions comparing political intrigue with writing a play. Rākṣasa reflects:

> At first arranging just a slight hint of the objective,
> desiring to extend it;
> then germinating the fruit of the embryonic seeds,
> which is hidden and very mysterious;
> Taking pause with intelligence, then again gathering
> in what was extended and become the objective:
> the maker of dramas, or one of our own kind,
> experiences this trouble. (IV.3)

In Act VI (before verse 3) one of Cāṇakya's agents, mystified by the effects of his policies, compares them with a drama by a bad writer, which has one thing as the opening and another thing as the conclusion. This, his colleague points out, is only because he does not understand them, their ways being unknown like destiny's. The techniques of the *Nāṭyaśāstra*, of course, were generally established long before Viśākhadatta's time, but it is interesting to find a great dramatist bearing them so much in mind when at work, confirming that dramatic practice in the +6 closely followed the theory and that the later critics are right in analysing the plays accordingly.

1633. Viśākhadatta's characterisation is extremely skilful. Cāṇakya was traditionally regarded as very irascible and this is demonstrated by the manner of his first entrance, at once recalling his legendary personality to the minds of the audience. But Viśākhadatta's Cāṇakya is a very much more complex character than this irascible but subtle politician. He sees a high ideal as the aim of his work and is without personal ambition except to the extent of repaying a humiliating insult with interest (his motive for destroying the Nandas). He serves his ideal for its own sake and not for self-glorification: apparently he will be happy to retire from active politics when Rākṣasa agrees to become minister of Candragupta. He is a connoisseur of good qualities in other people, for example in Rākṣasa and Candanadāsa. On the other hand he is absolutely single minded in his service of his ideal and thus capable of complete ruthlessness in dealing with opponents. He lives simply, his 'magnificence' being described as follows by the chamberlain as he approaches his house:

> This piece of rock is for splitting cakes of cowdung,
> this is the shed for the sacrifices offered by the boys,
> The shelter, too, with firewood being dried inside,
> is seen with its walls decayed and the end of its thatch broken down. (III.15)

The cowdung cakes are split into brickettes for use as fuel and the boys are Cāṇakya's young pupils. The magnificence of an orthodox brahman consists in the Vedic rituals he performs in this simple and very ancient style.

1634. Rākṣasa is perhaps slightly less ruthless than Cāṇakya, though he has tried repeatedly to have Candragupta assassinated. He goes steadfastly to his defeat, selfless and loyal to his principles. But he is human, more human than Cāṇakya, which probably is why he is defeated: as noted already he trusts too easily and in the relentless battle of intrigue he begins to show tiredness and finally loss of nerve when charged with treachery by Malayaketu. It is also a weakness that he seizes an opportunity of making an advantageous purchase of some jewellery, thus falling into Cāṇakya's trap. When defeated he still cannot be seduced from his principles, cannot compromise his honour, but is finally won over only by the force of a more immediate and practical form of honour: offering his life to save the faithful Candanadāsa.

1635. Candragupta Maurya regards himself humbly as the pupil of Cāṇakya, who incidentally calls him *vṛṣala*, 'helot' (*śūdra*), on account of his birth, not flattering him with royal titles. He plays his part conscientiously, but it is a carefully studied part, rather than his own character, which he displays. In this lies his wisdom as a prince and his fitness to become a mighty emperor — served ably by the ministers to whom he delegates the burden of administration.

1636. Malayaketu on the other hand is an adventurer, impatient and contemptuous of ministers except as junior officers in his own autocratic government. He is impetuous, thus somewhat careless, then too easily believes the faked evidence Cāṇakya piles into his hands, not having appreciated the true character of Rākṣasa or reflected sufficiently on the motives of others. Obviously he believes in war rather than intrigue, but he is not a good enough leader and destroys his allies because he knows he does not deserve their loyalty, or does not believe in any such thing. In short he lacks judgment. This is Viśākhadatta's idea of a 'barbarian' *mleccha.* K. P. Jayaswal (*Indian Antiquary* Vol. XL pp. 265 ff.) has conjectured that 'Malayaketu' is a corruption of 'Salayaketu', i.e. Seleukos, the Greek general and successor of Alexander of Macedon in Syria and Iran (confusion of *s* and *m* is easy in some Indian scripts, especially the *nāgarī*). Seleukos in fact attacked Candragupta in the war of —305 to —303, was defeated and forced to yield up not only the whole of NW India but also the Iranian province of Aria. Possibly the story which Viśākhadatta dramatised goes back to this war with the Greeks, whom the Indians regarded as barbarians, but with a chronological error (or aesthetic distortion) of ten years.

1637. The presentation of the minor characters is also excellent. Candanadāsa's defiance of Cāṇakya, when arrested, is well done. The time serving and obsequious old chamberlain at the Pāṭaliputra court, terrified when the King and the minister quarrel, is a notable sketch. Among the secret agents of Cāṇakya we should note Bhāgurāyaṇa, troubled by his conscience when deceiving Malayaketu (Act V, between verses 3 and 4). The other leading agents give displays of professional virtuosity, in which humour plays a conspicuous and very practical part, negotiating tricky situations. Since they are disguised as vagrant entertainers and the like (unlike Bhāgurāyaṇa, a man of aristocratic family who pretends to have become disaffected from Candragupta) and are not known to the ordinary associates of the ministers (or even to other secret agents on the same side, for that matter), it is naturally difficult for them to obtain access to their employers and they have to exercise considerable wit to penetrate close enough to them to be recognised and admitted. To their intimates, such as servants and pupils, both ministers must appear to be amateurs of charlatans of all kinds, such as prophets of doom and snake charmers. Assassins, on the other hand, are described as bunglers.

1638. Viśākhadatta is not a great poet: his descriptive verses, which are few, are forceful but do not always flow naturally or clearly. There are no striking effects of figurative language. But he is one of India's very greatest dramatists: the complete absence of lyricism or any kind of poetic effect from the Signet Rākṣasa enhances and concentrates its dramatic force. It can be appreciated only as a drama and there are no distractions from this purely dramatic enjoyment. The aesthetic experience is of course the heroic, generated by the intense energy of the characters in what is presented as a fast moving struggle. Their heroic acts are of various kinds, with most emphasis on self sacrifice.

1639. It has also been pointed out, by Kuntaka, that this is a highly instructive play. There are many aspects to this instruction. The play is a study of human character, as we have seen, and of human nature in a time of difficult struggle. Here there is much to ponder. It has always been regarded as a practical exemplification of political science (*Śṛṅgāraprakāśa* II 319) : thus the commentary of Vaṭeśvara of Tīrabhukti (+15), the *Mudrāprakāśa*, presents it as a system of the science as well as as a play. Then there are some significant special points. We have noted already Viśākhadatta's apparent preoccupation with 'barbarians' and his presumed lesson for India on the subject of the defence of civilisation from barbarism. Rākṣasa ought not, in his indignation on behalf of the Nandas, to have entered the service of a barbarian. He must now be won back, reconciled, because he is in fact a man of incontestable virtue despite this aberration. With so many of Cāṇakya's agents around him it would have been easy to assassinate him, but that is not the aim and he is even protected from possible danger, from Malayaketu, by these agents. The more difficult task is to bring him back. A civilised state needs such men, such virtue as is not to be found among ambitious barbarians loyal to no one and seeking only treasure and autocratic power.

1640. The varying appreciation and understanding of Viśākhadatta in India through the centuries might lead to an interesting enquiry in relation to the fortunes of civilisation. Thus there was a remarkable revival of interest in the Signet Rākṣasa in the Marāṭha Empire, resulting in the writing of commentaries on it and of narratives dealing with the events which preceded its action. These include the historian Ḍhuṇḍhirāja's (+18) commentary, sometimes regarded as the best, one by the Marāṭha King Śarabha of Tañjanagara and Ananta's (+17) introductory narrative on Nanda history. Ḍhuṇḍhirāja concentrates on an attempt at analysing the dramatic construction of the play, following the *Daśarūpaka*, in which he tries, for example, to point out all the sixty four 'limbs' of the conjunctions. Unfortunately the *paurāṇika* did not understand dramaturgy and goes wildly astray (thus he thinks the 'embryo' coincides with Act II, contrary to Rāmacandra and Guṇacandra [1629], and moreover contains the 'sub-plot', whilst the 'conclusion' occupies the whole of Acts V-VII). In the same rigidly pedantic spirit he tries to find all the thirteen limbs of the street play in the Prologue [325].

1641. As long as India could produce Cāṇakyas, her civilisation flourished, defended from the aggression of the *mlecchas*. When on the other hand she relied on simple, straightforward heroism and chivalry, as the ideal, her civilisation was gradually destroyed by barbarous invaders.

1642. Let us conclude with Rākṣasa's praise of the selfless and incorruptible Candanadāsa who sacrifices his life for others, contained in the message Rākṣasa sends to Cāṇakya when he gives himself up :

> Even in the evil Kali Age, which bad people like, this honourable one is protecting another with his own life,
> reducing the honour of Śivi to total insignificance;
> This pure one with his good deeds has made even the action of *buddhas* seem 'defiled' :
> here am I, for whose sake even he, worthy of honour, has been sentenced to death by you. (VII.6)

INDEX

(The numbers refer to paragraphs)

APPENDIX

(the numbers refer to the relevant paragraphs)

1297. Śārṅgadhara (3822) ascribes the following verse on 'the traveller in spring' to Rāmila and Somila:

Thinness from being ill, the blood of a wound,
the trickling spittle of a bite:/
here there is nothing of these; how then has
the poor traveller died?/

Ha! I know: the bees greedy for honey have
begun a clamour;/
surely he recklessly let his glance fall on
a mango bud./

The metre is *śārdūlavikrīḍita*.

1333. Tilaka in his Commentary (*Vivṛti*) on Udbhaṭa V. 14-5 (p. 43) quotes a *vasantatilaka* verse which suggests the context of Indra afraid of Hayagrīva or already defeated by him: it might have stood at the end of one of these early cantos. But as Indra's enemy is not named this is conjectural, it just seems to be in Meṇṭha's manner:

He touches Airāvaṇa, takes counsel with the Maruts,/
handles his thunderbolt, looks at his companies
of warriors;/

Great Indra finds the slopes of Meru dangerous:/
from fear of you, O King, he does not feel
sleepy at night./

This is quoted to illustrate praise of what is not the subject: Indra has abandoned the idea of setting out to fight, though the description at first seems to be of preparations to march.

1335. The anonymous *Kalpalatāviveka* (+12) criticizes the *Hayagrivavadha* (by name, p. 78) for introducing a matter which contradicts the aesthetic experience of its context. This tells us of another episode in the poem. Hayagrīva has sent his son to the demon Naraka to bring him to the festival. But on arrival he finds Naraka has just been killed by Viṣṇu [1148]. He hears Naraka's daughter, grieving for her father, has gone to the forest and goes to comfort her. However, instead of the compassionate, the sensitive is developed:

> For, slender one, asceticism is not suitable for you/
> in youth, fit for the festival of love;/
> Say, broad loins, whether causeways/
> over the rivers shall be made with the pollen of flowers?

The metre is *puṣpitāgra*. Perhaps this clumsy move at the wrong time is what one would expect of a demon. Rudraṭa (XI. 13) has paraphrased the verse.

1351. Jayanta [3345ff.] in his *Nyāyamañjarī* (p. 177) quotes a speech from a play: "It's me, the Witch become Sītā!" (omit the *na*, with Cakradhara's Commentary, p. 78). Jayanta is discussing 'error' *bhrama*, from a philosophical point of view, as where a piece of oyster shell is taken for silver. Cakradhara names the play as the *Kṛtyārāvaṇa* and says he mentions this as ridicule *upahāsa* (of Rāvaṇa?). For the Fire God has instigated the Witch to kill Rāvaṇa. So when it is time for him to come she takes on the appearance of Sītā. Cakradhara does not tell us what happens. But she does not succeed, for Rāvaṇa survives to be killed by Rāma, as is reported in Act VII. She presumably gains a respite for the real Sītā, who is hard pressed in this play. But the plot, with this intrigue by the Fire God, is still more complicated than had appeared. The centrality of Sītā is reinforced by this appearance of an illusory Sītā defending the real one.

1448. Varieties of *veḍha* (Sanskrit *veṣṭa*) are used later also, for example by Mānāṅka [2532f.], Haribhadra [2673], Svayambhū [3305] and Somadeva I [3977].